Electronic Payment Systems for E-Commerce

Second Edition

For quite a long time, computer security was a rather narrow field of study that was populated mainly by theoretical computer scientists, electrical engineers, and applied mathematicians. With the proliferation of open systems in general, and of the Internet and the World Wide Web (WWW) in particular, this situation has changed fundamentally. Today, computer and network practitioners are equally interested in computer security, since they require technologies and solutions that can be used to secure applications related to electronic commerce. Against this background, the field of computer security has become very broad and includes many topics of interest. The aim of this series is to publish state-of-the-art, high-standard technical books on topics related to computer security. Further information about the series can be found on the WWW at the following URL:

http://www.esecurity.ch/serieseditor.html

Also, if you'd like to contribute to the series and write a book about a topic related to computer security, feel free to contact either the Commissioning Editor or the Series Editor at Artech House.

Recent Titles in the Artech House Computer Security Series

Rolf Oppliger, Series Editor

For a listing of recent titles in the *Artech House Computing Library,* turn to the back of this book.

Electronic Payment Systems for E-Commerce

Second Edition

Donal O'Mahony
Michael Peirce
Hitesh Tewari

Artech House
Boston • London
www.artechhouse.com

Library of Congress Cataloging-in-Publication Data
O'Mahony, Donal, 1961–
   Electronic payment systems for e-commerce / Donal O'Mahony, Michael Peirce,
Hitesh Tewari.—2nd ed.
       p.   cm. — (Artech House computer security series)
   Rev. ed. of: Electronic payment systems, c1997.
   Includes bibliographical references and index.
   ISBN 1-58053-268-3 (alk. paper)
   1. Electronic funds transfers.   2. Data encryption (Computer science).
   3. Internet.   I. Peirce, M. E. (Michael E.)   II. Tewari, Hitesh.   III. O'Mahony,
   Donal, 1961– Electronic payment systems.   IV. Title.   V. Series.
HG1710 .O45   2001
332'.0285—dc21   2001022856

British Library Cataloguing in Publication Data
O'Mahony, Donal, 1961–
   Electronic payment systems for e-commerce.—2nd. ed.—
   (Artech House computer security series)
   1. Electronic funds transfers
   I. Title   II. Peirce, Michael, 1972–   III. Tewari, H.
   332.1'0285

   ISBN 1-58053-268-3

Cover design by Igor Valdman

© **2001 ARTECH HOUSE, INC.**
685 Canton Street
Norwood, MA 02062

International Standard Book Number: 1-58053-268-3
Library of Congress Catalog Card Number: 2001022856

10 9 8 7 6 5 4 3 2 1

Contents

Preface

This book is about the techniques and systems used to allow payments to be made across the Internet. It is written primarily for researchers and industry professionals who need to develop a broad understanding of the important technologies in this area. Anyone involved in electronic commerce will ultimately need to understand how payment can be incorporated into trading systems, and this book gives a comprehensive view of the best ways to achieve this today. It assumes that the reader has some knowledge of computers and networked systems, and the necessary cryptography required to understand the systems is fully explained in Chapter 3. Readers without a financial background will be introduced to the salient aspects of conventional (pre-Internet) systems in Chapter 2 as a background to Chapters 4–9, which cover each significant Internet-based payment category.

The three authors of this book have been actively engaged in research into electronic payment systems since 1994. They are all members of the Networks & Telecommunications Research Group (NTRG) at Trinity College, Dublin, Ireland, and in this context have been responsible for developing innovative new designs and prototypes for new check, cash, and micropayment schemes. In 1996, as e-commerce was beginning to emerge as a major phenomenon, they saw a need for a book to give a good overview of the different types of payment systems that were offered. The book, *Electronic Payment Systems*, published in 1997, was very well received and, appropriately, won a best-seller award in its category from the on-line bookseller Amazon.com. Many things have changed since 1996, and this second edition of *Electronic Payment Systems for E-Commerce* has been greatly revised. New encryption techniques such as the Advanced Encryption Standard (AES) have been covered as well as new coverage of elliptic curve cryptography. The main chapters have been updated to reflect the success or failure of systems that existed in 1996 and also any new significant systems that have been added. Perhaps the most significant change is a brand-new chapter on mobile payment for use in m-commerce. This is a commercially very hot topic at the time of writing and is likely to remain so in the medium-term future.

As with the first edition, this book can only hope to capture a snapshot of the technology as it progresses. Nevertheless, we believe that the core principles of payment exemplified by the systems in this book will be valid for many years to come.

Motivation for electronic payment

Everything must be assessed in money; for this enables men always to exchange their services, and so makes society possible.

—Aristotle (384–322 B.C.)

The idea of paying for goods and services electronically is not a new one. All around us we see evidence of transactions taking place where at least part of the process is carried on electronically. Since the late 1970s and early 1980s, a variety of schemes have been proposed to allow payment to be effected across a computer network. Few of these schemes got beyond the design stage since the schemes were of little use to those who were not connected to a network.

The arrival of the Internet has removed this obstacle to progress. This network of networks has grown dramatically from its inception in the late 1970s to today's truly global medium. It is not known how many people make regular use of the Internet, but

Figure 1.1 shows a graph of the number of host computers [1] connected at different points in its history.

By July 2000, after a period of exponential growth, the number of machines hooked up to the network had grown to over 93 million. In the early stages of the Internet evolution, it was common to make the assumption that each of these machines was used by around 10 people. This would mean that some 930 million people have Internet access worldwide. Most commentators would agree that this figure is much too high, and have used a variety of other estimating techniques to arrive at a better answer. The 2001 Nua Internet Survey [2] takes an average of such estimates and concludes that just over 400 million people were on-line by January 2001. Much of this growth has been driven by the avail-ability of World Wide Web (WWW) technology that allows information located on machines around the world to be accessed as a single multimedia-linked document with simple point-and-click interactions.

Surveys of Internet users [3] suggest that the profile is changing from the original university-centered user base to a more broadly based resi-dential population with a high spending power. These facts are not lost on commercial organizations wishing to offer goods and services for sale to a global consumer audience.

Initially the focus of electronic commerce (e-commerce) was on sell-ing goods to consumers. The most popular categories included computer goods and software, books, travel, and music CDs. This so-called business-to-consumer (B2C) e-commerce grew spectacularly. In the United States [4], such spending was estimated at $7.7 billion in 1998, $17.3 billion in 1999, and $28 billion in 2000.

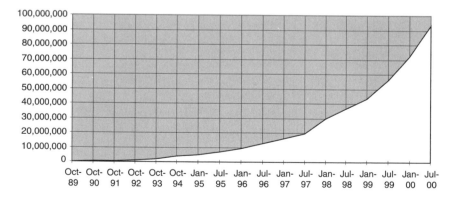

Figure 1.1   Count of host computers connected to the Internet over time.

Around 1999, the industry focus began to shift to the trade that companies do with each other. By building on-line electronic marketplaces, it became possible to bring together businesses such as car manufacturers and their component suppliers, or fruit wholesalers with primary producers. This business-to-business (B2B) e-commerce is thought to have the potential to become considerably larger than the B2C sector, and indeed some early estimates [5] suggest that B2B e-commerce reached $226 billion worldwide in 2000 and is projected to reach $2.7 trillion by 2004.

In both the B2C and B2B sectors, the Web was first used simply as a means of discovering products and services, with the payment being carried out off-line by some conventional payment method. In the case of B2C consumer purchases, merchants found they could capture credit card details from Web forms allowing the completion of the transaction off-line, albeit with a complete absence of security measures.

When the first edition of *Electronic Payment Systems* was released in 1997, a huge variety of different payment methods had been developed by both academic researchers and commercial interests. Some of these were launched on the market and failed to reach a critical mass. Early market leaders such as First Virtual Inc., CyberCash Inc., and Digicash launched payment systems that achieved some quite extensive deployment but failed to generate an economic return. At the same time, many new companies started up, offering new methods of payment for the B2C sector. The advent of B2B payments with their different requirements will give a greater impetus to payment methods that can cope with bank-mediated large-value transfers. A totally new market has also developed for people to make payments with the assistance of their mobile phone or handheld wireless device. Mobile commerce (m-commerce) has the potential to become a very large industry and many payment technology providers have appeared to fill this gap.

This book attempts to present the technology involved in the more important payment systems currently available to network users. Since the field is undergoing a major upheaval, this account will necessarily be a kind of snapshot of the current state of play.

The following chapter will look at the ways in which the world's population currently pays for goods and services in order to gain a good appreciation for the context in which the new systems are being introduced. Since most of the new schemes rely on cryptographic techniques for their security, Chapter 3 provides the necessary background information on cryptography required for a thorough understanding of how the new schemes operate.

Chapters 4, 5, and 6 survey the principal schemes used to effect payment electronically in a manner that is most similar to credit card, check, and cash, respectively, while Chapter 7 looks at micropayments, a new form of payment that has no counterpart in conventional commerce. In this edition, we have included a new Chapter 8, which deals with mobile payment systems for m-commerce. We conclude with a look at what lies ahead for payment systems in the years to come.

References

[1]   "Internet Host Count Maintained by the Internet Software Consortium," July 2000, http://www.isc.org/.

[2]   Nua Internet Surveys, "How Many Online?" February 2001, http://www.nua.ie.

[3]   Pitkow, J., "The WWW User Population: Emerging Trends," *GlobeCom '97*, November 1997, http://www.cc.gatech.edu/gvu/user_surveys/papers.

[4]   U.S. Department of Commerce, "Statistical Abstract of the United States: 2000," February 2001, http://www.census.gov/statab/www/.

[5]   Emarketer, *The eCommerce: B2B Report*, February 2001, http://www.emarketer.com.

CHAPTER

2

Characteristics of current payment systems

Payment in its most primitive form involves barter: the direct exchange of goods and services for other goods and services. Although still used in primitive economies and on the fringes of developed ones, this form of payment suffers from the need to establish what is known as a *double coincidence of wants*. This means, for example, that a person wishing to exchange food for a bicycle must first find another person who is both hungry and has a spare bicycle! Consequently, over the centuries, barter arrangements have been replaced with various forms of money.

The earliest money was called *commodity money*, where physical commodities (such as corn, salt, or gold) whose values were well known were used to effect payment. In order to acquire a number of desirable properties including portability and divisibility, gold and silver coins became the most

5

commonly used commodity money, particularly after the industrial revolution in the 1800s.

The next step in the progression of money was the use of tokens such as paper notes, which were backed by deposits of gold and silver held by the note issuer. This is referred to as adopting a *commodity standard*. As an economy becomes highly stable and governments (in the form of central banks) are trusted, it becomes unnecessary to have commodity backing for notes that are issued. This is referred to as *fiat money* since the tokens only have value by virtue of the fact that the government declares it to be so, and this assertion is widely accepted.

Cash payment is the most popular form of money transfer used today, but as amounts get larger and security becomes an issue, people are less inclined to hold their wealth in the form of cash and start to avail of the services of a financial institution such as a bank. If both parties to a payment hold accounts with the same bank, then a payment can be effected by making a transfer of funds from one account to another. This essential mechanism is at the root of a wide variety of payment schemes facilitated by the financial services industry today. The following sections will look at some of these and how they compare with traditional cash payment.

2.1 Cash payments

On first examination, payment by cash appears to be the simplest and most effective of all of the alternatives. It is easily transferred from one individual to another. In paper form, it is quite portable and large amounts can be carried in a pocket or briefcase. There are no transaction charges levied when a payment is made, which makes it very suitable for transactions with a low value, and no audit trail is left behind. This last attribute makes cash payment a favorite payment method for those engaged in criminal activity.

But contrary to appearances, cash is not *free*. There is a huge amount of cash in circulation. It was estimated in 1999, that $500 billion in U.S. currency [1] was in the hands of the public. This currency wears out—a $1 bill has a life expectancy of 18 months, while the less common $50 bill usually lasts about nine years. Each year, around 10 billion notes are destroyed and replaced with newly printed ones. Regardless of the denomination, each note costs some 4¢ to produce, and this cost is ultimately borne by the taxpayer. A similar situation exists in every country in the world.

Once the cash has been produced, it must then be transferred to and from banks or companies under very high security. Vaults must be built to store it, and heavy insurance premiums paid to cover losses due to theft. All of these costs are eventually passed on by a variety of indirect means to the cash user. With recent advances in color photocopying techniques, the risk from counterfeiters is also growing at an alarming rate.

Nevertheless, cash is the most commonly used form of payment, accounting for about 80% of all transactions. As an example, U.S. statistics and estimates [2] suggest that in 1993, nearly 300 billion cash transactions took place in the American economy with a total dollar value of some $3.4 trillion. The fact that this yields an average transaction value of around $11 reflects the fact that cash is mostly used to buy low-value goods.

One of the factors that has allowed cash to remain the dominant form of payment is the development of automated teller machines (ATMs), which allow consumers much easier access to money in cash form. The banking industry, which acts as the distributor of cash in the economy, has been attempting for many years to wean consumers off cash and into electronic bank mediated payments and in recent years has begun to have some success.

2.2 Payment through banks

Where both parties have lodged their cash with a bank for safekeeping, it becomes unnecessary for one party to withdraw notes in order to make a payment to another. Instead, they can write a check, which is an order to their bank to pay a specified amount to the named payee. The payee can collect the funds by going to the payer's bank and cashing the check. Alternatively, the payee can lodge the check so that the funds are transferred from the account of the payer to that of the payee.

2.2.1 Payment by check

If the parties hold accounts with separate banks, then the process gets more complicated. The cycle begins when A presents a check in payment to B. What happens next is shown in Figure 2.1. Party B lodges the check

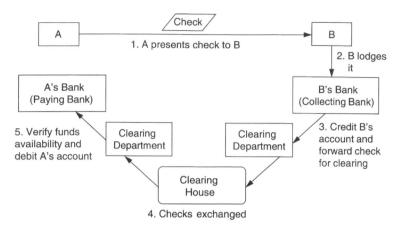

Figure 2.1   The check-clearing process.

with his bank (referred to as the *collecting bank*), which will collect the funds on his behalf. In most cases, a credit is made to B's account as soon as the check is lodged, but this *immediate funds* availability is not always the case. All checks lodged with bank B over the course of a day will be sent to the *clearing department*, where they are sorted in order of the banks on which they are drawn. The following day, they are brought to a *clearing house*, where a group of banks meet to exchange checks. The check in question will be given to bank A and (usually) one day later bank A will verify that the funds are available to meet the check and debit A's account for the sum involved.

If funds are not available, the signature on the check does not match with samples, or any other problem occurs, then the check must be returned to the collecting bank together with some indication as to why it could not be processed. Bank A must attend to this promptly, usually within one working day. These so-called *returned items* are the major problem with the check as a payment instrument in that their existence introduces uncertainty, and the fact that they need individual attention from banking staff means that they are very expensive to process. The principal loser in this situation is B, who finds himself in possession of a dishonored check with hefty bank charges to pay. In general, however, the bank's changes are seldom high enough to cover their processing expenses.

If funds are available to meet the check, then the following day the banks that are part of the clearing arrangement will calculate how much they owe to or are owed by the group of clearing banks as a whole. This amount is then *settled* by making a credit or debit from a special account usually maintained by the central bank.

The clearing of paper checks is a major operation, and in the United Kingdom over 2.8 billion items went through the system in 1999, with a value of £1.3 trillion [3]. Volumes have declined by between 2% and 4% per year since 1991. The cost to the member banks of operating the clearing system is very high and in the United Kingdom has been estimated at over £1.5 billion per year. One way to reduce the costs is to keep the check at the collecting bank and forward the transaction details electronically through the clearing system. These may be accompanied by a scanned image of the check to allow signatures to be verified. This process is known as *truncation*, and has been implemented in many countries since the early 1970s, but was forbidden by law in some jurisdictions. The United Kingdom, for example, until May 1996, required that a check be physically presented at the bank branch on which it was drawn.

2.2.2 Payment by giro or credit transfer

The returned items problem is the single biggest drawback with checks as a payment method. This problem is eliminated using a credit transfer or giro payment. A giro is an instruction to the payer's bank to transfer funds to the payee's bank. As Figure 2.2 shows, the processing of a giro is similar to a check, with the main difference being that the transaction cannot be initiated unless A has the funds available. This eliminates any uncertainty and extra cost imposed by the need to process returned items. It is an easier process to conduct electronically since the correct processing of the payment does not require sending the signed document through the clearing system.

This form of payment is quite popular in many European countries where national post offices rather than banks tend to operate the system. The payment method is not used in paper form in the United States, but credit transfers in electronic form are possible.

2.2.3 Automated clearing house (ACH) payments

From their inception, paper-based payments (checks and giros) grew in popularity and as the task of carrying out paper-based clearing grew, the banks began to look for more automated ways to make payments. In 1968, a group of Californian bankers came together to form the Special Committee on Paperless Entries (SCOPE), which led to the formation in

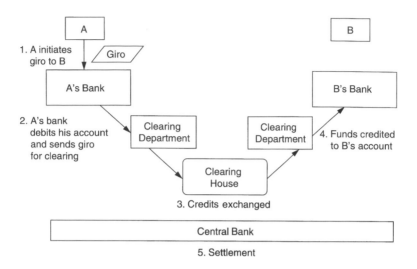

Figure 2.2 Payment by credit transfer or giro.

1972 of the California Clearing House Association, the first regional automated clearing house (ACH) in the United States. In the United Kingdom, similar moves were happening, and an automated clearing center was established in 1968, which was incorporated in 1971 as the Bankers Automated Clearing Service (BACS).

The ACH system operates in a similar way to paper clearing except that the payment instructions are in electronic form. In the early days of ACH, banks prepared magnetic tapes of these transactions that were transported to the ACH, sorted by destination bank, and distributed in much the same way as paper checks and giros, but increasingly this method is being replaced by real-time transactions sent on telecommunications links.

In the United States ACH system, the first message to be used was a corporate cash disbursement (CCD) message consisting of a 94-character message to identify the payee, amount, and any other details. In more recent years, more message formats have been added, and message formats have been changing from proprietary formats to ones that comply with open standards defined by the electronic data interchange (EDI) community [4].

The system is now used extensively by employers to pay wages directly into workers' bank accounts, to implement standing orders, direct debits, and direct credits. In the United Kingdom in 2000, BACS processed 3.2 billion transactions to the value of £1.8 trillion. In the United States [5], usage of ACH has been growing at between 9% and 22% per year and in 1999 processed 6.2 billion transactions with a value of $19.4 trillion. More than half of the recipients of Social Security use it for direct deposit, and nearly half of the private sector receive their wages by ACH.

There is considerable variation [6] in the operation of ACH payments systems in different countries around the world. In general, there is no compatibility between the messages used in individual countries, but there are major developments both in Europe and globally that are noteworthy. Spurred on by impending monetary union and the introduction of a common currency, many European countries came together in 1999 to form a high-value money transfer system called Trans-European Automated Real-Time Gross settlement Express Transfer (TARGET) [7] system, which links national payment systems together. Though TARGET is intended to cater for high-value payments, a similar low-value system called Straight Through Euro Processing (STEP) [8] is being proposed by the Euro Banking Association, with the first phase of this (called STEP1) carrying live transactions since November 1999. This system has a maximum transaction value of Euro 50,000 and a low processing fee of Euro 0.48. It is anticipated that as European Monetary Union progresses, demand for these kind of cross-border low-value transactions will mushroom.

On a more global level, a consortium of global banking players referred to as the Worldwide Automated Transaction Clearing House (WATCH) [9] came together in late 2000 to plan a global system that would bridge national ACH systems with a target of achieving live operation by July 2002. This would initially provide only credit transfers in six to eight currencies with more functions being added over time.

2.2.4　Wire transfer services

The ACH method of effecting payment is ideal for mid- to low-value transactions. In 1999, for example, the average value of a credit ACH payment in the United States was around $3,000. Where the value of payments is considerably higher, the risk level rises and different procedures involving more scrutiny are required. These high-value payments are referred to as wire transfers.

In the United States, the Federal Reserve (central bank) operates the Fedwire payment system, and a private sector organization called

Table 2.1
Volumes and Values of Noncash Payments in the United States in 1999
Source: Adapted from [10].

Payment Instrument	Transaction Volume	Transaction Value	Average Value
Check	71%	10%	$1,179
Credit/Debit Card	25%	0.1%	$59
Credit Transfer (ACH)	2%	1%	$2,845
Debit Transfer (ACH)	0.5%	1%	$1,583
Wire Transfer	0.1%	86%	$4,325,605

the Clearing House Interbank Payment System (CHIPS) is also in operation. Typically, these systems handle payments between corporations and banks and to and from government. In 1998, the average wire transfer payment was worth $4.3 million. As Table 2.1 shows, while wire transfers do not register in terms of the proportion of transactions that take place, they account for 86% of the value transferred.

2.3 Using payment cards

The idea of payment using cards first arose in 1915, when a small number of U.S. hotels and department stores began to issue what were then referred to as "shoppers plates" [11]. It was not until 1947 that the Flatbush National Bank issued cards to its local customers. This was followed in 1950 by the Diners Club, which was the first "travel & entertainment" or charge card, and eight years later the American Express card was born.

Over the years, many card companies have started up and failed, but two major card companies, made up of large numbers of member banks, have come to dominate this worldwide business. These are Visa International and MasterCard.

Credit cards are designed to cater for payments in the retail situation. This means that payments can only be made from a cardholder to a merchant who has preregistered to accept payments using the card. The card companies themselves do not deal with cardholders or merchants, but rather license member organizations (usually banks) to do this for them.

A bank that issues cards to its customers is called a card-issuing bank. This means that it registers the cardholder, produces a card incorporating the card association's logo, and operates a card account to which payments can be charged.

Merchants who wish to accept payments must also register with a bank. In this case, the bank is referred to as the *acquiring bank,* or simply the acquirer. In a paper-based credit card payment, a merchant prepares a sales voucher containing the payer's card number, the amount of the payment, the date, and a goods description. Depending on policy, the transaction may need to be authorized. This will involve contacting an authorization center operated by or on behalf of the acquiring bank to see if the payment can go ahead. This may simply involve verifying that the card does not appear in a blacklist of cards, or it may involve a reference to the card-issuing bank to ensure that funds are available to meet the payment. Assuming it can be authorized, the payment completes.

At the end of the day, the merchant will bring the sales vouchers to the acquiring bank, which will clear them using a clearing system not unlike that used for paper checks and giros but operated by or on behalf of the card associations. The merchant's account is credited, the card-holder's is debited, and the transaction details will appear on the next monthly statement.

In recent years, the card associations and their member banks have made great efforts to eliminate paper from credit card transactions. This has meant that sales vouchers with the cardholder's signature only come into play when a dispute arises, and most of the information flows in Figure 2.3 are entirely electronic.

All the costs associated with a credit card transaction are borne by the merchant involved. The cardholder will see only the amount of the transaction on his or her statement, but the merchant typically pays over a small percentage of the transaction value with some associated minimum charge that is divided between the acquiring bank and the card association. For this reason, credit cards are not worthwhile for transactions in which the amount is below a certain threshold (typically around $2).

The reason why a credit card is so named is that the balance owing on a cardholder's account need not necessarily be paid at the end of the monthly period. The cardholder can pay interest on the outstanding balance and use the card for credit. Other arrangements are possible; for example, if the balance must be paid in full at the end of the period, it is called a *charge card.*

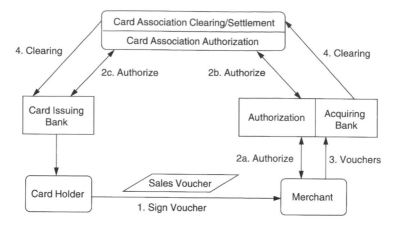

Figure 2.3 Stages in a credit card payment.

Another possibility is to link the card to a normal bank account, and to process the transaction in real time. This means that at the time the transaction takes place, the amount is transferred from the customer to the merchant bank account. This arrangement is called a *debit card*.

One final way to use a payment card is to incorporate a storage facility into the card that can be loaded with cash from the cardholder's bank account. This *electronic purse* facility will be fully discussed in Chapter 6. Bankers often classify payment cards into three types: pay before (electronic purse), pay now (debit cards), and pay later (credit cards).

2.4 Consumer preferences in payment systems

The sections above have described most methods commonly used to effect payment today. The degree to which they are used differs between countries for a variety of reasons including the level of development of the country and the state of the banking system.

Consumers in all countries use cash for somewhere between 70% and 80% of all of their transactions. Table 2.2 shows how the remaining 20% to 30% of transactions are made for a selection of countries. It can be seen that, of the developed countries, the United States is unusual in that checks are the most popular form of noncash payment with very little use of credit or debit transfers. The picture in Europe shows considerably less check usage with a more even spread of payment options.

Table 2.2
Consumer Preferences in Noncash Payment Methods by Country in 1998
Source: Adapted from [10].

Country	Use of Checks	Use of Credit Transfers (Giros)	Payment Cards	Direct Debits
United States	70%	3.7%	24.3%	2.0%
The Netherlands	1.9%	45.0%	24.5%	28.5%
United Kingdom	28%	19.3%	33.1%	19.4%
Germany	4.8%	50.6%	5.1%	39.5%
Turkey (1997 figures)	6.9%	2.6%	83.9%	—
Namibia (1996 figures)	75%	14%	Not provided by national banks	9%

Turkey, whose financial systems are perhaps less developed than the United States or European countries, shows an unusually high usage of payment cards, while the national banks in Namibia, at least during 1996, were not offering payment cards to their customers at all.

This represents the starting position before the electronic payment methods discussed in this book are introduced. All other things being equal, one would expect that an electronic payment method that was check-like would be popular in the United States, but may not have the same appeal in European countries. It would also be unlikely that an electronic payment scheme based on credit cards would find a ready market in Namibia. Of course, the market share of network payment methods may depart radically from the above in the event of one electronic payment scheme being immensely superior to others.

2.5 Regulatory framework

Payment systems are crucial to the efficient functioning of any economy, and consequently governments are keen to exert some control and regulation over how these systems operate. Conventional payment instruments have, in the past at least, been operated by banks that are subject to regulation by their national central bank. Typically, a bank must be licensed to operate, and in the course of obtaining this license will subject itself to scrutiny. This will include a test to ensure that the individuals representing the bank are "fit and proper" individuals, that the bank has a minimum level of capital, and that it meets the needs of some section of the community. These tests are mainly aimed at ensuring that consumers are protected from the consequences of bank failure. Indeed, in many countries banks are required to take out insurance to cover such an eventuality.

All conventional payment methods involving banks have been the subject of central bank regulation in the past. The newer electronic payment methods described in this book have only just started to attract the scrutiny of the central bank regulators. Many of the newer methods of payment are, to a certain extent, electronic extensions of existing bank-operated payment methods and thus can be covered by minor adjustments to existing regulations. For example, in the United States, the Electronic Funds Transfer Act of 1980 as implemented by the Federal Reserve Regulation E covers a variety of banking transactions including electronic bill payment, payment at the point of sale, and many others. It limits consumers' liability for unauthorized electronic withdrawals, provides procedures for resolving errors, and requires institutions to provide terminal receipts and account statements. This represents a good starting point for regulating any form of electronic payment.

The payment method that has caused most concern is the preloaded stored-value card. In Europe, a working group consisting of representatives of central banks from all countries in the European Union convened in 1993 and produced a report [12] detailing what changes in policy would be required to cope with the electronic purse. Their concerns would apply equally to any of the electronic cash schemes described later in this book. They distinguished between single-purpose electronic purses (e.g., cards for pay phones or public transport) and multipurpose cards. In the case of the latter, they recommended that only *credit institutions* (meaning financial institutions that are already subject to central bank regulation) should be allowed to issue such cards. It further suggested that central banks may wish to discourage some electronic purse initiatives if they were worried about the adequacy of the security features of the scheme. A more recent study [13] undertaken by the Bank for International Settlements reviewed the issues raised by electronic money but stopped short of making any definite recommendations.

In the United States, the policy on the new forms of payment has been to adopt a "wait-and-see" attitude. A landmark speech by Alan Blinder, a vice chairman of the Federal Reserve Board of Governors [14], in 1995 stated as follows: "The present is, we believe, an appropriate time for public debate and discussion, a poor time for regulation and legislation."

Another area where concern could be expected is in the area of monetary policy. If the government is the only issuer of cash in an economy, it can keep a tight rein on the amount of cash in circulation. Operators of stored-value cards or other electronic cash systems could, in principle, affect this balance, decreasing the amount of control a government can exert. This possibility is dismissed [15] by the U.S. Federal Reserve members who believe that the impact of electronic payment systems on the money supply will be insignificant in the short to medium term.

There are, of course many other issues relating to electronic payment that governments may wish to regulate. These include the question of the levying of taxes on transactions that take place electronically, protection against money laundering, and many others. It seems that both in Europe and the United States, the authorities have only begun to consider the issues involved.

References

[1]   Federal Reserve Bank of New York, *Fedpoint 1: How Currency Gets into Circulation*, 2000, http://www.ny.frb.org/pihome/fedpoint/fed01.html.

[2]   Miller, R., and D. VanHoose, *Modern Money and Banking*, 3rd ed., New York: McGraw-Hill International, 1993.

[3]   Association for Payment Clearing Services (APACS), *Yearbook of Payment Statistics*, London, APACS Statistical Unit, 2000.

[4]   O'Hanlon, J., *Financial EDI—Closing the Loop*, London, Banking Technology Ltd., April 1993.

[5]   National Automated Clearing House Association, "ACH Statistics Sheet: 1989–2000," http://www.nacha.org/news/Stats/stats.html.

[6]   Bank for International Settlements, "Clearing and Settlement Arrangements for Retail Payments in Selected Countries," Basel, Switzerland, September 2000, http://www.bis.org/publ.

[7] European Central Bank, "Welcome to the World of TARGET," August 2000, http://www.ecb.int.

[8] European Banking Association, "Straight Through Euro Payment System —Impact Document for STEP1 Banks," Version 0.3, June 2000, http://www.abe.org.

[9] NACHA Cross-Border Council Global ACH Working Group, "Concept Paper for a Global Automated Clearing House," Version 1.4, May 1999, http://www.globalach.org.

[10] Bank for International Settlements, "Statistics on Payment Systems in the Group of Ten Countries," Basel, Switzerland, February 2000, http://www.bis.org/publ.

[11] Members of the Bankers Clearing House, *Payment Clearing Systems: Review of Organisation, Membership and Control*, London, Banking Information Service, 1984.

[12] *Report of the Working Group on EU Payment Systems*, European Monetary Institute, Frankfurt, 1993.

[13] Bank for International Settlements, "Implications for Central Banks of the Development of Electronic Money," Basel, Switzerland, October 1996, http://www.bis.org/publ/bisp01.pdf.

[14] Blinder, A., *Statement by Vice Chairman of the Board of Governors of the Federal Reserve System before the Subcommittee on Domestic and International Monetary Policy, U.S. House of Representatives*, October 1995.

[15] Kelley, E., *Remarks by Edward W. Kelley, Jr., Member of the Board of Governors of the Federal Reserve System at the CyberPayments '96 Conference*, Dallas, TX, June 18, 1996, http://woodrow.mpls.frb.fed.us/info/sys/people.html.

CHAPTER

3

Contents

Cryptographic techniques

The payment systems outlined in the previous chapter rely on a number of different mechanisms for establishing the *identity* and *intent* of the various parties involved in a payment-related transaction. The most often-used method is the application of a human signature to a document that will serve as the legal basis for the transaction. The identity of the signer can be confirmed by comparison with a stored sample signature or, in case of subsequent dispute, a handwriting expert may later testify to its authenticity.

The essential elements of these mechanisms can be replicated across computer networks through the use of cryptographic techniques. In addition, cryptography is useful in protecting against a wide variety of other attacks on the communications between two parties. In this chapter we will give a basic introduction to the essential cryptographic techniques necessary to understand how electronic payment systems function. Readers who are already familiar with this material may skip ahead to Chapter 4 and refer back as required.

3.1 Encryption and decryption

A message in human readable form is referred to in cryptographic terms as *plaintext* or *cleartext*. The process of disguising a message in such a way as to hide its substance is called *encryption* and the resulting message is referred to as *ciphertext*. As Figure 3.1 shows, the reverse process (*decryption*) takes ciphertext as input and restores the original plaintext.

Plaintext is denoted by P, whereas ciphertext is denoted by C. The encryption function E operates on P to produce C:

$$E(P) = C$$

In the reverse process, the decryption function D operates on C to produce P:

$$D(C) = P$$

A cryptographic algorithm, also called a *cipher*, is a mathematical function used for encryption and decryption. A restricted cryptosystem requires the encryption and decryption algorithms to be kept secret. This method is called *security by obscurity* and should be used only in very specific cases. All modern encryption algorithms use a *key*, denoted by K. The value of this key affects the encryption and decryption functions, so that they can now be written as:

$$E(K, P) \; 5 \; C$$

$$D(K, C) \; 5 \; P$$

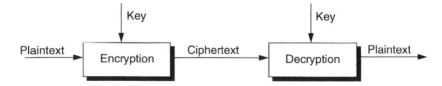

Figure 3.1 Encryption and decryption using a key.

The algorithms can now be made available for public scrutiny. This is the default case with the majority of cryptosystems.

Historically, the primary purpose of cryptography has been to keep the plaintext hidden from adversaries. *Cryptanalysis* is the science of recovering the plaintext message without knowledge of the key. One can categorize attacks on a cryptosystem as being of a number of different forms:

1. *Ciphertext-only attack:* In this attack, the cryptanalyst has the cipher-text of several messages, all of which have been encrypted using the same encryption key. From this the cryptanalyst attempts to derive either the plaintext or the key.

2. *Known-plaintext attack:* The cryptanalyst has access not only to the ciphertext of several messages but also to the corresponding plain-text. From this he or she may be able to derive the key used for encrypting the messages.

3. *Chosen-plaintext attack:* The cryptanalyst has access to the ciphertext and associated plaintext for several messages and he or she can gain access to ciphertext corresponding to plaintext that he or she has chosen. These blocks could be chosen to yield more information about the key or to pursue a particular line of attack.

Any cryptosystem may be *broken* by the "brute force" method, which simply involves testing all possible key values until the correct one is found. In practice this depends on the particular algorithm in question and the available computational resources. With rapid increases in computer processing power, coupled with the development of special purpose encryption hardware, this form of attack deserves more attention than it has merited in the past. This theme will be explored further in later sections.

3.2 Symmetric encryption

As the name suggests, symmetric encryption implies that both parties to a communication must first possess a copy of a single secret key, as shown in Figure 3.2. The most widely used algorithm in this category was, until recently, the Data Encryption Standard (DES).

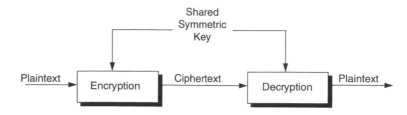

Figure 3.2   Operation of a symmetric cryptosystem.

3.2.1 Data Encryption Standard (DES)

In January 1977, a standard encryption method called the Data Encryption Standard [1, 2] was adopted by the U.S. government. Its origins lay in an internal IBM project to develop an algorithm codenamed *Lucifer* that could not be broken, even by the fastest machines available at the time. The terms of the Federal Information Processing Standard (FIPS) under which it was adopted were that it should be used for sensitive, but not classified, information. Though the algorithm used is complex, it is easily implemented in hardware, and software implementations are widely available. The American National Standards Institute (ANSI) approved DES as an industry standard [3], calling it the Data Encryption Algorithm (DEA).

3.2.1.1 Algorithm

DES is a *block cipher*. This means that it operates on a single chunk of data at a time, encrypting 64 bits (8 bytes) of plaintext to produce 64 bits of ciphertext. The key length is 56 bits, often expressed as an eight-character string with the extra bits used as a parity check. The algorithm has 19 distinct stages. The first stage reorders the bits of the 64-bit input block by applying a fixed permutation. The last stage is the exact inverse of this permutation. The stage penultimate to the last one exchanges the leftmost 32 bits with the rightmost 32 bits. The remaining 16 stages (called *rounds*) are functionally identical but take as an input a quantity computed from the key K_i and the old right half R_i, where i is the current round number. K_i is derived from the original 56-bit key passed as input to the algorithm. Figure 3.3 shows the overall process.

At each iteration, the algorithm takes in two 32-bit inputs and produces two 32-bit outputs. The left output is simply a copy of the right input. The right output is an exclusive OR (XOR) of the left input and a function of the right input and the key for the stage K_i. All the complexity lies in the function *f*, which does a number of substitutions and permutations using simple hardware elements called S-boxes (for substitution) and P-boxes (for permutation). Decryption in the DES algorithm uses the same sequence of steps, but the keys used at each of the 16 stages (K_1 to K_{16}) are applied in reverse order.

In addition to the fundamental DES algorithm, the standards [4] specify a number of different modes of operation. These include electronic codebook, cipher block chaining, output feedback, and cipher feedback. The electronic codebook mode is that outlined in Figure 3.3 and is the most widely used (because of its simplicity), but it is also the most vulnerable to attack. We shall briefly discuss the cipher feedback mode.

3.2.1.2 DES cipher feedback (CFB) mode
Another way to make cryptanalysis of DES much harder is to operate it as a so-called *stream cipher*. Stream ciphers treat the plaintext as a continuous stream of information, where the ciphertext produced depends on

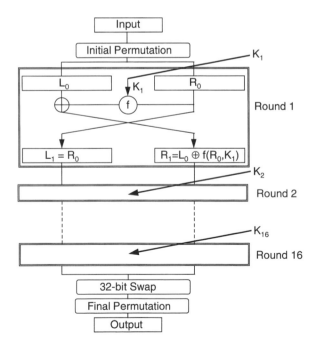

Figure 3.3 The DES algorithm.

the entire history of the stream. When using stream cipher mode, both sender and receiver operate their DES chips in encryption mode. Figure 3.4 shows this process in action. Each DES chip has a 64-bit input register, which operates as a shift register, and a 64-bit output register, which does not. Both parties must start off with identical contents in their input registers. When a plaintext character arrives, it is XORed with 8 bits of output register O_1. The ciphertext thus created is both transmitted to the receiver and shifted into the input register, pushing I_8 off the end. The chip is then activated and the output computed for the new input.

At the receiving end, the incoming character is first XORed with O_1. This will reverse the effect of the XOR operation applied by the sender, yielding the plaintext. The arriving ciphertext is simultaneously shifted into I_1 so that the input registers at both ends of the link are synchronized. If the sender and receiver start out with identical registers, they should remain identical forever.

3.2.1.3 Cracking DES and U.S. export restrictions

All encryption algorithms can theoretically be broken using the so-called "brute-force" attack. This form of attack involves simply applying every possible key until the correct one is found. When DES was first conceived, the idea of breaking a cipher by making 2^{56} attempts was not considered practical, but machines have become considerably faster since then, and the availability of even greater computing power can be expected in the future. On average a brute-force attack requires one to test 50% of the key space.

By 1996, by using application specific integrated circuits (ASICs), a single chip could be produced that was capable of testing 30 million DES

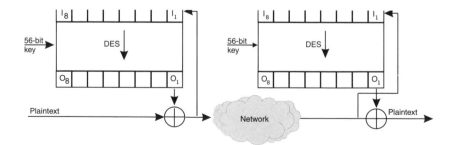

Figure 3.4 DES stream encryption.

keys per second [5]. Estimates are that a determined government agency that was willing to spend $300 million on building a massively parallel array of such chips could recover a single DES key in 12 seconds. In light of these facts, designers of cryptographic protocols need to ensure that the safety of their schemes cannot be compromised by successful brute-force attacks.

In terms of attacks other than brute force, DES has proved to be highly resilient. Using a technique known as *differential cryptanalysis,* Biham and Shamir [6] mounted an attack on 16-round DES that was somewhat more effective than a brute-force attack. A related technique known as *linear cryptanalysis* was applied by Matsui [7] to some effect. Neither attack has caused too much concern to those using the DES algorithm.

The U.S. government, mindful of the fact that cryptographic techniques can be used against the American national interest, has taken steps to ensure that crytographic products are treated in much the same way as munitions for export purposes. The International Traffic in Arms Regulations (ITAR) states that products involving cryptography must be individually licensed before they can be exported from the United States. Applicants for export licenses have found that, in general, licenses will not be granted where a software or hardware product uses strong algorithms to encrypt the message content, whereas using cryptography to assure message integrity is not a problem. Exceptions to the above are frequently made where the encrypted data is purely concerned with financial data.

In 1992, under an agreement with the American Software Publishers Association (SPA), the U.S. State Department eased the restrictions on two algorithms, RC2 and RC4 (described in Section 3.2.5), provided the key length was 40 bits or less. It was clear that this would leave products using these small keys open to brute-force attacks. In January 1996, a group of eminent cryptographers produced a report [5] that stated that 40-bit keys offer "virtually no protection" against such attacks. They went on to state that cryptosystems that expect to protect information adequately for the next 20 years should use keys that are at least 90 bits long. The U.S. government responded to this in October 1996 by permitting the export of software using 56-bit keys on the condition that the companies involved produced a plan to implement some form of key-escrow scheme that would allow government agencies to gain access to such keys in accordance with national policies. Since then, U.S. government policy has softened, and in December 2000, the key length restriction for symmetric encryption algorithms was removed completely.

3.2.2 Triple DES

Triple DES [8] is a more secure alternative to DES and is appealing in that it requires no new algorithms or hardware over and above conventional DES. Figure 3.5 shows three 56-bit DES keys being used as input to an array of three DES chips (or software blocks). The pattern used for the encryption step is encrypt-decrypt-encrypt (EDE) with a DED pattern being used to reverse the process. Using these combinations allows us to be backwardly compatible with the single version of the DES algorithm. In one variation of Triple DES, $K1$ is set to be equal to $K3$, giving a 112-bit key length. The latter mode is sometimes referred to as *2 key Triple DES*, as opposed to *3 key Triple DES* when $K1$, $K2$, and $K3$ are distinct, yielding a total key length of 168 bits.

Its greatest appeal will be for the very large number of financial institutions that have an installed base of equipment with DES hardware. However, software implementations of Triple DES are slow in comparison, as we have to compute three DES functions. Also, Triple DES uses the same 64-bit block size as DES, which is considered to be weak.

3.2.3 IDEA

Like DES, the International Data Encryption Algorithm (IDEA) is a block cipher, using secret-key symmetric encryption. It is defined in [9] and a good description is given in [10]. It was originally developed in Zurich by

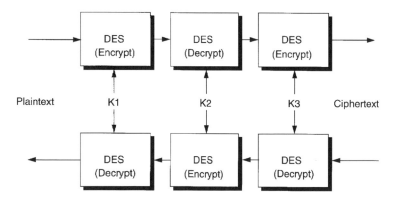

Figure 3.5 The Triple DES algorithm.

Massey and Lai in 1990 [11]. It was strengthened against Biham and Shamir's *differential cryptanalysis* attack to become IDEA in 1992.

IDEA uses a 128-bit key to operate on 64-bit plaintext blocks. The same algorithm is used for both encryption and decryption and consists of eight main iterations. It is based on the design concept of "mixing operations from different algebraic groups." The three algebraic groups whose operations are being mixed are:

▸ XOR;

▸ Addition, ignoring any overflow (addition modulo 2^{16});

▸ Multiplication, ignoring any overflow (multiplication modulo $2^{16}+1$).

As shown in Figure 3.6, these operations operate on 16-bit subblocks, making the algorithm efficient even on 16-bit processors. IDEA runs much faster in software than DES.

3.2.3.1 Cracking IDEA

IDEA's key length is 128 bits, over twice as long as DES, which means that trying out half the keys would take 2^{127} encryptions. This is such a large number that breaking IDEA by brute force is obviously out of the question.

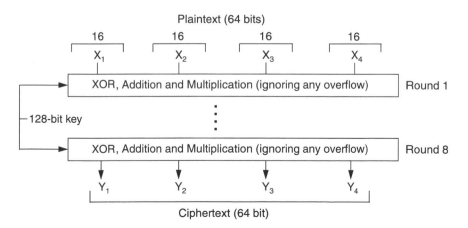

Figure 3.6 The workings of the IDEA cipher.

Biham and Shamir have been examining the IDEA cipher for weaknesses, without success. As many formidable academic and military cryptanalyst groups still attempt to attack it, confidence in IDEA is growing. To date, it appears IDEA is significantly more secure than DES. The algorithm is covered by patents in both the United States and Europe, and license fees must be paid if it is to be used commercially.

3.2.4 Advanced Encryption Standard (AES)

Recent advances in the field of cryptanalysis, combined with the continuing increases in the processing power of CPUs, have resulted in the long-term security of the DES algorithm being put into question. For some time now, the U.S. National Institute of Standards and Technology (NIST) has been looking into replacing DES with a new algorithm. The Advanced Encryption Standard (AES) will be a new FIPS that will specify a cryptographic algorithm for use by U.S. government organizations to protect sensitive (unclassified) information. NIST also anticipates that the AES will be widely used by organizations, institutions, and individuals outside the United States.

On January 2, 1997, NIST announced its intention to develop the AES and made a formal call for proposals in September 1997. The criteria set out by NIST were that AES would specify an unclassified, publicly disclosed algorithm, available royalty-free worldwide; in addition, the algorithm must be a symmetric block cipher and support block sizes of 128 bits (minimum) and key sizes of 128, 192, and 256 bits. On August 20, 1998, NIST announced a group of 15 AES candidate algorithms at the first AES Candidate Conference (AES1). NIST selected five algorithms from the original 15 submissions. The candidate algorithms were MARS, RC6, Rijndael, Serpent, and Twofish [12]. These finalist algorithms received further analysis during a second, more in-depth review period prior to the selection of the final algorithm.

3.2.4.1 Rijndael

On October 2, 2000, NIST announced that Rijndael (pronounced "rain doll") had been selected as the proposed AES. Rijndael is a symmetric block cipher with variable key and block sizes of 128, 192, and 256 bits. However, since most of the cryptanalytic study during the standards process focused on the 128-bit block size, this will be the preferred block size included in the standard. Rijndael has considerable speed improvements over DES in both hardware and software implementations.

Encryption and decryption speeds of 243 Mbps can be achieved on a 450-MHz Pentium II machine [13]. It can also be implemented efficiently in small 8-bit devices such as smart cards [14].

The cipher consists of between 10 or 14 rounds (Nr), depending on the key length (Nk) and the block length (Nb). A plaintext block X undergoes n rounds of operations to produce an output block Y. Each operation is based on the value of the nth round key. The round keys are derived from the cipher key by first expanding the key and then selecting parts of the expanded key for each round. Figure 3.7 shows an overview of the process.

3.2.4.2 The round transformations

Each round except the last is composed of four different operations. The last round is equivalent to the other rounds with the MixColumn step removed. The round operations guarantee that there are no linear relationships between the input and the output of a round. It also guarantees that there is a very small correlation between the bytes of the round input and the bytes of the output.

ByteSub: Each byte at the input of a round undergoes an S-box substitution.

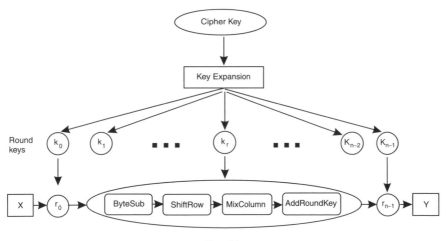

Figure 3.7 Overall structure of Rijndael cipher.

ShiftRow: Assuming a block length (Nb) of 128 bits where the individual bytes are arranged in a 4 × 4 grid, each "row" of the grid is cyclically shifted, as shown in Figure 3.8.

MixColumn: Each column is multiplied by a fixed polynomial c(x) = '03' x^3 + '01' x^2 + '01' x + '02'.

AddRoundKey: Each row is simply XOR'ed with the expanded round key.

Rijndael is a fast, state-of-the-art, and secure algorithm. It has efficient implementations in both hardware and software across a wide range of computing environments. The algorithm is currently under public review and comment. If all the steps of the AES development process proceed as planned, it is anticipated that the standard will be completed by mid-2001.

3.2.5 RC2, RC4, and RC5

In anticipation of the demise of DES, Ron Rivest, a noted cryptographer, has been developing a family of ciphers for RSA Data Security, Inc., that might be used to replace it. Unofficially, RC stands for Ron's Code, but officially it is an abbreviation of "Rivest Cipher." It appears as though RC1 never got beyond the design stage, and RC3 was broken before it was released. RC2, however, was released and is used in a number of commercial products. It is a 64-bit block cipher with a variable-length key. RC4 can also use a variable-length key, but operates as a stream cipher. A commodity export license was obtained for 40-bit versions of RC2 and RC4, and the latter was used as the stream cipher in the first secure Web browsers that became available in 1995. No patents have been applied for, and the details of the algorithms are only available subject to a non-disclosure agreement with RSA Data Security, Inc. In September 1994,

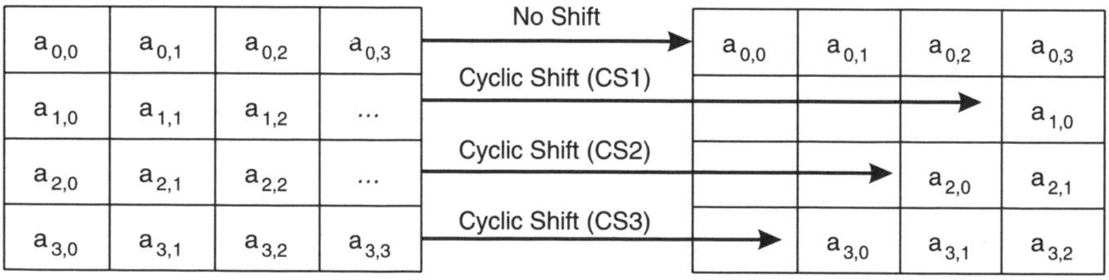

$a_{0,0}$	$a_{0,1}$	$a_{0,2}$	$a_{0,3}$	No Shift	$a_{0,0}$	$a_{0,1}$	$a_{0,2}$	$a_{0,3}$
$a_{1,0}$	$a_{1,1}$	$a_{1,2}$	...	Cyclic Shift (CS1)				$a_{1,0}$
$a_{2,0}$	$a_{2,1}$	$a_{2,2}$	...	Cyclic Shift (CS2)			$a_{2,0}$	$a_{2,1}$
$a_{3,0}$	$a_{3,1}$	$a_{3,2}$	$a_{3,3}$	Cyclic Shift (CS3)		$a_{3,0}$	$a_{3,1}$	$a_{3,2}$

Figure 3.8 ShiftRow transformation.

however, code to implement RC4 was posted to a network newsgroup and implementations can now be easily obtained. This knowledge was used in 1995 [15] to mount a successful brute-force attack against a single ciphertext message encrypted with 40-bit RC4.

The penultimate algorithm in the series is RC5 [16], which is a totally parameterized system. Among the items that may be changed are the block size, the key length, and the number of rounds. The basic algorithm is a block cipher, but stream versions [17] are also defined. The details of this algorithm have been published, the name RC5 has been trade-marked, and patents have been granted.

3.2.5.1 RC6

RC6 is the most recent block cipher designed by Ronald Rivest et al. [18] and was among the five finalist candidate algorithms for the AES. The main goal for the inventors was to meet the requirements for the AES. RC6 is based on RC5 [19] and, like RC5, it is a parameterized algorithm in which the block size, key size, and number of rounds are variable. The upper limit to the key size for RC6 is 2,040 bits.

RC6 is more accurately specified as RC6-$w/r/b$ where the word size is w bits. Encryption consists of a non-negative number of rounds r, and b denotes the length of the encryption key in bytes. Since RC6 is targeted for the AES, $w = 32$ and $r = 20$ are the default values in that context. The algorithm operates on blocks of four w-bit words using the following six basic operations. The base-two logarithm of w is denoted by $lg\ w$. For $w = 32$ bits, this equates to 5.

a + b	integer addition modulo 2^w;
a − b	integer subtraction modulo 2^w;
a ⊕ b	bitwise exclusive-or of w-bit words;
a * b	integer multiplication modulo 2^w;
a <<< b	rotate the w-bit word a to the left by the amount given by the least significant $lg\ w$ bits of b;
a >>> b	rotate the w-bit word a to the right by the amount given by the least significant $lg\ w$ bits of b.

The user supplies a key of b bytes, where $0 \le b \le 255$. From this key, $2r + 4$ words (w bits each) are derived and stored in an array $K[0, ...,$

$2r + 3$]. This array is used in both the encryption and decryption processes.

3.2.5.2 Encryption and decryption

RC6 works with four w-bit registers, W, X, Y, Z, which contain the initial input plaintext as well as the output ciphertext at the end of the encryption process. Figure 3.9 shows the overall process of encryption.

At the beginning and end of the r rounds, prewhitening and post-whitening steps are performed. Without these steps, the plaintext reveals part of the input to the first round of the encryption, and the ciphertext reveals part of the input to the last round of the encryption. Instead of using X and Z directly, transformed versions of these registers are used during the integer multiplication step. This ensures that the rotation amount derived from the output of this transformation depends on all the bits of the input and provides good mixing within the word.

A bitwise XOR transformation based on a function $f(x) = x(2x + 1)$ (mod 2^w) followed by a left rotation by 5-bit positions is performed.

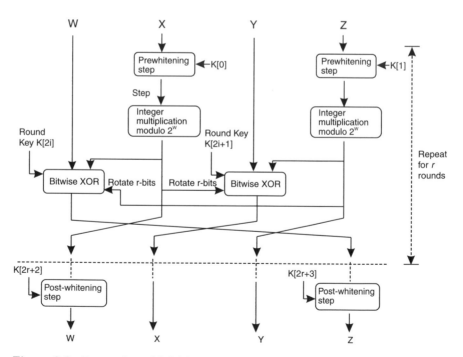

Figure 3.9 Encryption with RC6.

Finally, a permutation of the registers $(W, X, Y, Z) = (X, Y, Z, W)$ is performed, so that the WX computation is mixed with the YZ computation. Similarly there is a corresponding decryption function. RC6 is a secure, compact, and simple block cipher. It offers good performance on a variety of hardware platforms. On a 450-MHz Pentium II machine, one can get speeds of 258 Mbps for encryption [13].

3.3 Message digesting or hashing

When the symmetric algorithms in Section 3.2 are applied to a message, they provide two main services. First, the message contents are kept confidential from eavesdroppers, who cannot unscramble the encrypted message, and second, the integrity of the message is assured. This can be guaranteed since no alteration can be made to the message unless one is in possession of the key.

In many cases, a check on the message integrity is all that is required, and time spent in providing message confidentiality is wasted. In many business applications, users are not concerned with attackers eavesdropping on the message, but would be very worried if their contents could be altered in transit. Export restrictions applied by the U.S. government are primarily concerned with the ability of law enforcement agencies to intercept the contents of messages. If a system uses encryption strictly for message integrity checks only, then exportability is assured.

One way to provide integrity without confidentiality is to use a technique known as a message digest. This involves applying a digesting or *one-way* hash function to the (long) message to produce a (short) message digest. The secret key can be applied to this hash and the result sent with the message across the network. Figure 3.10 shows how the hashing algorithm is first applied to the complete message. The hash is then encrypted to become a message authentication code (MAC), which is appended to the message before transmission. Since the encryption is only being applied to a very small quantity, and message digesting is faster than, encryption, this process can be considerably faster than encrypting the entire message.

When the message arrives, the receiver computes a hash of the message using the same algorithm. If this matches the decrypted MAC that came with the message, then the message has not been tampered with.

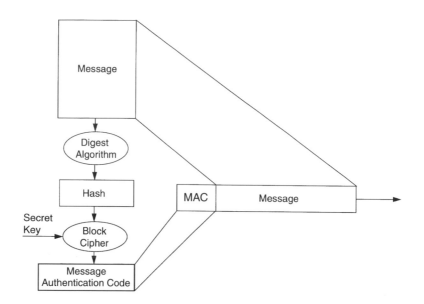

Figure 3.10 Computing a message authentication code (MAC).

A good one-way hash function will have two properties. First, it will be difficult to invert. This means that attempting to produce a message that would yield a given hash should be completely unfeasible. It should also be resistant to collision, which means that there should be a low probability of finding two messages with the same hash.

Two well-known hash functions that have found a place in payment protocols are MD5 and SHA.

3.3.1 MD5

The MD5 algorithm [20] is one of a series (including MD2 and MD4) of message digest algorithms developed by Ron Rivest. It involves appending a length field to a message and padding it up to a multiple of 512-bit blocks. Each of these 512-bit blocks is then fed through a four-round process involving rotation and a range of Boolean operations producing a chaining value that is input into the processing of the next 512-bit block. The hashed output is the 128-bit chaining value produced in processing the last block of the message.

3.3.2 The Secure Hash Algorithm (SHA)

NIST released a series of cryptographic standards in 1993, one of which [21] specified the secure hash algorithm. It is based quite heavily on the work of Ron Rivest in the MD series of algorithms. The message is first padded as with MD5, and then fed through four rounds, which are more complex than those used in MD5. The chaining value passed from one round to the next is 160 bits in length, which means that the resulting message digest is also 160 bits.

3.4 Kerberos

Using just the symmetric encryption algorithms outlined in Section 3.2 together with message digest algorithms, some quite sophisticated security protocols can be devised. One such protocol is Kerberos, which provides message authentication and confidentiality facilities for communicating parties and is used as the basis for a number of payment systems outlined in later chapters. It is based on the trusted third-party model presented by Needham and Schroeder [22]. The Kerberos authentication service was developed at the Massachusetts Institute of Technology (MIT) for Project Athena and the following discussion is based on version 5 of the protocol [23]. Kerberos allows a client to prove its identity to a third-party server without sending any sensitive information across the network and also encrypts the channel between the two. This section presents an overview of the protocol from the payment systems point of view.

3.4.1 Overview of the Kerberos model

Network services that require authentication are required to register with Kerberos, as are the clients that wish to use those services. The Kerberos model consists of a Kerberos server (A), which securely stores the keys of each principal on the network. These shared keys are symmetric keys that are established out-of-band and have a long lifetime. The model is also responsible for generating session keys that are used to exchange messages between two principals with a lifetime limited to the duration of a single communication session.

Two types of credentials are used in Kerberos: *tickets* and *authenticators*. A ticket is used to authenticate a client (C) to a server (S) when used in conjunction with an authenticator. A ticket consists of two parts, one encrypted and the other in plaintext. A Kerberos ticket has the form:

$$T_{CS} = [S, [C, \text{Addr}, N, \text{Validity}, K_{CS}]K_S]$$

A ticket contains:

> The name of the server (S) in plaintext;

> The name of the client (C);

> The network address of the client (Addr);

> A timestamp in the form of a nonce (N) to prevent replays;

> The period of validity of the ticket;

> A session key (K_{CS}) that will be used to secure dialogues between the client and the server.

A ticket is only valid for a single server and a single client. The secret part of the ticket is encrypted with the key of the server (K_S) for which the ticket is issued. Once a ticket has been issued, it may be used multiple times by the named client to gain access to the named server until the ticket expires.

An authenticator is generated by a client and contains client-specific information that is encrypted with the session key (K_{CS}). In comparing the authenticator fields with the corresponding ticket, it proves beyond doubt that the client presenting the ticket is the same one to whom the ticket was issued. An authenticator has the form:

$$\text{Auth}_C = \{C, \text{Addr}, \text{Timestamp}\}\, K_{CS}$$

It contains:

> The name of client (C);

> The network address of the client (Addr);

> A timestamp in the form of a nonce to prevent replays.

The authenticator proves that the client has knowledge of the session key (K_{CS}) included in the ticket.

Figure 3.11 shows an overview of the Kerberos authentication protocol. A client initiates the protocol by requesting the Kerberos server (A) to generate a ticket for a specific server (S). The Kerberos server responds by returning a ticket encrypted with the key of the server. The client presents this ticket to the server along with an authenticator. Assuming that

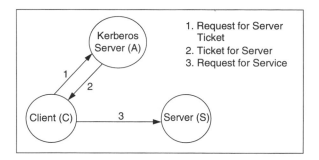

Figure 3.11 Overview of the Kerberos authentication protocol.

each of the above steps is successful, the client will gain access to the service.

3.4.2 Obtaining a ticket

When a user requires a service, he or she sends a request (see Figure 3.12) to the Kerberos server requesting it to grant the user a ticket for a server. The user sends an identity (C), the name of the server (S) for whom the ticket is required, and a nonce (N).

The Kerberos server checks that it knows about the identity of the client and generates a session key (K_{CS}) and another nonce. It encrypts these two fields with the *secret key* (K_C) of the user, which it obtains from its secure database.

It then creates a ticket for the end-server (T_{CS}) that includes the session key (K_{CS}). The contents of the ticket are encrypted using the shared key of the end-server (K_S) that the Kerberos server obtains from its secure database. The Kerberos server sends the ticket along with an encrypted copy of the session key back to the client. Once the response has been received by the client, the client uses his or her key (K_C) to decrypt it.

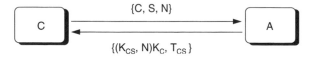

Figure 3.12 Request for ticket.

3.4.3 Service request

Once the client has obtained a ticket for a specific service, the client builds an authenticator containing the name of the client, the network address of the client, and a timestamp. The authenticator is encrypted with the session key (K_{CS}) obtained as part of the procedure in Section 3.4.2.

As Figure 3.13 shows, the client sends the encrypted authenticator and the service ticket to the server. The server decrypts the ticket using its key (K_S) and recovers the session key (K_{CS}). It then decrypts the authenticator (Auth$_C$) and matches the fields contained within the authenticator to that in the ticket (T_{CS}). If all the fields match, then the server allows the request to proceed. Optionally, a client can request a server to verify its identity. The server adds one to the timestamp sent by the client in the authenticator, encrypts the result with the session key (K_{CS}), and returns it to the client.

3.5 Asymmetric or public-key encryption

The greatest problem with the use of symmetric cryptosystems is that before any communication can occur, both parties must somehow acquire a shared, common key. For closed applications (e.g., within a single company), this problem can be addressed using protocols such as Kerberos or by employing human couriers to distribute the keys. A special *key distribution key* may also be employed, which is used only to distribute new values for the more frequently used working key.

The problem is much more severe in an open network, where parties that have never before had any kind of relationship may wish to enter into a spontaneous communication. A good example of this is when a user wishes to buy goods across a network from a merchant to whom the user is completely unknown.

Public-key cryptography was first proposed in 1976 by Whitfield Diffie and Martin Hellman [24] in order to solve the key management problem highlighted above. In public-key cryptography, each person gets a

Figure 3.13 Service request.

pair of keys, called the *public key* and the *secret key*. The public key is published and widely distributed, while the secret key is never revealed. The need for exchanging secret keys is eliminated as all communications only involve public keys. No secret key is ever transmitted or shared.

Thus, when user Alice wishes to send an encrypted message to Bob, she looks up Bob's public key (PK_B) in a public directory or obtains it by some other means, uses it to encrypt the message, and sends it off to Bob (see Figure 3.14). Bob then uses his secret key (SK_B) to decrypt the message. Anyone who has access to Bob's public key can send him an encrypted message, but no one else apart from Bob can decrypt it.

3.5.1 Properties of a public-key cryptosystem
Assume that PK is the encryption key and that SK is the decryption key. A public-key cryptosystem will have the following general properties:

1. Encipherment (applying the algorithm with the encryption key) followed by decipherment of a message M results in M:

$$SK\,(PK\,(M)) = M$$

2. Given PK and SK, it is easy to perform encryption and decryption, respectively.

3. By publicly revealing PK, the user does not reveal an easy way to compute SK.

A function satisfying properties (1) to (3) above is known as a "trapdoor one-way function" and fulfills the basic criteria for public-key cryptosystems. In addition, some systems can operate in reverse where a message M is first deciphered and then subsequently enciphered, producing the original M as the result:

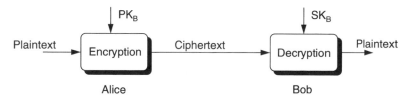

Figure 3.14 Public-key cryptosystem.

$$PK \ (SK \ (M)) = M$$

This is known as a "trapdoor one-way permutation" and can be used to implement *digital signatures*. This process will be described below.

3.5.2 Trapdoor one-way functions

The notion of *one-way functions* is central to public-key cryptography. A one-way function is a function that is relatively easy to compute in one direction, but (apparently) very difficult to compute in the other direction. As they stand, they are not of much use for encryption purposes since it would be impossible to decrypt the resulting ciphertext. For encryption, we need something called a *trapdoor one-way function*. They are called "trapdoor" functions, since the inverse function is easy to compute once certain private trapdoor information is known.

3.5.3 Using public-key cryptosystems for authentication

Authentication is the process whereby the receiver of a digital message can be confident of the identity of the sender. If Bob receives a message that purports to come from Alice, he may like to have some means of proving the message's authenticity (i.e., a check that the message was indeed sent by Alice).

One way to achieve this is for Alice to apply her secret key (SK_{Alice}) to the message before it is sent. The resulting ciphertext can be read by anyone (including Bob) by simply obtaining and applying Alice's public key, but the only person capable of producing it is the person who possesses Alice's secret key (i.e., Alice).

3.6 Digital signatures and enveloping

These examples have shown how public-key systems can be used for two purposes: encrypting a message with the recipient's public key to achieve confidentiality, or encrypting a message with the sender's secret key to achieve message authentication. Both of these involve applying the public-key algorithm to the entire message. The public-key algorithms in use today are computation-intensive, and with large messages they may be too expensive or too slow for the application, but alternative solutions are available.

If message authentication is the focus of attention, a simple way to achieve this is to compute a message digest using an algorithm such as MD5 or SHA, and apply the sender's secret key to this. The resulting quantity can be thought of as a digital signature and be appended to the message before it is transmitted.

Figure 3.15 shows this process. At the destination, the receiver uses the same hashing algorithm to produce a message digest, and using the sender's public key verifies that the computed digest matches the decrypted signature. In the case of a match, the receiver can be assured that the message emanated from the purported sender and that it was not been altered in transit.

If message confidentiality is what is required, then the message can be *enveloped*. To achieve this, the sender can invent a key at random and use this message key in conjunction with a (fast) symmetric encryption algorithm to encrypt the message. As shown in Figure 3.16, this will protect the message from eavesdroppers. In order to transport this message key to the recipient, it is encrypted with the recipient's public key and included with the message that is transmitted.

When the message arrives, the recipient uses his or her secret key to unlock the content encryption key, thus allowing him or her access to the message in plaintext.

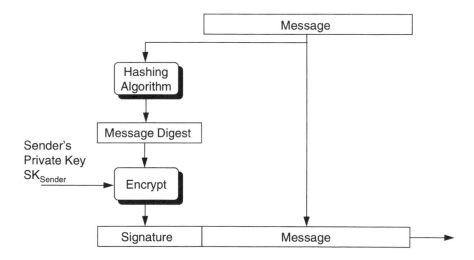

Figure 3.15 Appending a digital signature to a message before transmission.

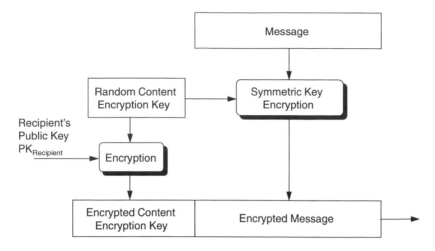

Figure 3.16   Enveloping a message for a recipient.

3.7   RSA

The de facto standard algorithm for implementing public-key cryptography can be used for both encryption and authentication and is called the RSA algorithm. It is named after its inventors, Rivest, Shamir, and Adleman [25], who developed it in 1978 while working at MIT. Its security is based on the difficulty of factoring very large numbers. The basic algorithm is outlined next. First, the public and matching secret key must be generated. This is done in the following manner:

1.   Choose two large distinct primes, p and q;

2.   Compute the product (modulus) $n = p * q$;

3.   Compute Euler's totient function $\Phi(n) = (p - 1) * (q - 1)$;

4.   Randomly choose an encryption key e, such that e and $\Phi(n)$ are relatively prime.

     Two numbers are relatively prime when they share no factors in common other than 1 (i.e., gcd $(e, \Phi(n)) = 1$);

5.   Finally, calculate the decryption key d, the multiplicative inverse of e mod $\Phi(n)$ such that

$$d = e^{-1} \bmod \Phi(n)$$

$$d = e^{-1} \bmod (p - 1) * (q - 1)$$

Note that d and n are also relatively prime. The numbers e and n are the public key. The number d is the secret key. The two primes p and q are never needed again. They should be discarded and never revealed.

To encrypt a message M, we first break the message into a series of blocks and represent each block as an integer. The block size is chosen to ensure that this integer will be smaller than n. We then raise it to the power of e modulo n:

$$C = M^e \bmod n$$

To decrypt the resulting ciphertext C, we raise to another power d modulo n:

$$M = C^d \bmod n$$

Thus with RSA, each owner of a key pair holds d secret, and issues e and n as his or her public key. The owner does not need to know about p and q, although knowledge of these factors may be used to speed up calculations. The security of RSA depends on the problem of factoring large numbers. For RSA this entails factoring the modulus n into its prime factors p and q. Substituting these values into the equation $d = e^{-1} \bmod (p - 1) * (q - 1)$ will result in the decryption key. As an example, for a human to factor the number 29,083 by hand would take perhaps an hour, but confirming that the factors are indeed 127 and 229 takes only about a minute. The disparity between the effort required to compute the factors and that required to confirm them gets wider as the size of the numbers is increased. Another method to attack the cipher would be to mount a brute-force attack by trying all possible values of d. This is more inefficient than factorizing the modulus n.

The size of key used in RSA is completely variable, but for normal use a key size of 1,024 bits is typically used. In applications where key compromise would have very serious consequences or where the security must remain valid for many years into the future, key lengths of 2,048 bits are used. Note that performing exponentiation with numbers of this size is expensive in terms of computing resources. A typical software implementation of a symmetric encryption algorithm (e.g., DES) would be around 100 times faster than RSA, while hardware implementations would be between 1,000 to 10,000 times as fast.

3.8 Elliptic curve cryptography

In 1985, Victor Miller [26] and Neil Koblitz [27] independently proposed the use of elliptic curves for use in public-key algorithms. The elliptic curve cryptosystem (ECC) is an analog of existing public-key cryptosystems in which the security of the system depends on the *discrete logarithm problem* over points on an elliptic curve. An elliptic curve is a member of a class of mathematical functions similar to those used to calculate the circumference of an ellipse. Given two points G and Y on an elliptic curve such that $Y = k.G$ (i.e., the operator represents multiplication or repeated addition over an elliptic curve—thus Y is G added to itself k times over an elliptic curve) it is easy to calculate Y given k and G. However, deducing k given Y and G is very difficult. This form of addition constitutes a one-way function.

Choosing an appropriate elliptic curve and selecting appropriate points on the curve are complex problems. However, once this has been done, the resulting curve parameters may be used for multiple users within a group. Each user has a public-key pair where k is the private key and $k.G$ is the public-key component that can be published widely. Current known methods for computing elliptic curve logarithms are much less efficient than those for factoring integers or computing conventional logarithms. As a result, shorter key sizes can be used to achieve the same level of security as that of public-key cryptosystems [28]. Other associated advantages are that applications can compute signatures faster than before and that they occupy less space.

In recent years more people have begun to show an interest in elliptic curve cryptosystems. Elliptic curve equivalents of popular public-key algorithms have been proposed [29]. Mathematicians and number theorists have been studying elliptic curves for well over 100 years. The mathematics of elliptic curves is considerably more complex and harder to explain than that of RSA and is beyond the scope of this book. For more information on the topic, the reader is referred to [30].

3.9 Public-key infrastructure (PKI)

Public-key cryptography is based on the idea that an individual will generate a key pair, keep one component secret, and publish the other component. Other users on the network must be able to retrieve this public key, associate it with an identity of some sort, and use it to communicate securely with, or authenticate messages from, the user claiming that identity.

If an attacker can convince a user that a bogus public key is associated with a valid identity, then the attacker can easily masquerade as the person with that identity. The simplicity of this attack demonstrates that public-key cryptography can only work when users can associate a public key with an identity in a trusted fashion.

3.9.1 Certificates

One way to form a trusted association between a key and an identity is to enlist the services of a trusted third party (TTP). This is an individual or organization that all users of a system can trust. In an identification scheme, it could be a government organization; in a payment system, it is likely to be a financial institution. As Figure 3.17 shows, the TTP will construct a message, referred to as a *certificate,* that contains a number of fields, the most important of which are a user identity and the associated public key. The TTP signs this certificate using its private (secret) key, in the process guaranteeing that the public key is associated with the named user.

This guarantee is made subject to a defined security policy. This could be quite lax and involve the user forwarding the public key to the TTP for certification, or it could be an involved process requiring the physical presence of the user together with the presentation of multiple forms of identification.

Subject (Identity of User)	Public Key	Validity Period	Issuer (Identity of TTP)	Other fields	Signature of TTP

Figure 3.17 Typical set of fields found in a certificate.

The certificate is used when a message recipient wishes to gain access to the sender's public key. The recipient can either consult some on-line directory service to obtain this or, alternatively, the sender may append their certificate to the message. It is assumed that every user in the system is first equipped with the public key of the TTP. Using this, the signature on the certificate can be verified, and if it passes the test, the public key contained in the certificate can be trusted.

3.9.2 Certification authorities

TTPs that issue certificates are referred to as certification authorities (CAs), and when the population of users becomes large, it is unlikely that a single CA can serve the entire user base. This means that either each user must acquire the public keys of each independent CA or the CAs can be organized into a hierarchy.

The root of the hierarchy is a CA that issues certificates only to other CAs, which then certify users of the system. There may, of course, be more levels than this, but the principles are the same. User of the system need only hold the public key of the root CA, and when sending a message they include a copy of all certificates in the path between them and the root.

Figure 3.18 shows a simple certification hierarchy where Alice has been certified by CA1 and Bob by CA2. The two CAs use a common root CA that has issued certificates for both CA1 and CA2, and all users of the system are equipped with the public key of this root CA. When Alice sends a message to Bob, she includes her own certificate, signed by CA1 and CA1's certificate signed by the root CA. When Bob receives this message, he uses the PK_{Root} to verify PK_{CA1}, PK_{CA1} to verify PK_{Alice}, and PK_{Alice} to authenticate the message. This is called traversing the trust chain of certificates, and a similar process can be undergone for messages sent in the reverse direction.

In cases where the certification hierarchy is extensive, including all certificates with each message can be a substantial overhead. This can be alleviated by each user keeping a copy of the certificates they receive. Rather than including the certificates in the message, the sender includes a message digest of the certificate, called a "thumbprint," in its place. The receiver compares this thumbprint with a digest of each certificate of which it has a copy, and if it cannot find a match, it will ask the sender to forward a copy.

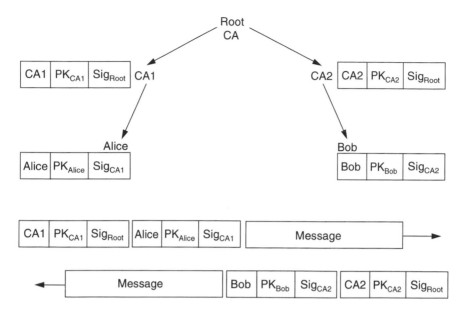

Figure 3.18 Certification hierarchy in action.

If a user's secret key becomes compromised, then the certificate associated with the public key must be revoked. CAs keep certificate revocation lists (CRLs) that are available for users of the system. In order to completely trust the authenticity of the message, the CA for each certificate in the trust chain must be contacted to check that none have been revoked since they were issued. The extent of this problem will depend on two things: first, the number of compromised keys, and second, the normal period of validity of a certificate.

3.9.3 Attribute certificates

X.509 public-key certificates are long-lived objects, which provide evidence of a person's identity. The X.509 version 3 standard [31] has an EXTENSIONS field that can be used to provide attributes or privileges to the owner of the certificate. These privileges could be linked to their role within their organization (e.g., a stand-in manager may be given "signing authority" for things normally covered by a manager on vacation). However, privileges will often have a much shorter lifetime than those of a public-key certificate (i.e., a user's name is far less likely to change than the user's job specification). One way to do this is to separate the attribute information into a separate object called an attribute certificate (AC).

An AC is a separate structure from a person's public-key certificate. The main differences are that the AC does not contain a public key, so it cannot be used to establish identity, and it is usually short-lived. Lifetimes of a day or even hours may be assigned. Since ACs are short-lived, they do not need to be revoked and simply expire. This feature can be used to eliminate the need for CRLs, which has been one of the stumbling blocks in establishing large PKIs. A person's AC is linked to his or her public-key certificate by including a hash of the person's public key or a hash of his or her public-key certificate within one of the attribute certificate fields.

A person may have multiple ACs associated with his or her public-key certificate (e.g., one for each role that the person may be associated with within his or her organization). There is no requirement that the CA must also act as the attribute authority (AA). In fact, it is recommended that these roles be separated into two distinct entities. The CA could be some TTP, which requires a formal procedure to be undertaken before it can issue a public-key certificate. However, an AA could be an organizational entity which has local knowledge of a person's requirements and privileges.

ACs may be distributed in two ways. The first is where the AA assigns privileges to a person through the creation of an attribute certificate. For example, an AC would be generated by the system each morning when a user logs into his or her machine. The AC would give the user access to resources on the corporate network. Alternatively, a user may request a privilege from an attribute authority server. The user would then supply the AC to the application or resource that he or she wishes to use. The application would first use the user's public-key certificate to establish his or her identity. If successful, it would then verify that the user has been granted privileges to access the specified resources by examining his or her AC.

3.10 Transport of security information

The previous sections have outlined a number of different security algorithms and techniques. If these techniques are to be implemented across a global network, then they will involve communication between a wide diversity of machine architectures and software development environments. This is particularly the case in the area of electronic payments, where the machines participating in dialogues will range from handheld personal machines to large transaction-processing mainframes in financial institutions. For this to work, there must be a standardized means of representing cryptographic information before it is sent across the network.

3.10.1 Abstract syntax notation (ASN.1)

The problem of communicating between heterogeneous computer systems is twofold. First, there must be some means of agreeing on what information is to be communicated. Ideally, this information could be specified in a machine-independent manner. Second, there is a need for a standard means of representing this information as it flows through the network. This means that a machine receiving such a stream should be able to make sense of the information that arrives and relate it to the machine-independent specification.

The approach adopted by the International Standards Organization (ISO) to this was to define an abstract syntax notation (ASN) in which data could be described in just such a machine-independent fashion. The first such notation to be developed was called ASN.1 [32] and although some changes have been made to the original document, it has not been necessary to create an ASN.2 thus far.

The notation contains some built-in types such as INTEGER and OCTET STRING to describe a whole number (of any size) or an arbitrary string of bytes, respectively. There are also structuring mechanisms such as SEQUENCE to denote an ordered grouping of basic fields or SET where no order is defined.

One of the more novel basic types is called an OBJECT IDENTIFIER. This is a sequence of numbers that is used to uniquely identify something. The numbers are the path through a naming tree, where the owner of each node has naming authority from that point in the tree downwards.

Figure 3.19 shows the naming tree for the object identifier that uniquely identifies the MD5 message digest algorithm. The first-level branches of the tree are under the control of the ISO and CCITT standards bodies. ISO has defined branch number 2 for national standards bodies and branch 840 of that to the United States. The national naming body

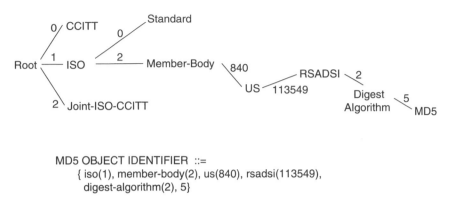

MD5 OBJECT IDENTIFIER ::=
    { iso(1), member-body(2), us(840), rsadsi(113549),
    digest-algorithm(2), 5}

Figure 3.19   The object identifier for MD5 in ASN.1 and naming-tree form.

for the United States has assigned branch number 113549 to RSA Data
Security Inc., which can assign as many globally unique object identifiers
as they wish, beginning with the prefix 1.2.840.113549. They have built
a subtree for digest algorithms and assigned branch 5 of this to represent
the MD5 algorithm. Figure 3.19 also shows how this is specified in ASN.1
notation.

Figure 3.20 shows a hypothetical example of how two communicating parties may define a hashed message to be sent across a network. The
new type will have three fields: *contents* is an arbitrary length string of
bytes containing the message itself, *digestAlgorithm* will identify which
algorithm is used to create the message digest, and *digest* will hold the
output of the designated algorithm.

When it comes to expressing this or any other ASN.1 specified data
stream as a sequence of bytes, an encoding scheme must be chosen. The
scheme most commonly used with ASN.1 is called the basic encoding
rules (BER) [33], but this is unsuitable for cryptographic applications, as
it allows for more than one way to encode some of the basic types. Where

```
HashedMessage ::= SEQUENCE
        { contents  OCTET STRING,
          digestAlgorithm  OBJECT IDENTIFIER,
          digest  OCTET STRING }
```

Figure 3.20   Example definition of a new ASN.1 data type.

cryptography is used, a constrained subset of the BER called the *distinguished encoding rules* (DER) is used instead. Each element of an ASN.1 data type is encoded as three fields: a tag identifying the data type involved (e.g., INTEGER, OCTET STRING, and SEQUENCE), a length, and the value of the data element. In this way, the receiver of the information stream can reconstruct a data element of arbitrary complexity.

Using ASN.1 as the specification mechanism, it is possible to define payment protocols that can be implemented by many different organizations across the world on a variety of machine architectures and still have a very high probability of successful interworking.

3.10.2   The X.509 directory authentication framework

In payment protocols, it is often a critical requirement that various parties to a payment establish their identity. Since we are dealing with entities such as people, payment servers, and so forth that may be distributed across many different countries, it is important that we have some scheme for assigning globally unique names to people and processes.

In 1988, the CCITT—an organization representing the operators of the world's telephone networks—produced a series of recommendations [34] that described how to build a global distributed database containing details on people and processes. This database was to be called the X.500 directory. The CCITT has now been superseded by the International Telecommunication Union Technical Standards (ITU-TS), which is now responsible for X.500, and the standards are also coissued by the International Standards Organizations (ISO) [35].

The X.500 recommendations are based on the idea of a single global distributed database containing objects representing people and processes. The objects are arranged in a tree structure that at the top level would hold a single object for each country in the world together with objects representing organizations of global standing (e.g., the United Nations). The countries are identified by a standardized two-letter code [e.g., US (United States), GB (Great Britain), FR (France), JP (Japan)]. Under each country, there would be objects representing significant organizations at a national level together with objects representing each main region in a country, and this hierarchy would continue as required. At each level, one attribute of each object must give a name that is unique at that level. For example, at the global level, there can only be one country with a country attribute having the value FR (c = FR). This attribute is used to distinguish that object at that level and is called the relative distinguished name (RDN). If all the RDNs on the path from the root to a particular object are concatenated, the result globally identifies an object and is called a distinguished name (DN).

Figure 3.21 shows a part of the global X.500 information tree. An organization (o) named "Universal Export" is registered under the Great Britain country object and under it is registered a "person" object whose common name (cn) attribute is "James Bond." The X.500 DN for this entity would be the concatenation of these: c = GB, o = Universal Exports, cn = James Bond. Similarly, the server number 24 operated by the Home Shopping Network in the United States could be identified as c = US, o = Home Shopping Network, cn = Secure Server 24. The X.500 scheme also allows for individuals to be named relative to the locality in which they reside and to have two or more entries in the directory tree.

3.10.2.1 X.509 certificates

Earlier in this chapter, we discussed how an identity could be linked to a public key by using a certificate. The X.509 recommendation specifies the exact syntax for a certificate that can link a public key to an X.500 DN where the trusted third party is also identified by an X.500 DN.

Figure 3.22 shows a fragment of ASN.1 adapted from the X.500 standards. The *certificate* data element is defined with the most important fields in italics. Using a macro capability of ASN.1, the entire data unit is defined as having a signature appended to it. The meaning of the certificate is to bind the entity identified by SUBJECT with the public key held in the SUBJECTPUBLICKEYINFO field for a period specified by VALIDITY. This binding is certified by the entity identified by ISSUER.

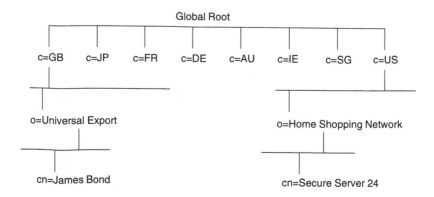

Figure 3.21 The X.500 directory hierarchy.

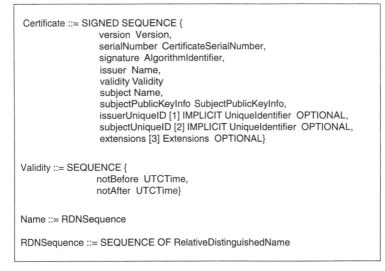

```
Certificate ::= SIGNED SEQUENCE {
              version Version,
              serialNumber CertificateSerialNumber,
              signature AlgorithmIdentifier,
              issuer Name,
              validity Validity
              subject Name,
              subjectPublicKeyInfo SubjectPublicKeyInfo,
              issuerUniqueID [1] IMPLICIT UniqueIdentifier OPTIONAL,
              subjectUniqueID [2] IMPLICIT UniqueIdentifier OPTIONAL,
              extensions [3] Extensions OPTIONAL}


Validity ::= SEQUENCE {
              notBefore UTCTime,
              notAfter UTCTime}


Name ::= RDNSequence

RDNSequence ::= SEQUENCE OF RelativeDistinguishedName
```

Figure 3.22   The specification for an X.500 certification in ASN.1.

The most recent version of the standard was X.509 version 3, and in it the EXTENSIONS field has been added to provide much more information related to the policy governing the certified binding.

Many of the payment systems outlined in later chapters will employ X.500 DNs to identify entities, with X.509 certificates being used to link these identities with the corresponding public keys. The availability of the ASN.1 specification means that developers of diverse software will be able to exchange certificates without the need for bilateral agreement.

3.10.3   PKCS cryptographic message syntax

Another family of quasi-standards that are of interest for payment system applications are the Public Key Cryptography Standards (PKCS) [36] developed by RSA Laboratories. These are a group of documents defining in ASN.1 how a variety of cryptographic exchanges that commonly occur should be performed. One of the series that is of particular interest is PKCS#7 [37], which describes how signed and enveloped data should be transferred across networks.

The simplest data type defined in the standard is SignedData, and an excerpt from the ASN.1 is shown in Figure 3.23. This allows multiple signers (each described by an individual SignerInfo) to sign a message held in the ContentInfo field in parallel. Fields are present to determine

```
SignedData ::=SEQUENCE {
                version Version,
                digestAlgorithms DigestAlgorithmIdentifiers,
                contentInfo ContentInfo,
                certificates [0] IMPLICIT ExtendedCertificatesAndCertificates
                        OPTIONAL,
                crls [1] IMPLICIT CertificateRevocationLists OPTIONAL,
                signerInfos SignerInfos}
```

Figure 3.23   The PKCS#7 specification for sending signed data across a
network.

what digest algorithms have been used by each signer. Optional fields are
included to enclose such certificates and certificate revocation lists as are
necessary to verify the signatures.

Enveloping is specified in a similar manner. Figure 3.24 shows how
an arbitrary chunk of data (EncryptedContent) can be encrypted using a
symmetric cipher with the key chosen at random. For each recipient of
the data, a RecipientInfo field is constructed that contains the symmetric
key encrypted with the public key of the recipient.

The PKCS#7 standards also include much ancillary information necessary to fully construct the data elements described above, and also to
define a SignedandEnvelopedData type that combines both security functions into one type.

3.11   Dual signatures

Digital signatures are used to link an identity with the content of a particular message. In order to verify the message, the recipient must also be
able to access the message content. In protocols involving three parties,
such as a credit card transaction, a cryptographic technique that is sometimes employed is the dual signature. This provides a link between a message and an identity, without the need to be able to see the message
contents. As the name implies, it is used in applications in which two
related messages are being sent. Whenever a payment is made, a separa-
tion can be made between financial details required to effect the transaction and the details of what is being purchased. These can be separated
into two distinct messages.

Figure 3.25 shows how a dual signature is constructed. First, the two
related messages are individually hashed using some message digest

```
EnvelopedData ::= SEQUENCE {
                version  Version,
                recipientInfos  RecipientInfos,
                encryptedContentInfo  EncryptedContentInfo }


EncryptedContentInfo ::= SEQUENCE {
                contentType  ContentType,
                contentEncryptionAlgorithm
                        ContentEncryptionAlgorithmIdentifier,
                encryptedContent [0] IMPLICIT EncryptedContent
                        OPTIONAL}

EncryptedContent ::= OCTET STRING

RecipientInfo ::= SEQUENCE {
                version  Version,
                issuerandSerialNumber  IssuerandSerialNumber,
                keyEncryptionAlgorithm  KeyEncryptionAlgorithmIdentifier,
                encryptedKey  EncryptedKey }

EncryptedKey ::= OCTET STRING
```

Figure 3.24   The PKCS#7 specification for sending enveloped data across a network.

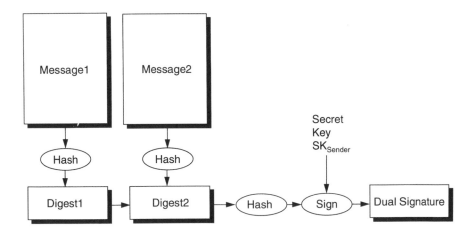

Figure 3.25   Constructing a dual signature on a pair of messages.

algorithm. Next, the two digests are concatenated and a new digest computed, which is then signed with the sender's private key.

If Alice had two such messages and wanted to send Message1 to Bob
and Message2 to Carol while assuring both Bob and Carol that a second
linked message existed, she could send Message1, Digest2, and the dual
signature to Bob with Message2, Digest1, and the dual signature going
to Carol. When Bob receives this data, he can apply the hash algorithm to
Message1, concatcnate this with Digest2, hash the result, and check that
this matches the dual signature. Thus, although he can only see the contents of Message1, he can be confident that a Message2 exists that hashes
to Digest2 and that the dual signature links these two documents. Carol is
in a similar position in that she can only see Message2, but can verify that
the dual signature links this to Message1. As an additional benefit, the
sender need only compute one dual signature for the pair of messages,
which saves some computing resources.

The use of this technique in a payment application will be demonstrated in later chapters.

3.12 Nonces

When using cryptographic protocols, a form of attack that is often
neglected is the so-called *replay attack*. This type of attack does not
attempt to break the cryptographic algorithms used; rather, it records
valid messages and plays them back in a different context. A classic example is the recording of messages from an automated teller machine. An
attacker can record the (crytographically protected) dialogues that occur
when a withdrawal is made and then replay these repeatedly at a later
time to make multiple unauthorized withdrawals.

This can be guarded against by including a quantity in each message
that will never be used again in subsequent messages. Such a quantity is
called a *nonce*. A simple nonce would be an ever-increasing integer,
where the party contacted could keep track of the numbers that had been
used to date. A more general system would involve including some form
of timestamp (expressed as time since some epoch) together with a randomly generated quantity. Nonces containing timestamps can also be
used to limit the period of validity of the message. For example, participants could agree that a message is only valid for a fixed period beyond
the timestamp.

Many of the payment systems outlined in later chapters will make extensive use of nonces.

3.13 Blind signatures

The use of blind signatures is a method for allowing a person to sign a message without being able to see its contents. The method has been used for implementing voting and digital cash protocols. Blind signatures were first proposed by David Chaum [38], who also developed their first implementation [39] using the RSA algorithm.

The process of blinding a message can be thought of as putting it in an envelope along with a piece of carbon paper. Nobody can read the message through the envelope. A blind signature is made by signing the outside of the envelope. The signature goes through the carbon paper and onto the message as well. When the message is taken out of the envelope, it will be signed, and the signer will not have known what he or she has signed. This blind signature analogy is shown in Figure 3.26.

In the steps below, a user, Alice, uses the blind signature protocol to get another user, Bob, to sign a message without knowing its contents.

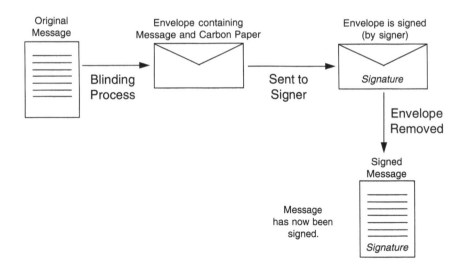

Figure 3.26 Blind signature analogy.

1. Alice takes the message and multiplies it by a random value, called a blinding factor. This blinds the message so its contents cannot be read.

2. Alice sends the blinded message to Bob.

3. Bob digitally signs the blinded document and returns it to Alice.

4. Alice divides out the blinding factor, leaving the original message now signed by Bob.

For this to work, the signature function and the multiplication function should be commutative. The properties of blind signatures are the following.

1. The signature on the document after it has been unblinded is a normal valid digital signature. It has the same properties of any digital signature.

2. It can't be proved in any way that the digital signature was placed on the message using the blind signature protocol. If a record is kept of every blind signature made, given an unblinded signed message, it cannot be linked to any of the signing records.

Mathematically, the blind signature protocol works as follows. Bob has a public key e, a private key d, and a public modulus n. Alice wants Bob to blindly sign message M.

1. Alice chooses the blinding factor, k, as a random value between 1 and n. Then M is blinded by computing

$$T = Mk^e \bmod n$$

2. Bob signs T:

$$T^d = (Mk^e)^d \bmod n = M^d k \bmod n$$

3. Alice unblinds T^d by computing

$$S = \frac{T^d}{k} = \frac{M^d k}{k} \bmod n$$

4. The result is

$$S = M^d \bmod n$$

This result is the message encrypted (signed) with Bob's secret key. In essence, this scheme demands that Bob sign a message without knowing anything of its contents. Blind signatures are generally applied using a special-purpose key that is only used for signing one kind of document. A specific example is given in Chapter 6, where a digital quantity may be signed by a bank with its $1 secret key. The resulting signed quantity can only be used to represent a $1 bill regardless of the message contents.

3.14 Chip cards/smart cards

All of the techniques that have been described so far in this chapter have centered on software implementations of algorithms or protocols. In many applications, particularly in payment, secure hardware devices can play an important role. One of the most important secure hardware devices is the chip card (popularly referred to as a *smart card*), which is a portable data storage device with intelligence and provisions for identity and security. It most often resembles a traditional credit or bank card in size and dimensions, and embedded within the card is a customized integrated circuit. The physical characteristics of a chip card are defined by [40, 41].

By demanding that the user provide a password, usually in the form of a personal identification number (PIN), before making any meaningful response, a chip card is equipped to identify positively its authorized bearer on each occasion. Second-generation chip cards are characterized by the presence of a magnetic stripe, as shown in Figure 3.27(a). In addition, an *active* or *super* smart card may consist of a keyboard, a liquid crystal display, and an onboard power supply, as shown in Figure 3.27(b). Such devices are also referred to as *electronic wallets* in the context of electronic payment systems.

Such a card allows a user to enter his or her PIN directly on the card and further limits the chance of an adversary gaining knowledge of the user's PIN. All data passing between the card and the external system

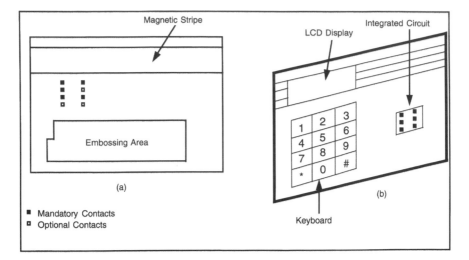

Figure 3.27   (a) Smart card with magnetic stripe, and (b) third-generation super smart card.

(which may be local or at the end of a network link) may be encrypted to render all transmissions unreadable to any intruders attempting to intercept sensitive material.

3.14.1   Card types

There are a number of card types in use today, namely:

> • *Magnetic stripe cards:* This type of card most resembles the credit card of today. It has a magnetic stripe at the back of the card that holds the details about the user, such as name, the card number, and so forth. Anyone with an appropriate card reader device can read the information stored on the card.

> • *Memory cards:* These are used for simple applications such as the pre-paid telephone card, which has a chip with 60 or 120 memory cells, one for each telephone unit. Each cell can be switched on/off. A memory cell is cleared each time a telephone unit is used. Once all the memory units are used, the card becomes useless and is thrown away. The hard-wired security provides enough protection for rela-tively low-value applications.

 ▸ *Processor cards:* Processor cards are characterized by the presence of a microprocessor onboard that controls access to information on the card. It operates under the control of an operating system also housed on the chip (a chip card operating system is usually unique to the chip and the card supplier). The microprocessor card increases protection against fraud and can be used in high-value or security-critical applications. An example application could be storage of cryptographic keys, and the chip card would act as a secure hardware device. Processor cards can be further classified as:

1. Contact cards: The integrated chip (IC) on the card requires an external power source and clock to drive the chip and an input/output path for the transmission of data. The card achieves this through a direct connection to an external device, such as a card reader. The IC on the chip is connected to a contact plate on the surface of the card, which is the interface presented to the outside world. When the card is placed on the card reader device, the contact plate comes in contact with its opposite number and the circuit is complete.

2. Contactless cards: This type of card provides added flexibility in the sense that the user's card does not need to come into direct contact with a third-party external device (e.g., a card reader device). The card uses some form of electrical coupling to communicate with a card reader device. Generally, contactless chip cards have to be placed in close proximity to the reader. There is ongoing research to extend the distance between the two devices. One application has been in a toll system, where each driver carries a contactless chip card in the car, which can be used to automatically pay the toll charge. Some forms of contactless cards use radiowave energy to operate over longer distances.

3.14.2 Memory types and capacity

Processor and nonprocessor chip cards contain data storage or memory, as shown in Figure 3.28. This comes in the following forms:

 ▸ *ROM:* Read-only memory (ROM) is memory programmed by means of masks and is integrated at the time the chip is manufactured. The data contained in it can subsequently be read by the

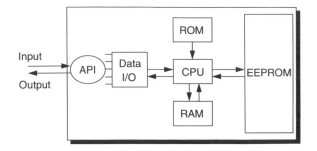

Figure 3.28 Basic chip card configuration.

microprocessor, but not altered. Into this memory is put the card operating system (COS), the input/output routines, routines for data logging, and basic functions such as algorithms for PIN checking and authentication.

» *EPROM:* An electrically programmable read-only memory (EPROM) can generally be erased with ultraviolet light after it has been programmed. In order to do this, normal EPROM chips have a small window that, when placed under an ultraviolet light source for about half an hour, erases the information contained within the chip. Since a chip card has no window, it is not possible to erase this type of memory. For this reason, an EPROM contained in a chip card can only be programmed once (i.e., data can only be written to it). The first thing to be written here is personalization information. This includes data specific to the card and to certain applications. When the card is used, other data is stored here such as transaction monitoring or error data. Since it is not possible to erase the data, an increasing amount of memory space is written to until such time as the memory is full and the card becomes unusable.

» *EEPROM:* Unlike the EPROM, an electrically erasable programmable read-only memory (EEPROM) allows memory cells to be erased electrically. This has considerable advantages for the chip card, as it removes virtually all limitations on the use of the card. The memory cells can be reprogrammed at least 10,000 times. Data can be retained in the memory for at least 10 years. The EEPROM also offers advantages in the realm of security.

▸ *RAM:* Random access memory (RAM) serves as high-speed working storage for the processor. It is used as a scratch pad by the microprocessor. The amount of RAM has a lot of influence on the overall performance of the card. If more RAM is available, larger blocks of data can be exchanged in one single message between the card and the external world, reducing communication overheads.

3.14.3 Physical specifications

There is considerable variation in the specification of the microprocessors and memory technology used in contact cards by the various vendors. Below is a typical specification for a chip card:

▸ Clock rates: 1 to 5 MHz;

▸ EPROM: 8 to 16 KB (for data storage, nonvolatile);

▸ RAM: 256 to 500 bytes (for operating system computation);

▸ EEPROM: 2 to 8 KB (nonvolatile).

An EPROM usually takes up a lot less physical storage space than an EEPROM. Since a chip card that conforms to the ISO standard [40] can only use a single storage chip that cannot be greater than 20 mm², this limits the amount of EEPROM memory that a chip card may contain. Current chip card architectures may use both EPROM and EEPROM memories.

3.14.4 Security

There are two types of security associated with a chip card: logical security and physical security.

▸ *Logical security:* The chip card is designed such that no single function or a combination of functions can result in disclosure of sensitive data except as allowed by the security procedures implemented in the card. This can be achieved by internal monitoring of all operations performed by the card user and by imposing an upper limit on the number of function calls that can be made within a time period [42]. Recent advances made by researchers at Bellcore [43] cast some doubt on this security. Their attack was based on heating the card to induce it to produce an incorrect output. By examining this output, attacks on the key became easier.

▸ *Physical security:* Chip cards incorporate not only logical but physical security features as well. Special layers of oxide over the chip protect against analysis of the contents of the memory. Even if the protective layers were removed and the silicon exposed, further difficulties make analysis virtually impossible. Another barrier protecting the contents of the memory against unauthorized reading results from the fact that the electrical charges at the memory gates of an EEPROM are very small. This means that they are lost if a probe is put close to them, thus making any attempt to probe the memory contents impossible. Although it is theoretically possible to analyze the memory contents of a secure chip, the enormous effort involved is out of proportion to any possible advantage to be gained.

A category of attacks that has received attention over the past few years has been based on the idea of observing and analyzing the power consumption of smart cards during a cryptographic operation. It is generally assumed that the smart card is a secure device and will not reveal any sensitive key or PIN information across the hardware interface in cleartext form. However, current-generation smart cards have minimal shielding and it is possible to attach a probe to the card to monitor the electromagnetic activity of the device. Cryptographic Research, Inc., a U.S.-based company, has been leading the research in this area and has developed techniques for monitoring and analyzing the power consumption of such devices in order to mount a cryptanalysis attack. These attacks are classified under the categories of simple power analysis (SPA) and differential power analysis (DPA) [44]. The DPA attack is the more sophisticated of the two and requires statistical analysis of the collected data and knowledge of the cryptographic algorithms to be able to extract information about the secret keys.

3.14.5 Public-key processing capabilities

Asymmetric cryptography is fast becoming the norm in the cryptographic world today as it alleviates key distribution problems associated with symmetric key cryptosystems. However, public-key cryptosystems require far greater processing capabilities. At present, the predominant architecture in the chip card world is 8-bit, which does not have the processing power to run public-key algorithms in an acceptable time. Hence the need to move to 32- or even 64-bit architectures. Early developments in the area concentrated on generating a 512-bit signature in less than a second. This was later revised to three signatures in less than one second.

3.14.6 Multiapplication cards

Multiservice or multiapplication capability, in essence, means the capability to take a chip card hosting one or more different applications and add another application without reference to those existing on the card and without disturbing them. This capability will help in reducing the overall number of cards in the consumer's hands.

3.14.7 Java Card

A Java Card is a smart card that is capable of running a program written in the Java programming language. Like the Java programming language, the Java Card effort has been developed and promoted by Sun Microsystems. Java Card technology is compatible with existing smart card technology and at the physical, electrical, and link levels conforms to the international smart card standard [45].

The Java Card allows application developers to take advantage of Java's "write-once-and-run-anywhere" features. Also the object-oriented features of Java allow for greater modularity and code reuse.

The Java Card specification consists of three main components:

- The Java Card Virtual Machine (JCVM) sits on top of the native card operating system and executes Java byte code. It hides the underlying specifics of the smart card hardware from the application programmer, as shown in Figure 3.29.

- The Java Card Run-time Environment (JCRE) describes memory management, security enforcement, and other procedures.

- The Java Card Application Programming Interface (API) specifies a subset of the Java language tailored for use on smart cards and allows for programming smart card applications.

The JCVM frees the application developer from having to worry about the internal hardware specification of a particular smart card

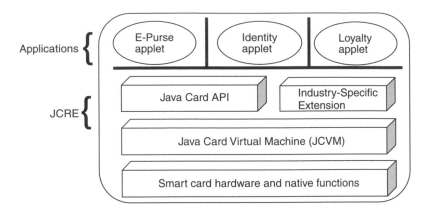

Figure 3.29　Java Card system architecture.

platform and such issues as memory management. Instead it allows him or her to concentrate on the core task of developing end-user applications. In the past, application developers had to sign nondisclosure agreements with various card manufacturers before they were given access to the low-level card API.

A Java Card applet, unlike a regular Java applet, is not intended to run within a Web browser. The reason the name applet was chosen for Java Card applications is that Java Card applets can be loaded into the JCRE after the card has been manufactured. The JCRE allows for multiple applets residing on the same card simultaneously (e.g., an electronic purse, authentication, and loyalty scheme all on the same Java Card). Each applet runs within a designated space and is isolated by an applet firewall. The existence and operation of one applet have no effect on other applets on the card. The JCVM enforces the applet firewall on the card.

The Java Card 1.0 specification was released in November 1996 and was followed a year later by version 2.0 of the specification. There are a number of development environments, most of which have simulators, that allow the application developer to simulate his or her application before loading it onto the card. This allows faster debugging and testing of applications. This in turn results in faster development cycles and lower development costs. The Java Card concept is an important step on the road to greater acceptance of smart card technology in the electronic payments arena.

implies that if the issuing organization places a malicious observer in the chip card, there is no way that it can divulge any information about the owner.

Thus, the interests of both the cardholder and the card issuer are protected.

References

[1] National Bureau of Standards, *Federal Information Processing Standard (FIPS) Publication 46: The Data Encryption Standard*, 1977.

[2] National Institute of Standards and Technology (NIST), *Federal Information Processing Standard (FIPS) Publication 46-1: Data Encryption Standard*, January 1988.

[3] American National Standards Institute (ANSI), *ANSI X3.92—Data Encryption Algorithm*, 1981.

[4] National Bureau of Standards, *Federal Information Processing Standard (FIPS) Publication 81: DES Modes of Operation*, December 1980.

[5] Blaze, M., et al., *Minimal Key Lengths for Symmetric Ciphers to Provide Adequate Commercial Security: A Report by an Ad hoc Group of Cryptographers and Computer Scientists*, January 1996, ftp://coast.cs.purdue.edu/pub/doc/cryptography/Symmetric-Cipher-Keylength.ps.Z.

[6] Biham, E., and A. Shamir, "Differential Cryptanalysis of the Full 16-Round DES," *Advances in Cryptology—CRYPTO '92, Proc. 12th Annual Int. Cryptology Conference*, Lecture Notes in Computer Science, Vol. 740, Berlin: Springer-Verlag, 1993, pp. 487–496.

[7] Matsui, M., "Linear Cryptanalysis Method for DES Cipher," *Advances in Cryptology—EUROCRYPT '93 Proc.*, Lecture Notes in Computer Science, Vol. 765, Berlin: Springer-Verlag, 1994.

[8] American National Standards Institute (ANSI), *ANSI X9.17-1985: Financial Institution Key Management*, 1985.

[9] Lai, X., *On the Design and Security of Block Ciphers*, ETH Series in Information Processing, Vol. 1, Konstanz, Hartung-Gorre Verlag, 1992.

[10] Schneier, B., *Applied Cryptography: Protocols, Algorithms, and Source Code in C*, 2nd ed., New York: John Wiley and Sons, Inc., 1996, p. 145.

[11] Lai, X., and J. Massey, "A Proposal for a New Block Encryption Standard," *Advances in Cryptology—EUROCRYPT '90, Workshop on the Theory and Application of Cryptographic Techniques Proc.*, Lecture Notes in Computer Science, Vol. 473, Berlin: Springer-Verlag, 1991, pp. 389–404.

[12]   Advanced Encryption Standard, NIST, http://csrc.nist.gov/encryption/aes.

[13]   Aoki, K., and H. Lipmaa, "Fast Implementations of AES Candidates," *3rd AES Candidate Conference*, New York, April 2000.

[14]   Daemen, J., and V. Rijmen, *AES Proposal: Rijndael*, September 1999, http://csrc.nist.gov/encryption/aes/rijndael/Rijndael.pdf.

[15]   Doligez, D., *Account of the Successful Breaking of the SSL Challenge*, INRIA, August 1995, http://pauillac.inria.fr/~doligez/ssl/.

[16]   Rivest, R., "The RC5 Encryption Algorithm," *Dr. Dobbs Journal*, Iss. 225, January 1995, pp. 146–148.

[17]   Baldwin, R., and R. Rivest, *The RC5, RC5-CBC, RC5-CBC-Pad, and RC5-CTS Algorithms*, MIT Laboratory for Computer Science and RSA Data Security Inc., Internet Draft:draft-rsadsi-rc5-00.txt, March 1996, ftp://ftp.rsa.com/pub/rsalabs/rc5.

[18]   Rivest, R., et al., *The RC6 Block Cipher*, MIT Lab for Computer Science, Cambridge, MA, 1998, http://theory.lcs.mit.edu/~rivest/publications.html.

[19]   Rivest, R., "The RC5 Encryption Algorithm," *Proc. 1994 Leuven Workshop on Fast Software Encryption*, Berlin: Springer-Verlag, 1995, pp. 86–96, http://theory.lcs.mit.edu/~rivest/publications.html.

[20]   Rivest, R., *The MD5 Message-Digest Algorithm*, RFC 1321, Internet Activities Board, April 1992, http://www.ietf.org/rfc.html.

[21]   National Institute of Standards and Technology (NIST), *Secure Hash Standard*, May 1993.

[22]   Steiner, J. G., B. Clifford Neuman, and J. I. Schiller, "Kerberos: An Authentication Service for Open Network Systems," *Proc. Usenix Conference*, Dallas, TX, February 1988, pp. 191–202, http://nii.isi.edu/info/kerberos/documentation.html.

[23]   Khol, J., and B. Clifford Neuman, *The Kerberos Network Authentication Service: Version 5 Protocol Specification*, RFC 1510, September 1993, http://www.ietf.org/rfc.html.

[24]   Diffie, W., and M. Hellman, "New Directions in Cryptography" *IEEE Trans. on Information Theory*, No. 22, 1976, pp. 644–654.

[25]   Rivest, R., A. Shamir, and L. Adleman, "A Method for Obtaining Digital Signatures and Public-Key Cryptosystems," *Communications of the ACM*, Vol. 21, No. 2, 1978, pp. 120–126.

[26]   Miller, V., "Use of Elliptic Curves in Cryptography," *Advances in Cryptology—Crypto '85*, Berlin: Springer-Verlag, 1986, pp. 417–426.

[27]   Koblitz, N., "Elliptic Curve Cryptosystems," *Mathematics of Computation*, Vol. 48, 1997, pp. 203–209,

[28] Certicom white paper, "Current Public Key Cryptographic Systems," April 1997 (Updated July 2000), http://www.certicom.com/research.html.

[29] ANSI X9.62, "Public Key Cryptography for the Financial Services Industry—The Elliptic Curve Digital Signature Algorithm (ECDSA)," January 1999.

[30] Menezes, A., *Elliptic Curve Public Key Cryptosystems*, Norwell, MA: Kluwer Academic Publishers, 1993.

[31] "ITU-T Recommendation X.509 (1997 E): Information Technology—Open Systems Interconnection—The Directory: Authentication Framework," June 1997.

[32] ISO/IEC, *Information Processing—Open Systems Interconnection—Specification of Abstract Syntax Notation One (ASN.1)*, IS 8824, 1987.

[33] ISO/IEC, *Information Processing—Open Systems Interconnection—Specification of Basic Encoding Rules for Abstract Syntax Notation One (ASN.1)*, IS 8825, 1987.

[34] International Telegraph and Telephone Consultative Committee, *X.500—The Directory—Overview of Concepts, Models and Service*, 1988.

[35] ISO/IEC, *Information Technology—Open Systems Interconnection—The Directory: The Models*, IS 9594-2, 1995.

[36] Kaliski, B., *An Overview of the PKCS Standards*, RSA Laboratories, November 1993, ftp://ftp.rsa.com/pub/pkcs/doc/overview.doc.

[37] RSA Laboratories, *PKCS #7: Cryptographic Message Syntax Standard*, November 1993, ftp://ftp.rsa.com/pub/pkcs/doc/pkcs-7.doc.

[38] Chaum, D., "Blind Signatures for Untraceable Payments," *Advances in Cryptology: Proceedings of CRYPTO '82*, New York: Plenum, 1983, pp. 199–203.

[39] Chaum, D., "Security Without Identification: Transaction Systems to Make Big Brother Obsolete," *Communications of the ACM*, Vol. 28, No. 10, October 1985, pp. 1030–1044.

[40] ISO/IEC, *Identification Cards—Physical Characteristics*, ISO Central Secretariat, Geneva, IS 7810 1985.

[41] Europay International S.A., MasterCard International Incorporated, and Visa International Service Association, *EMV '96: Integrated Circuit Card Specification for Payment Systems*, June 1996, http://www.mastercard.com/emv/.

[42] Europay International S.A., MasterCard International Incorporated, and Visa International Service Association, *EMV '96, Integrated Circuit Card Terminal Specification for Payment Systems*, June 1996, http://www.mastercard.com/emv/.

[43] Boneh, D., R. DeMillo, and R. Lipton, "On the Importance of Checking Cryptographic Protocols for Faults," *Proc. Eurocrypt '97*, Lecture Notes in Computer Science, Vol. 1233, Berlin: Springer-Verlag, 1997, pp. 35–51.

[44] Kocher, P., J. Jaffe, and B. Jun, "Differential Power Analysis," *Advances in Cryptology—Proceedings of Crypto '99*, Springer-Verlag, 1999, pp. 388–397.

[45] ISO/IEC, *Information Technology—Identification Cards—Integrated Circuit(s) Cards with Contacts—Part 4: Interindustry Commands for Interchange*, IS 7816-4:1995.

[46] MULTOS, http://www.multos.com.

[47] Chaum, D., and T. Pedersen, "Wallet Databases with Observers," *Advances in Cryptology—CRYPTO '92, Proc. 12th Annual Intl. Cryptology Conference*, Lecture Notes in Computer Science, Vol. 740, Berlin: Springer-Verlag, 1993, pp. 89–105.

[48] Chaum, D., "Achieving Electronic Privacy," *Scientific American*, Vol. 267, No. 2, August 1992, pp. 76–81, http://www.chaum.com/articles/ Achieving_Electronic_Privacy.htm.

Credit card–based systems

Credit card schemes have been in use as a payment method since the early 1960s and the two major international brands, Visa and MasterCard, are household names all over the world. The Visa brand grew from a scheme launched by the Bank of America, which was subsequently licensed by Barclaycard in the United Kingdom in 1966. By the spring of 2000, this organization, owned by its 21,000 member financial institutions, had issued more than 1 billion cards and is now accepted by more than 19 million merchants in 300 countries.

Its principal competitor, MasterCard, is of comparable size with 19 million merchants in 210 countries and 22,000 member organizations. As Table 4.1 shows, they collectively account for a total of more than 1.3 billion cards issued and $2.3 trillion of sales each year.

Table 4.1
Usage of Two Main Branded Credit Cards in 1999

Region	Visa		MasterCard	
	Sales volume, billions of dollars (U.S.)	Number of cards (millions)	Sales volume billions of dollars (U.S.)	Number of cards (millions)
United States	$721.1	488.5	$352.2	212.8
Europe	$496.1	158.2	$186.4	60.9
Asia-Pacific	$165.8	183.6	$136.8	73.2
Canada	$54.4	50.4	$421.5	15.5
Middle East, Africa	$34.7	16.2	$6.4	2.3
Latin America	$117.9	100.5	$22.7	25.5
Totals	$1,590	997.4	$726	390.2
Combined	$2.3 trillion sales		1.3 billion cards	

Since their inception, the introduction of more payment options has led to the development of a number of different *payment card* schemes. These include the following:

▶ *Credit cards* have payments set against a special-purpose account associated with some form of installment-based repayment scheme or a revolving line of credit. Cards typically have a spending limit set by the card issuer, and the interest rate levied on unpaid balances is typically many times the base lending rate.

▶ *Debit cards* are linked to a checking/savings account. Normally, a payment cannot be made unless there are funds available to meet it. In effect, this type of payment can be considered a paperless check.

▶ *Charge cards* work in a similar way to credit cards in that payments are set against a special-purpose account. The principal difference is that the entire bill for a charge card must be paid at the end of the billing period. Often, there is no associated spending limit.

▶ *Travel and entertainment cards* are charge cards whose usage is linked to airlines, hotels, restaurants, car rental companies, or particular retail outlets.

With the exception of debit cards, where funds transfer takes place at the moment of payment, these schemes all operate in a similar fashion. Figure 4.1 shows the actors involved. Banks that belong to the card association may act as *card issuers* to their personal or business clients. This will involve the provision of a card and maintenance of a credit card account for that individual, to which transactions can be posted as they occur. Another or the same bank will act as an *acquirer* for clients of theirs who wish to accept credit card payments. This will usually involve providing equipment and/or software to process payments at the merchant's premises. Arrangements to perform on-line verification of transactions, as well as the policy for requiring on-line verification, are set by the acquirer. This may involve the setting of a *floor limit*, where any transaction exceeding this limit requires an on-line check as to the card status.

In a typical purchase, a merchant will capture the cardholder's details at the point of sale. Depending on the policy in force, the transaction may be completed straightaway or an on-line check may be made. Batched transactions are later sent to the acquirer for processing.

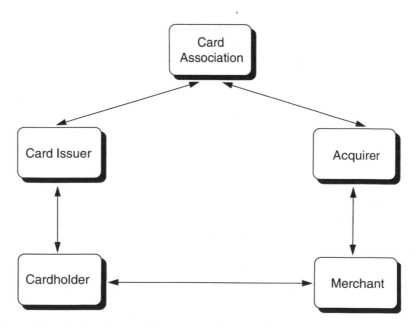

Figure 4.1 Entities involved in a conventional credit card transaction.

4.1   Mail order/telephone order (MOTO) transactions

For many years now it has been possible to make payments with credit cards without requiring the buyer and merchant to be colocated. Credit card companies have for some time allowed orders to be taken either by post or by telephone. These orders are referred to as mail order/telephone order (MOTO) transactions, and special rules have been imposed by the card companies on how these transactions are processed. Of necessity, in a mail-order situation, the credit card is not physically present when the transaction has been made. This means that the merchant cannot tell if the buyer is (or ever was) in possession of the card or check that a signature matches the sample on the card itself.

Normally, cardholders are asked to supply additional information, such as their name and address, that can be used to verify their identity. If goods that require physical delivery are being ordered, they must be dispatched to the address associated with the card. This gives limited protection against bogus orders. Since there is no cardholder signature involved, the processing rules allow the buyer to opt out of any transaction if they claim that they did not agree to the purchase. Clearly, this increases the risk borne by merchants.

Although there are more possibilities for fraud associated with this type of ordering, it is still a very popular form of payment, and it is clear that the benefits outweigh the fraud risks involved.

4.2   Unsecured network payments

Using credit cards to make payments across computer networks has similar associated risks as are experienced with MOTO transactions. Attackers eavesdropping on network traffic may intercept messages and capture credit card details as well as any associated verification information (e.g., name and address). Because of the distinctive structure of credit card numbers, with their inbuilt check digits, programs can be written to scan a data stream for occurrences of such patterns. The data stream could be either an intercepted transmission, a file on disk, reclaimed disk space on a shared system, or even the stream of keystrokes produced by someone typing at their workstation.

What makes the risks considerably higher than MOTO transactions is the speed with which transactions can be conducted. If merchants are processing orders electronically, then fraudsters can generate vast numbers of orders before the fraud is detected. The global scope of the network means that transactions can be carried out at locations that are far removed from where the card was issued. Thus, the gap between the card details being intercepted and blacklist notifications reaching all relevant merchants can be very significant.

Despite the increased risk, the absence of commonly accepted network payment schemes in a period when the Internet was rapidly expanding meant that many people resorted to this method of effecting payment. Some buyers adopted simple security measures such as spelling out the numbers of the credit card, or splitting the number across multiple messages. At the merchant end, the orders were processed in the same way as a MOTO transaction, using existing point of sale clearing systems.

4.3 First Virtual

One of the earliest credit card–based payment systems launched for the Internet was the product of a company called First Virtual Holdings, Inc. In October 1994, the company commenced operation of a payment system called the VirtualPIN that did not involve the use of encryption. The goal was to allow the selling of low-value information items across the network without the need for special-purpose client software or hardware to be in place. The system was not entirely fraudproof, but in the context of its target market this was not of such great importance.

Both merchants and buyers were required to register with First Virtual (FV) before any transactions could take place. The First Virtual server also had an involvement in every transaction and at intervals lodged the proceeds to the merchant's bank account.

A buyer registering with FV forwards his or her credit card details and electronic mail address to FV and in exchange receives a pass phrase, called a VirtualPIN. The initial part of this exchange can take place across the network, with the user filling in a Web form and inventing a pass phrase. FV acknowledges this and adds a suffix to the pass phrase to form the VirtualPIN. The next step involves the buyer making a telephone call to FV to tender his or her credit card number. This allows FV to establish a link between the VirtualPIN and the credit card without ever using the credit card number on the network.

Merchants must go through a similar registration process in which they give their bank details to FV and are given a merchant VirtualPIN. The normal method of transferring the bank details is to send a conventional check drawn on the bank account associated with the merchant. FV takes all account identifier information from the check itself. Once this is done, the merchant can request FV to process transactions from registered FV customers and, after deducting a per-transaction charge, deposit the funds in the merchant's bank account using the conventional bank automated clearing house (ACH) service.

Figure 4.2 shows a buyer using FV to make a purchase. Initially, the buyer browses the FV InfoHaus (FV Web server) or another Web server, where an FV merchant is selling goods. The buyer selects the item he or she wishes to purchase. The buyer is asked to enter his or her FV account identifier (Virtual PIN), which is forwarded to the merchant. The merchant checks that this account identifier is valid by querying the FV server. This can be done in a number of ways, ranging from manual queries to automated dialogues with an FV server. If the VirtualPIN has not been blacklisted, then the merchant will deliver the information to the buyer, either by e-mail, Web reply, or other means.

The merchant forwards information about the transaction, including the buyer's VirtualPIN, to the First Virtual Internet payment system server. No payment has yet been made, since the system is based on a

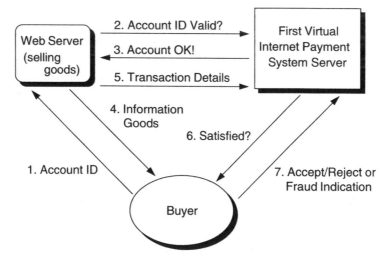

Figure 4.2 Buying with First Virtual.

"try before you buy" philosophy. Accordingly, the next step is for the FV server to send electronic mail to the buyer asking if the information was satisfactory.

There are three possible replies to this request:

▸ *Accept*, in which case the payment proceeds;

▸ *Reject*, indicating that the goods either were not received or that the buyer is not happy to pay for them;

▸ *Fraud*, which means that these goods were not ordered by the buyer. Upon receipt of this message, the FV server will immediately blacklist the VirtualPIN.

At the end of every 90 days, the buyer's credit card account is billed for the charges that have accumulated during the time period. The merchant's checking accounts are then credited with payments for items sold. FV performs the accounting for both the buyer and merchant, taking a percentage of the transaction as commission.

It is quite clear that if a VirtualPIN becomes compromised by attackers eavesdropping on network traffic, bogus purchases can be made from then until such time as the VirtualPIN is blacklisted. Since payment authorization requests are sent to the buyer by e-mail, this time period could range from a few minutes to perhaps a day or so. Also, denial of service or masquerade attacks on the e-mail system could prolong this period quite substantially.

In addition, a stolen credit card number could be used to set up VirtualPINs associated with e-mail addresses controlled by the attacker, which may also allow long periods where bogus transactions can be carried out.

The exposure to fraud is of lesser importance if the payment system is used for information items. In this context, although a fraud has been committed, the seller will have lost a sale rather than incurred a large financial loss. Experience of operation of the system showed a very low fraud rate. The overall model of how credit card payments work has been modified somewhat by the FV system. From the card company's point of view, FV takes on the role of merchant in that they are the ones that establish the relationship with the acquirer, and the value of all transactions is credited to their account in the first instance before being distributed using ACH bank transfers.

Perhaps the major advantage of the FV system was its simplicity. Since it makes no use of encryption, there were no export problems, and the simple exchanges that make up the protocol mean that no special software is needed at the front end, and the back-end software is not complex.

Its major disadvantage is that before either merchants or buyers could use the system, they had to preregister and have either a bank account (in the case of a merchant) or a credit card (in the case of a buyer). There were, however, no other qualifications demanded of merchants, in contrast with the stipulations typically made by credit card acquirers, and this made the system more attractive for merchants who were likely to have limited turnover.

Despite its appealing simplicity, the First Virtual system failed to build a sufficient base of registered merchants and buyers and after a few attempts to refocus their business wound up operations in July 1998. There are undoubtedly many reasons why this system failed to succeed. One might be related to timing, since the First Virtual system was in operation a year or two before the volumes of e-commerce transactions began to grow substantially. The most obvious reason, though, is the fact that the preregistration process put customers off.

4.4 Once-off credit card numbers

One reason for keeping the credit card number secret from attackers is that, if compromised, the card number, name, expiry date, and other information may be used again by a fraudster to carry out further transactions. One way around this is to generate a new disposable credit card number each time something is purchased. This system was first brought to the market by Orbiscom in a product called O-card in early 2000. This product was sold through credit card issuers who then offered it to their account holders. A somewhat similar system called Private Payments was announced by American Express in September 2000 for users of that brand of payment card, while in Israel, a company called Cyota offers a product called SecureClick that works in much the same way.

Before the O-card system can be used, the user must first contact his or her card issuer, enable the card for this type of transaction, and download the O-card application. When an Internet purchase is to be made, the local O-card application is run—selecting PAY on this application offers a screen that allows the user to place an upper limit on the value of this transaction. After this is done, the O-card securely establishes a link with the card issuer system and generates a new credit card number for this transaction—these generated numbers will be from a range allocated globally to the card issuer, but are distinct from those used when issuing real credit cards. The generated number has a fixed validity period of 1 month and is stored both by the card issuer and by the O-card application. The O-card system is illustrated in Figure 4.3.

Buying something at a merchant site proceeds as normal except that the one-time credit card number is entered into the merchant's form instead of the real credit card number. The merchant is unaware that there is anything unusual about this and processes the card in the normal way. Once a single transaction has completed, the card issuer will mark the number as invalid and refuse to process further transactions against that credit card number. If the transaction does not complete, the number will expire at the end of its validity period.

A major advantage of this system is that, from the merchant's point of view, this is a normal credit card transaction. This means that all on-line merchants who accept credit cards automatically accept the O-card. The user is protected against unscrupulous merchants who may try to

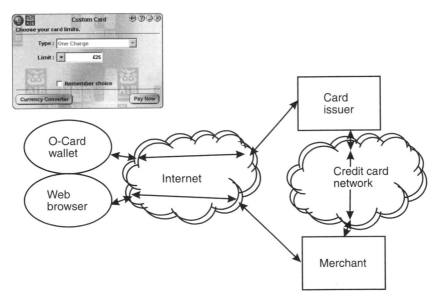

Figure 4.3 Orbiscom's O-card one-time credit card system.

retain the card number and perform further transactions at a later stage. On the negative side, the users must go through a fairly lengthy setup and download process and be sufficiently security conscious to run the O-card software every time they make a transaction.

4.5 The secure socket layer (SSL)

Both FV and O-card effect payment using the transfer of a semisecret quantity (VirtualPIN or once-off number) without the use of cryptography. An alternative approach is to securely transfer the credit card details across the network and then treat the transaction in the same way as a mail order/telephone order (MOTO) transaction.

For this to occur, two basic security services are required. First, some means must be found to encrypt the buyer-to-merchant communications link so that attackers cannot intercept the credit card details. Second, the merchant must be authenticated in some way to prevent attackers posing as merchants in order to capture card details. Although it would be desirable for the merchant to have some assurance that the person tendering the card details is in fact the cardholder, this is not strictly necessary in a MOTO type of transaction.

The security services alluded to above can be provided using the secure socket layer (SSL) [1] which is a general-purpose protocol designed to be used to secure any dialogue taking place between applications communicating across a "socket" interprocess communications mechanism, though its primary use to date has been to enable secure credit card transactions on the Web. The protocol was developed by staff at Netscape Corporation in 1994 and although patented by them, they have made it available to all on a royalty-free basis. SSL progressed to version 3.0 and the Internet Engineering Task Force incorporated this into their new standard for transport layer security (TLS) [2]. The two standards are virtually identical, but it is likely that TLS will develop further in the future.

Parties to an SSL exchange identify themselves by using certificates that link their *name* to a public key. No trust hierarchy is specified, so software agents taking part in SSL dialogues must be initialized with the certificates of certification authorities that are trusted. Most popular Web servers and browsers today have support for carrying out SSL dialogues.

Merchants who wish to use this must first apply to a public certification authority to be given an X.509 certificate attesting to their identity and ownership of their Internet domain name. This certificate and the accompanying private key are configured into the Web server before it is ready to engage in SSL dialogues. On the other side of the link, popular Web browser software typically comes preconfigured to trust certificates from a number of authorities. This list of trusted third parties can be modified if necessary. This common trust of the certification authority is the basis for the trust that is subsequently established in the SSL session and enables a merchant Web site to authenticate itself to the visitor in advance of payments being made.

The SSL protocol is transparent to the application using it. Once both sides are equipped with an SSL implementation, application data should pass through the secure socket in the same way as it would a normal (insecure) socket. Secured applications can exist side by side with normal applications. For example, calls to port 80 of a machine running a Web server can expect to have a dialogue with a Web server in an unsecured fashion, whereas calls to port 443 of the same machine will talk to the server over a secure socket connection.

Figure 4.4 shows the major components of the SSL protocol. When a socket connection for the SSL protocol is being set up, the *handshake* protocol does some initial work to establish the identities of the parties

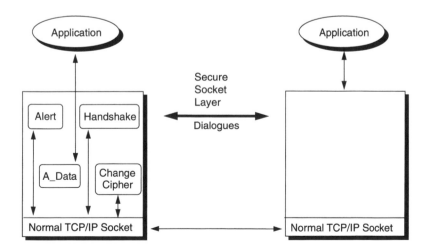

Figure 4.4 The main protocol components of the secure socket layer (SSL).

and negotiate cryptographic parameters for the session. Thereafter, application data is manipulated in accordance with these parameters and sent in *Application_Data* packets across the underlying socket connection. If the need arises to change the cryptographic parameters midsession, then the *Change_Cipher* primitives come into play. Similarly, any problems that may occur are dealt with by the *alert* protocol.

Within the handshake protocol, there are a wide variety of options depending on whether the client, the server, or both are to be authenticated, and which encryption and key-exchange algorithms should be used. In the following description, we will concentrate on the one most commonly used to effect electronic payment. In this configuration, only the server side is authenticated and subsequent payment dialogues must be encrypted.

Figure 4.5 shows a typical handshake process. When the client application initiates a connection to the server, the SSL layer emits a Client_Hello message. This contains 28 bytes of data generated by a secure random number generator in addition to a list of client-supported cryptographic and compression methods listed in order of preference. A unique session ID is also established that can be used to allow this session to be resumed later in a subsequent connection.

The server picks a cipher suite and a compression method from those offered and sends this back to the client in the Server_Hello message. The server also generates a random value that must be different from, and independent of, that included in the Client_Hello message. This is sent as part of the Server_Hello message. Following this, the server sends a Certificate message that contains a list of X.509 version 3 certificates beginning with its own certificate and including all certs as far as the root of the certification hierarchy. This part of the exchange is terminated with a Server_Hello_Done message.

Using the certificate path, the client can now extract the public key of the server and verify it's authenticity by following the trust path as far as the root. It computes a quantity called the *PreMasterSecret.* This is 48 bytes long and consists of 2 bytes giving the protocol version and 46 bytes of randomly generated data. The client encrypts this with the server's public key and sends it in a Client_Key_Exchange message. This PreMaster-Secret contains all of the information necessary to secure the SSL dialogue, and after this message is sent, both the client and server perform an identical set of computations (given here) on it to generate the *MasterSecret:*

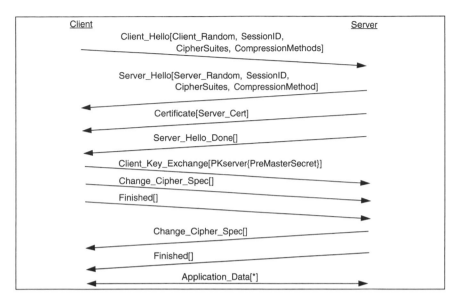

Figure 4.5 The main exchanges in the handshake protocol.

MasterSecret = MD5(PreMasterSecret + SHA('A' +PreMasterSecret +
ClientHello.Random + ServerHello.Random)) +
MD5(PreMasterSecret + SHA('BB' + PreMasterSecret +
CleintHello.Random + ServerHello.Random)) +
MD5(PreMasterSecret + SHA('CCC' + PreMasterSecret +
ClientHello.Random + ServerHello.Random))

This computation combines the PreMasterSecret with the random quantities sent in the Client_Hello and Server_Hello messages using concatenation (+), the message digest algorithm MD5, and the secure hash algorithm (SHA). Once the MasterSecret has been generated, a similar computation, shown here, is performed repeatedly to generate a stream, called a KeyBlock, until sufficient material has been generated for the partitioning process that follows:

KeyBlock = MD5(MasterSecret + SHA('A' + MasterSecret + SecretHello.Random +
ClientHello.Random))
+ MD5(Mastersecret + SHA('BB' + MasterSecret +
ServerHello.Random + ClientHello.Random))
+ MD5(MasterSecret + SHA('CCC' + MasterSecret + ServerHello.Random +
ClientHello.Random)) + [...]

Depending on the cipher suite agreed to in the negotiating process, key lengths for signing and encryption will vary. Figure 4.6 shows the sequence in which these are extracted from the KeyBlock. The first two quantities (client and server Write_MAC_Secret) will be used to generate message authentication codes (MACs) for messages. The remaining material is used to provide the encryption key (Write_Key) and initialization vector (IV) for whatever symmetric algorithm is used for bulk encryption of the dialogue. If there is material remaining after all keys have been generated, it is simply discarded.

At this point, both sides are equipped with all the necessary quantities to implement the agreed cryptographic regime. The client signals this by first sending a Change_Cipher_Spec message to indicate a changeover to the specification that has just been negotiated. This is followed by a Finished message, which is sent under this new specification. To signal its agreement, the server sends a similar Change_Cipher_Spec and Finished message pair.

At this point, the handshake protocol has terminated, the client and server application processes will be informed that a socket connection has been initiated, and they will start to exchange user data. This data is encapsulated in Application_Data units that vary in form depending on the cipher specification in force.

Figure 4.7 shows how user data to be sent on the secure socket is fragmented first into chunks of up to 2^{14} bytes (16 KB) in size. If both ends have agreed to use compression, then this fragment is passed through the agreed upon algorithm before proceeding. Depending on the cipher specification in force, the sender of data will want to do one of two things. Either the sender will want to produce a GenericStreamCipher unit sending the data in cleartext with a MAC appended, or a GenericBlockCipher will be produced in which the data is fully encrypted as well as having a MAC appended. The length of the MAC field will depend on which algorithm is used to generate it. Similarly, the PAD fields included in the GenericBlockCipher serve to bring the size of the overall data unit up to some multiple of the block size associated with the ciphering algorithm.

The cipher suites that can be used in an SSL connection are given names that are of the form:

SSL_KeyExchangeAlg_WITH_BulkCipherAlg_MACAlgorithm

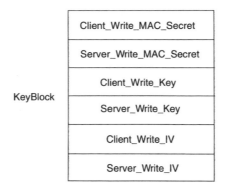

Figure 4.6 Partitioning the KeyBlock to obtain the individual keys.

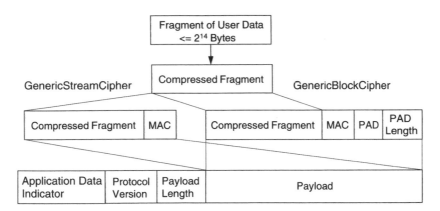

Figure 4.7 Encapsulating user data into application data protocol data units.

where the algorithms used for key exchange, bulk enciphering, and generation of message signatures are individually specified. Some examples include:

                SSL_RSA_WITH_NULL_MD5
                SSL_RSA_EXPORT_WITH_RC4_40_MD5
                SSL_RSA_WITH_IDEA_CBC_SHA
                SSL_DHE_RSA_WITH_3DES_EDE_CBC_SHA
                SSL_DH_ANON_EXPORT_WITH_DES40_CBC_SHA
                SSL_FORTEZZA_DMS_WITH_FORTEZZA_CBC_SHA

It can be seen from these examples that a large number of different algorithms are catered for in the SSL version 3.0 specification. This list has been further extended in the TLS document and at the time of writing, proposals have been made to extend this to incorporate the new AES into the list of algorithms that can be applied. In order to comply with the U.S. export restrictions on strong cryptography, versions of the popular Internet browsers that are available outside of the United States typically only support RC4 with a 40-bit key for content encryption, while those obtained within the United States use 128-bit RC4 by default. At the time of writing, this situation is changing, and while it is possible for non-U.S. browsers to use the stronger cryptography, it typically requires the user to apply a software patch to the European software to enable this.

When SSL is used to effect payment, the merchant operates an SSL-enabled Web server loaded with a certificate signed by an authority trusted by the Web client software. The client software will request a Web page whose address begins with *https* rather than the usual *http*. This indicates that SSL is to be used to secure the http dialogue. The server first authenticates itself, bulk encryption parameters are established, and the buyer's credit card details are sent in a Web form to the server, where they can be decrypted and processed. Eavesdroppers will be unable to access the encrypted network traffic, and the merchant processes the credit card details in the same way as for a MOTO order.

From a payment perspective, the use of SSL offers very little protection from many of the risks involved in a payment transaction. There is some assurance that the merchant Web site does represent a bona fide business since they authenticate themselves with respect to an X.509 certificate issued by a public authority. Since the dialogue is encrypted, there is little danger that an attacker can eavesdrop on the credit card details. Outside of that, there is no protection afforded on the amount of the transaction, the number of separate transactions, the assent of the card holder, or the creditworthiness of the card. In spite of this, SSL has been enormously successful and the vast majority of credit card–based Internet transactions today takes place across a link secured by SSL.

Probably the main reasons for the success of SSL lie in the fact that there is no need for any registration or sign-up procedure on behalf of the cardholder. Those who don't care about security are unaware that SSL is being applied to the dialogue. Those who are aware will notice the visual indicators (usually a padlock icon or a joined-up key that appears in the corner of the browser window) and can, using the browser menus, verify the certified identity of the merchant Web site. For the merchant, obtaining a certificate is a once-off and quite straightforward procedure. When SSL is coupled with a separate real-time system to check the creditworthiness of the card, it proves to be a very simple and robust payment solution.

4.6 *i*-Key protocol (*i*KP)

*i*KP [3] (where *i* = 1, 2, 3) is a family of secure payment protocols developed at IBM Research Labs in Zurich and Watson Research Center in the United States. The *i*KP protocols are based on public-key cryptography and differ from each other based on the number of parties that possess their own public-key pairs. This number is indicated by the name of the individual protocols: 1KP, 2KP, 3KP. The greater the number of parties that hold public-key pairs, the greater the level of security provided. The 1KP protocol is based on what security infrastructure already exists today. The 2KP and 3KP protocols can be phased in gradually to achieve full multiparty payment security as a more sophisticated certification infrastructure is put into place. This allows for gradual deployment of the system.

The current emphasis of the protocols is on credit card payments, as this is envisaged to be the most popular form of payment in the near future due to a large user base in place already. The entities involved in the system are the customer, the merchant, the customer's bank, and the merchant's bank. In the context of credit card systems, the merchant's bank is known as the *acquirer* because it acquires paper charge slips from the merchants. The customer's bank is known as an *issuer* because it issues credit cards to users. In the *i*KP protocols, the acquirer acts as a gateway between the Internet and the existing financial networks that support transactions between banks. The *i*KP protocols deal with *payment* transactions only (i.e., the solid lines in Figure 4.8). Therefore, the main parties involved in the transaction are the Customer (C), the Merchant (M), and the Acquirer gateway (A).

An important point to note is that the *i*KP suite of protocols are not a *shopping protocol* (i.e., the protocols do not provide encryption of the order information and assume that the order and price details have already been agreed upon by the customer and the merchant). Their sole function is to *enable* payment transactions between the various parties

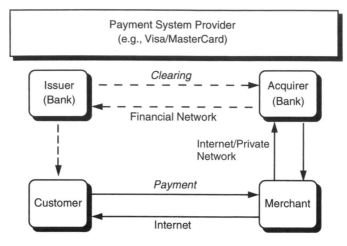

Figure 4.8 Payment protocol.

involved. This allows the protocols to be compatible with different browsing mechanisms.

4.6.1 Framework of *i*KP protocols

Each of the protocols consists of the seven basic steps shown in Figure 4.9. The contents of these steps may differ in each case:

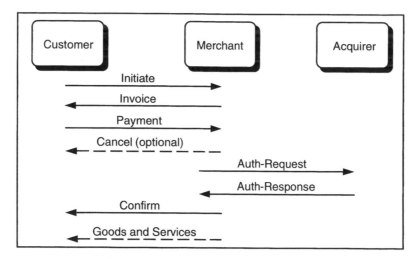

Figure 4.9 Overview of iKP protocol exchanges.

1. *Initiate:* The customer initiates the protocol flow.

2. *Invoice:* The merchant responds by providing an invoice.

3. *Payment:* The customer generates a payment instruction and sends it to the merchant.

4. *Cancel:* The merchant can refuse to further process the transaction.

5. *Auth-Request:* The merchant sends an authorization request to the acquirer.

6. *Auth-Response:* The acquirer uses existing networked clearing systems to obtain the authorization and returns an authorization response.

7. *Confirm:* The merchant forwards the acquirers signed response and any other additional parameters to the customer.

Table 4.2 lists a number of fundamental data elements that are exchanged in the course of an *i*KP transaction. Table 4.3 lists a number of fields that are formed by combining one or more of the atomic fields listed in Table 4.2. The quantities surrounded by square brackets are either optional or may occur in individual *i*KP protocols.

4.6.2 1KP

The 1KP protocol is the most basic of the protocols. Only the acquirer needs to possess and distribute its public-key certificate, $CERT_A$. Public-key encryption is required from the customer only, while decryption is required from the acquirer only. Both customer and merchant are required to verify the signature generated by the acquirer. Each entity participating in the protocol is assumed to possess some starting information.

Table 4.4 lists the starting information for each of the entities in the system. It is assumed that the customer and merchant have agreed on the description of the goods (DESC) prior to initiating the protocol (i.e., DESC is not carried within any *i*KP flow). It is also assumed that both the cardholder and merchant are in possession of the public key of the certification authority (CA) and the acquirer's certificate from which they can extract its public key.

All parties in 1KP must perform certain public-key computations. Each cardholder has a customer account number (CAN). This is normally

Table 4.2

Quantities Occurring in the iKP Protocols

Item	Description
CAN	Customer's account number (e.g., credit card number)
ID_M	Merchant ID; identifies merchant to acquirer
TID_M	Transaction ID; uniquely identifies the transaction
DESC	Description of the goods; includes payment information such as credit card holder's name and bank identification number
$SALT_C$	Random number generated by C; used to randomize DESC and thus ensure privacy of DESC on the M to A link
$NONCE_M$	Random number generated by a merchant to protect against replay
DATE	Merchant's current date/time
PIN	Customer's PIN which, if present, can be optionally used in 1KP to enhance security
Y/N	Response from card issuer; Yes/No or authorization code
R_C	Random number chosen by C to form CID
CID	A customer pseudo-ID which uniquely identifies C; computed as $CID = H(R_C, CAN)$
V	Random number generated in 2KP and 3KP by merchant; used to bind the Confirm and Invoice message flows

the customer's credit card number and is kept secret from the merchant. The following sections describe each of the steps shown in Figure 4.10.

4.6.2.1 Initiate composition

1. The customer forms a one-time cardholder ID (CID) that uniquely identifies the customer. It is computed as the hash of the customer's account number (CAN), and a random value R_C. CID = $H(R_C, CAN)$. (This avoids revealing the CAN to the merchant.)

2. Generates another random number $SALT_C$ that will be used by the merchant to randomize the goods' description information to avoid revealing it to the acquirer.

Table 4.3
Composite Field

Item	Description
Common	Information held in common by all parties: PRICE, ID_M, TID_M, DATE, $NONCE_M$, CID, H(DESC, $SALT_C$), [H(V)]
Clear	Information transmitted in the clear: ID_M, TID_M, DATE, $NONCE_M$, H(Common), [H(V)]
SLIP	Payment instructions: PRICE, H(Common), CAN, R_C, [PIN]
EncSlip	Payment instruction encrypted with the public key of the acquirer: PK_A (SLIP)
$CERT_X$	Public-key certificate of X, issued by a CA
Sig_A	Acquirer's signature: $SK_A[H(Y/N, H(Common))]$
Sig_M	Merchant's signature in Auth-Request: $SK_M[H(H(Common), [H(V)])]$
Sig_C	Cardholder's signature: $SK_C[H(EncSlip, H(Common))]$

Table 4.4
Starting Information for 1KP

Actor	Information Items
Customer	DESC, CAN, PK_{CA}, [PIN], $CERT_A$
Merchant	DESC, PK_{CA}, $CERT_A$
Acquirer	SK_A, $CERT_A$

3. The customer transfers the two quantities to the merchant as part of the Initiate message.

$$\text{Initiate: } (SALT_C, CID)$$

4.6.2.2 Initiate processing and invoice composition

1. The merchant generates $NONCE_M$ and DATE. This allows the acquirer to uniquely identify an order. The acquirer also chooses a transaction ID (TID_M) to identify the context.

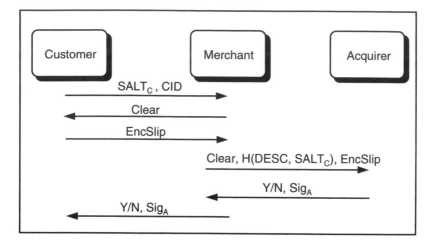

Figure 4.10   The 1KP protocol flows.

2.   Computes $H(\text{DESC, SALT}_C)$ and is now in a position to form Common. The merchant then computes $H(\text{Common})$ (see Table 4.3).

3.   Sends Clear in the Invoice flow to the customer. (The fields in Clear are sent as cleartext.)

Invoice: $(\text{ID}_M, \text{TID}_M, \text{DATE}, \text{NONCE}_M, H(\text{Common}))$

4.6.2.3   Invoice processing

1.   The customer already has DESC and SALT_C as part of the customer's starting information and computes $H(\text{DESC, SALT}_C)$. This quantity is included in Common by the merchant and is used by the customer to form Common in the next step.

2.   Computes $H(\text{Common})$ and verifies that this matches the value of $H(\text{Common})$ in Clear generated by the merchant. This confirms that the customer and merchant agree upon the contents of Clear.

3.   Generates a payment instruction (SLIP). The customer also includes the random number R_C, which was used to create the CID. This allows the acquirer to check that the CID given to the merchant corresponds to the CAN in the Payment message, but

not the merchant to recover the customer's account number. The customer then encrypts the SLIP using the acquirer's public key.

4. Transfers the encrypted SLIP (EncSlip) to the merchant as part of the payment flow.

$$\text{Payment: } (PK_A \ (SLIP))$$

4.6.2.4 Payment processing

1. If for some reason the merchant decides not to further process the message, the merchant sends a Cancel message to the customer.

2. The merchant now performs an authorization. The merchant forms an Auth-Request message. The merchant includes Clear and $H(DESC, SALT_C)$ along with EncSlip, which the merchant received as part of the payment instruction. This allows the acquirer to form Common and verify $H(Common)$ generated by both the merchant and customer.

$$\text{Auth-Request: } (EncSlip, \ Clear, \ H(DESC, SALT_C))$$

4.6.2.5 Auth-Request processing

1. The acquirer extracts from Clear the value $H(Common)$ as computed by the merchant. This is referred to as h_1. It also checks for replays using the values ID_M, TID_M, DATE, and $NONCE_M$.

2. Decrypts EncSlip and extracts $H(Common)$ from Slip as computed by the customer. This is referred to as h_2.

3. Checks that $h_1 = h_2$. This ensures that both customer and merchant agree on the order information.

4. Reforms Common from the various fields it receives in the Auth-Request and ensures that $H(Common) = h_1 = h_2$. In short, Common consists of a number of fields and $H(Common)$ allows each of the participants in the protocol to verify that they all agree on the details (e.g., the price and description of the goods) of the transaction. However, quantities such as the description information (DESC) and the cardholder's account number (CAN) are

disguised/salted in such a manner that only the parties that need to know that information are given access to it.

5. The acquirer then contacts the card issuer and obtains clearance for the transaction.

Upon receipt of a response from the issuer, the acquirer computes a digital signature on the response (Y/N) and H(Common) and sends the Auth-Response to the merchant. [Note that both the merchant and customer are already in possession of H(Common) and thus it is not sent as part of the Auth-Response message flow.]

$$\text{Auth-Response: } (Y/N, \text{Sig}_A)$$

4.6.2.6 Auth-Response processing

1. The merchant verifies the signature (Sig_A).

2. The merchant forwards the response and the acquirer's signature to the customer as part of the Confirm message flow. The customer in turn verifies the acquirer's signature, and the transaction is complete.

The 1KP protocol is simple and efficient for effecting electronic payments over open networks such as the Internet with minimal requirements for additional certification infrastructure. Its main weaknesses are the following:

▸ A customer authenticates himself or herself to a merchant only using a credit card number and optional PIN as opposed to using digital signatures.

▸ The merchant does not authenticate himself or herself to the customer or acquirer.

▸ Neither the merchant nor customer provide undeniable receipts for the transaction.

4.6.3 2KP

In 2KP, in addition to the acquirer, each merchant needs to possess a public-key pair and is required to distribute the public key contained in its certificate CERT_M to both customer and acquirer. This enables the customer and acquirer to verify the authenticity of the merchant. We now describe the additions to the basic flows that are required in 2KP.

The starting information for each of the parties is shown in Table 4.5. There are now three new elements in the Invoice:

1. The merchant generates a random number V and creates a message digest $H(V)$, and then adds $H(V)$ to Clear. [Note that Common now also contains $H(V)$.] The inclusion of V in Confirm later acts as a receipt of proof to the customer that the merchant has accepted the authorization response.

2. The merchant uses his or her secret key (SK_M) to sign the pair $H(\text{Common})$ and $H(V)$ to produce Sig_M.

3. The merchant also includes his or her public-key certificate $CERT_M$ so that the customer can verify the signature Sig_M.

The transaction message flow is shown in Figure 4.11. On receipt of the Invoice, the customer checks the merchant's signature Sig_M and generates a Payment message flow as before. The merchant appends the same signature Sig_M that he or she sent to the customer as well as his or her public-key certificate $CERT_M$ to Auth-Request. The acquirer checks the merchant's signature before authorizing the transaction. Finally, the value of V is sent in Confirm to the customer, who in turn computes $H(V)$ and verifies that this matches the value in Invoice.

The 2KP protocol satisfies all the requirements of 1KP as well as:

▸ The customer and the acquirer can verify the authenticity of the merchant due to the inclusion of the merchant's signature Sig_M and $CERT_M$.

Table 4.5
Starting Information for 2KP

Actor	Information Items
Customer	DESC, CAN, PK_{CA}, $CERT_A$
Merchant	DESC, PK_{CA}, $CERT_A$, SK_M, $CERT_M$
Acquirer	PK_{CA}, SK_A, $CERT_A$

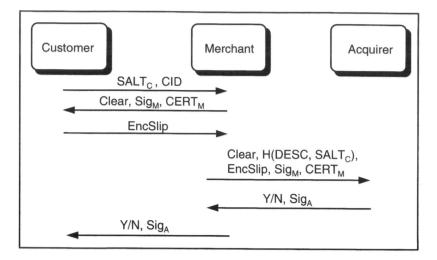

Figure 4.11   2KP protocol flows.

▶ The merchant generates a random number V and includes a message digest of the number $H(V)$ in Common. The merchant also signs the pair $H(V)$ and $H(\text{Common})$ to form Sig_M. This signature and $H(\text{Common})$ are verified by both the customer and the acquirer. The acquirer also signs $H(\text{Common})$ in Sig_A. When the customer receives V as part of the Confirm message flow, the customer is able to verify that $H(V)$ contained in Sig_M and Sig_A matches $H(V)$ that he or she has computed. Also, no other party is capable of finding V as this would involve inverting a strong one-way function. In effect, the customer receives a receipt of the transaction that assures the customer that the merchant has received and accepted the payment.

4.6.4   3KP

In 3KP, all the parties possess public-key pairs and corresponding certificates. This allows for nonrepudiation of all protocol exchanges. The protocol is modified to have the customer send a certificate to a merchant, who forwards it onto the acquirer. We describe the additions that are required to the flows of 2KP.

As Figure 4.12 shows, the customer now sends his or her public-key certificate to the merchant as part of the Initiate message. As a part of the

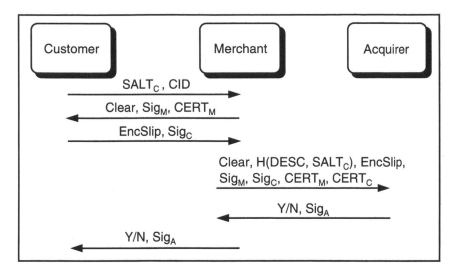

Figure 4.12   3KP protocol flows.

Payment, the customer sends his signature Sig_C to the merchant, where Sig_C is computed by encrypting EncSlip and H(Common). The merchant is able to verify the customer's signature, as the merchant already possesses the customer's certificate $CERT_C$. The merchant forwards Sig_C as part of the Auth-Request to the acquirer, who verifies the signature in turn.

The starting information for each of the parties is shown in Table 4.6. In 3KP, the customer's signature provides undeniable proof of the transaction authorization by the customer. This can be verified by both the merchant and the acquirer.

Table 4.6
Starting Information for 3KP

Actor	Information Items
Customer	DESC, CAN, PK_{CA}, SK_C, $CERT_A$
Merchant	DESC, PK_{CA}, $CERT_A$, SK_M, $CERT_M$
Acquirer	PK_{CA}, SK_A, $CERT_A$

The *i*KP protocols provide varying degrees of protection depending upon the number of entities that possess public-key pairs. In the initial stages of a deployment, 1KP could be used with a steady migration to 2KP and ultimately 3KP as the number of parties equipped with a public-/private-key pair increased.

IBM did implement the *i*KP system as a software suite referred to as the Zurich *i*KP Prototype (ZiP) [4] which was deployed in a number of payment trials in Spain, Japan, and The Netherlands. These deployments, however, were intended as precursors to the adoption of the industry-standard credit card payment system SET, which is discussed in Section 4.7.

4.7 Secure Electronic Transactions (SET)

By 1995, many different players in the credit card and software industries were applying their minds to the problem of securing credit card payments on the Internet. CyberCash, Inc. of Reston, Virginia, was a company founded in 1994 which developed its own set of protocols [5] and deployed wallet and cash-register software successfully for a number of years. Two major competing consortia were also formed, each led by a major credit card company. MasterCard combined with Netscape Corporation, IBM, and others to produce a fully specified system called the Secure Electronic Payment Protocol (SEPP) in October 1995. Within days of this launch, the second consortium led by Visa and Microsoft released a different and incompatible system called Secure Transaction Technology (STT). Both consortia proceeded to develop reference implementations of their efforts and formulate global rollout plans. Had this situation persisted, it would have led to an unfortunate situation in which transactions would need to be processed differently depending on which card-association brand they were associated with.

Ultimately, good sense prevailed, and in January 1996, the companies announced that they would come together to develop a unified system that would be called Secure Electronic Transactions (SET).

In February 1996, two documents were issued, the first of which [6] gave a business overview of the protocols, and the second of which [7] gave more technical details. This was followed by a public comment period during which interested parties discussed the specifications, and identified flaws. Following this, a revised book 3 protocol description was released [8] that defines the production SET protocol.

In order to coordinate the development of the SET standard, the two leading proponents, Visa and MasterCard, formed an independent company called Secure Electronic Transaction LLC (SETCo) in December 1997. Among the things that this company does are proposing and approving extensions and modifications to the SET standard. At the time of writing, eight different extensions had been approved.

The scope of the SET protocols was quite restricted from the outset. First, it was intended only as a payment protocol. The specification documents make clear that protocols would be developed by other parties to address on-line shopping, price negotiation, payment-method selection, and other electronic commerce functions. SET would only come into play after the customer had decided what to buy, for how much, and that the customer wanted to pay with a payment card.

In a conventional MOTO credit card transaction, a cardholder forwards his or her details to the merchant, who will then contact his or her (the merchant's) acquirer to obtain clearance for the payment. The acquirer can obtain this authorization from the institution that issued the card via a financial network operated by the card association (e.g., MasterCard or Visa). These private networks have existed for some time and have their own set of proprietary protocols operating on dedicated links with appropriate security mechanisms in operation. Thus, an infrastructure of links and transaction-processing computer hardware exists to electronically authorize credit card payments. SET assumes the existence of such a facility and only specifies the subset of dialogues between the customer and merchant and between the merchant and an entity known as the payment gateway.

An overview of the payment process is shown in Figure 4.13. The cardholder initiates a payment with the merchant using SET. The merchant then uses SET to have the payment authorized. The entity involved is called the payment gateway and it may be operated by an acquirer or could be some shared facility operated by a group of acquirers (or, indeed, the card association). The payment gateway acts as the front end to the existing financial network, and through this the card issuer can be contacted to explicitly authorize each and every transaction that takes place.

It is clear from the diagrams that SET is not intended to be a general-purpose payment protocol and is restricted to payment card or similar applications where parties will take on the role of buyer, merchant, or acquirer. It does not address transfer of funds from one individual to

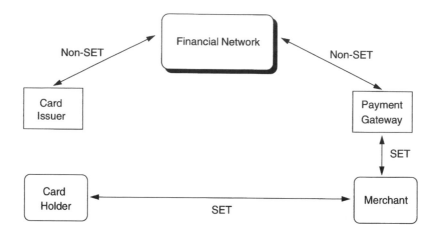

Figure 4.13 Phases of a credit card payment addressed by SET standards.

another and relies on the existing credit card infrastructure to effect the payment. The cardholder will see SET transactions on his or her credit card statement side by side with more conventional credit card payments, and the acquirer will see this as an extension of the current relationship he or she has with his or her merchant customers.

4.7.1 The SET trust model

Each of the parties that participates in a SET payment, with the possible exception of the cardholder, is required to authenticate himself or herself at some point in the payment process. He or she will do this by using the private part of a public-key pair. For this to operate satisfactorily, the corresponding public keys must be certified by some trusted third party.

In SET, bindings between identities and their corresponding public keys are stored using certificates in X.509 version 3 format. Figure 4.14 shows the format of such a certificate expressed in abstract syntax notation 1 (ASN.1). The principal purpose of this certificate is to bind the identity given by the *subject* field to the public key held in *subjectPublicKeyInfo* where the binding is certified by *issuer*: the authority that applies the signature to the certificate. In SET, a hierarchy of certification authorities shown in Figure 4.15 is used.

The first self-signed SET root certificate was produced in July 1997, and when SETCo came into existence, it took over its administration. The root authority uses its 2,048-bit private key to sign certificates for each

```
Certificate ::= SIGNED { SEQUENCE {
                        version [0]Version DEFAULT v1,
                        serialNumber CertificateSerialNumber,
                        signature AlgorithmIdentifier,
                        issuer Name,
                        validity Validity,
                        subject Name,
                        subjectPublicKeyInfo SubjectPublicKeyInfo,
                        issuerUniqueID  [1] IMPLICIT UniqueIdentifier OPTIONAL,
                        subjectUniqueID [2] IMPLICIT UniqueIdentifier OPTIONAL,
                        extensions [3] Extensions OPTIONAL }
```

Figure 4.14   The certificate definition in X.509 version 3.

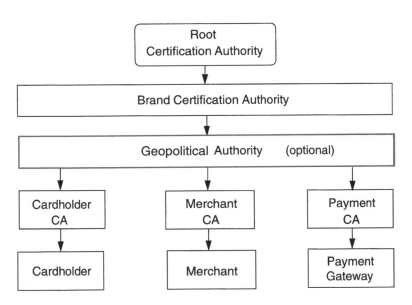

Figure 4.15   Certification authority hierarchy used in SET.

card brand (Visa, MasterCard, American Express, etc.). Procedures are defined to change from one root key to another before the root certificate reaches the end of its validity period. Each of the brands will then either deal directly with member financial institutions in individual countries or they will delegate this to some kind of geopolitical organization (e.g., Visa Europe). The certificates issued by the brand CAs and those lower down in the hierarchy are all signed using a 1,024-bit key length, reflecting the less onerous security regime required at the lower levels.

Cardholders must also be issued with certificates that they can use to assert their identity and the task of issuing these falls to the card-issuing banks. Payment gateways may be operated by an acquirer, who would already act as a merchant CA, but nevertheless, these gateways must use a certificate that has been signed by the payment CA before they can participate in a transaction.

SET also makes use of the *Extensions* field that became available in version 3 of the X.509 certificate definition. In particular, each certificate has a *Key Usage Restriction* field that specifies what tasks (e.g., signature verification and data encipherment) the key is approved for by the issuing CA. Cardholders are normally issued with a signature generation key certificate and they should not use the associated key pair for message confidentiality purposes.

The entities (cardholder, merchant, etc.) involved in SET transactions are identified in the certificates using an X.500 distinguished name. This is a collection of attributes that, taken together, uniquely identify the entity. Some examples of these attributes include country (c) and organization (o). Subdivisions of an organization can be identified by including one or more organizational units (ou) in the distinguished name. Normally, the last attribute used is the common name (cn), which would ordinarily give the individual name of an entity. In the case of SET cardholder certificates, neither the person's name nor the credit card number (often referred to as the primary account number or PAN) is shown in the certificate. Instead, a numeric quantity, computed by concatenating the PAN with a nonce as well as some fixed-character strings and computing the resulting hash, is used. This value is never regenerated, but is stored by the card issuer, and when a payment is attempted, the stored value is compared with the blinded account number contained in the request for payment authorization.

Figure 4.16 shows some examples of the kind of names that may be assigned to SET entities. The overall root of the hierarchy is operated by SETCo, as described earlier. Other examples shown in the figure are for a cardholder who has been issued a "European Express Card" from the Bank of Ireland, where the local promotional name used is "Fun Card." The common name attribute is a blinded version of the card number. This cardholder is shown interacting with a merchant called "Wolf a Pizza,"

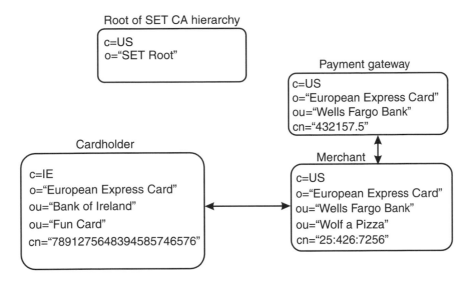

Figure 4.16 Some typical names assigned to SET entities.

whose acquiring organization is the Wells Fargo Bank. The payment gateway is operated by the same financial institution.

4.7.2 SET message structure

The SET protocol consists of request/response message pairs, such as the PReq and PRes messages shown in Figure 4.17. In this section, the contents and flow of the messages required to complete a purchase transaction are presented. To allow interoperability, the messages are defined in a machine-independent format in the specification. This will allow clients produced by one software company to perform a SET transaction with a server developed by a completely different company.

Encryption is performed on parts of certain messages. This end-to-end solution allows information contained with the message to be selectively revealed to parties as required. For example, the financial data about a credit card is not revealed to the merchant, and data about the purchased product is concealed from the acquirer. Point-to-point encryption of a connection link would not allow such selection to occur.

The messages needed to perform a complete purchase transaction (Figure 4.17) usually include:

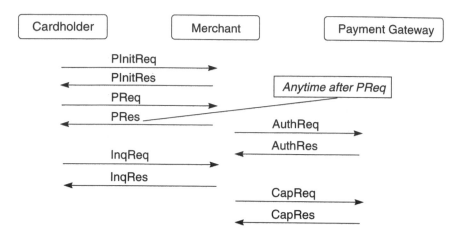

Figure 4.17   Steps in a SET transaction.

- Initialization (PInitReq/PInitRes);

- Purchase order (PReq/PRes);

- Authorization (AuthReq/AuthRes);

- Capture of payment (CapReq/CapRes);

- Cardholder inquiry (InqReq/InqRes) [optional].

These messages are not necessarily in this order. The contents and function of each pair are now examined in turn.

4.7.3   Payment initialization (PInitReq/PInitRes)

The SET payment starts after the cardholder has been presented with a completed order form and approved its contents. The way in which goods are selected and presented in an order form is outside the scope of SET, but it is likely that shopping protocols will be designed to handle this.

The PInitReq message is sent to the merchant to indicate that the cardholder is ready to pay for the goods. As shown in Figure 4.18, it contains:

- Brand of card that will be used in the payment, such as Visa or MasterCard (Brand_ID);

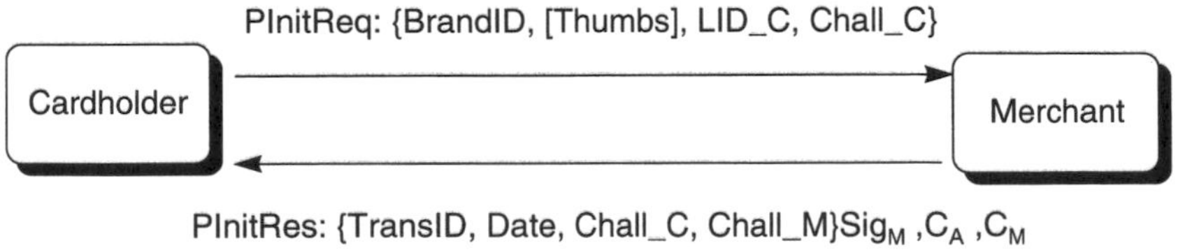

PInitReq: {BrandID, [Thumbs], LID_C, Chall_C}

```
┌──────────────┐                                      ┌──────────────┐
│  Cardholder  │ ──────────────────────────────────▶  │   Merchant   │
│              │ ◀──────────────────────────────────  │              │
└──────────────┘                                      └──────────────┘
```

PInitRes: {TransID, Date, Chall_C, Chall_M}Sig_M ,C_A ,C_M

Figure 4.18 Initialization messages.

› A local ID for the transaction (LID_C);

› Optional list of certificates (Thumbs) already stored by the cardholder software. This list consists of a thumbprint (SHA hash) of each certificate held;

› Challenge variable (Chall_C), which will be used in the merchant's response, to guarantee the freshness of the communication.

Upon receipt of the PInitReq, the merchant generates a globally unique ID that is combined with the LID_C to form the complete transaction ID (TransID). This is used to identify a specific purchase from other purchase messages received.

The merchant's response contains this TransID along with certificates and the current date. The cardholder's challenge is included along with a new merchant challenge (Chall_M). The certificates include those keys that are needed in the payment and that the cardholder doesn't already hold, such as the merchant and acquirer public keys.

Since the cardholder has now received an appropriate response to his challenge, he or she can be confident that the merchant is an accredited retailer.

4.7.4 Purchase order (PReq/PRes)

The purchase order messages fulfill the actual purchase by the cardholder from the merchant. It is the most complex message pair in the payment protocol. The cardholder sends two elements, the order information (OI) and payment instructions (PI), to the merchant, as shown in Figure 4.19:

› The OI holds data that identifies the order description at the merchant.

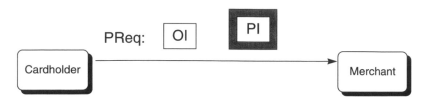

Figure 4.19   Purchase request.

- The PI contains the actual card data, purchase amount, and order and transaction identifiers. The PI is encrypted with the acquirer's public key so that the merchant cannot view its contents. It is forwarded to the acquirer later as part of the authorization.

4.7.4.1   Order information (OI)

The construction of the OI is shown in Figure 4.20. OIData consists of data from the initialization phase. The merchant challenge, Chall_M, is returned, demonstrating the freshness of the message to the merchant. ODsalt is a nonce that is used when creating a hash of the order description. By including this random nonce within the hash, dictionary attacks are prevented. That is, the nonce stops an attacker from guessing the hash value, H(OIData), by trying all possible combinations of dictionary words in the order description.

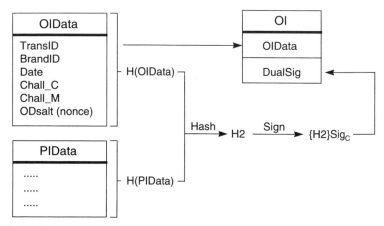

Note: No Encryption

Figure 4.20   Construction of the order info (OI) element.

A dual signature is created using the hashes of OIData and PIData (the data contents of the PI). The signature links OIData and PIData, which links the cardholder's order to the authorization payment instructions by showing that they were signed together. Anyone possessing either OIData or PIData and the dual signature can verify the signature without having to know the other. The dual signature is also a speed optimization since only one signature is needed instead of having to separately sign OIData and PIData. The cardholder signature certificate is also included with the signature so that the merchant can verify it.

4.7.4.2 SET dual signatures

While the dual signatures in SET are created in the normal way, as described in Chapter 3, a further optimization is applied. The result of XORing the hash of message 1 with the hash of message 2 is included with the signature. The signature can be verified with this value and either message 1 or message 2. This prevents having to include $H(M1)$ in one copy of the signature, and $H(M2)$ in the second copy of the signature when distributing to the two parties involved, as is normally the case. Instead, these values can be extracted from the XOR value and the single version of the dual signature can then be verified. The following example clarifies this:

- Take two messages, M1 and M2.

- Create a dual signature in the normal way:
  $H2 = H(H(M1), H(M2))$. Then Sign H2.

- Normal dual signature:
  $\{H2\}\text{Sig}_X$, $H(M1)$ for holder of M2.
  $\{H2\}\text{Sig}_X$, $H(M2)$ for holder of M1.

- But now include $Y = H(M1) \text{ XOR } H(M2)$ in signature.

- SET dual signature: $\{H2\}\text{Sig}_X$, Y for all parties.

- The holder of M1 verifies the dual signature by extracting $H(M2)$ from Y:
  $H(M1)$ is first obtained by applying the hash algorithm to M1
  $H(M2) = H(M1) \text{ XOR } Y$

- Having obtained $H(M2)$ from Y, the dual signature is validated in the normal way:

$H(M1)$ and $H(M2)$ are concatenated, and the result then hashed. $H3 = H(H(M1), H(M2))$. The resulting hash, $H3$, should match $H2$ in the signature.

$H3 = H2$ if signature valid.

The SET dual signature optimization allows the same signature material to be sent to both parties ($\{H2\}Sig_X$, Y), instead of having to replace Y with different values for each receiver. From the SET dual signature message, both parties can verify the signature that links message 1 and message 2 together.

4.7.4.3 Payment instructions (PI)

The PI is constructed as shown in Figure 4.21. Remember, the contents of the PI are never seen by the merchant, but are forwarded to the acquirer. The actual credit card data is included with nonces to defeat playback and dictionary attacks. The card data is protected by using extra-strong encryption as described in the following section. A hash of the order, $H(\text{Order})$, is included, which identifies the unique order the cardholder is referring to without giving away what that order is.

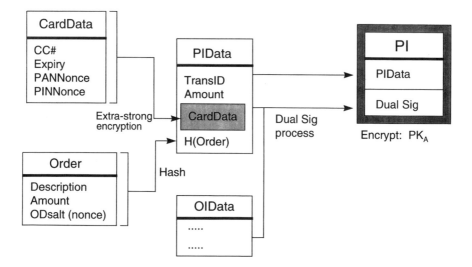

Figure 4.21 Construction of payment instructions (PI).

The same dual signature already created for OI is used as the signature on the PI. The PI is encrypted with the public-key of the acquirer. This prevents the merchant, or anyone else, from viewing its contents.

The payment request embodies the actual credit card payment from the cardholder's point of view. It is at the core of the SET payment protocol and once sent, the cardholder has shown an agreement to pay that cannot be easily reversed.

4.7.4.4 SET extra-strong encryption

Instead of encrypting with a symmetric DES key and then encrypting this symmetric key using RSA, the data is directly encrypted with RSA. This is illustrated in Figure 4.22 where extra-strong encryption is used on the card data and is much stronger than the normal SET hybrid encryption.

4.7.4.5 Processing PReq

When the merchant receives a purchase request from a cardholder, the OI and PI parts are extracted. The merchant verifies the cardholder's dual signature on OI using the cardholder's certificate by traversing the certificate trust chain to the root.

Before sending a purchase response (PRes) to the cardholder, the merchant will normally perform the authorization and perhaps capture steps of the payment. Authorization and capture are described in the following sections. However, PRes may be returned before capture or before both capture and authorization. The option chosen will affect the contents of the messages.

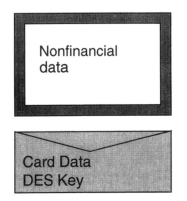

Nonfinancial data — Normal Encryption DES Encrypt (56 bit)

Card Data DES Key — Extra-Strong Encryption RSA Encrypt (1,024 bit)

Figure 4.22 SET extra-strong encryption.

If authorization is delayed, the merchant will return a purchase response indicating that the cardholder should inquire later about transaction status. The cardholder inquiry messages are described in Section 4.7.7.

When the merchant does send the purchase response to the cardholder, it will contain the transaction status and any result codes available. The message format is shown in Figure 4.23. The CompletionCode indicates whether the authorization or capture steps have been completed. Results contain the authorization or capture codes for the transaction if these steps have been performed. These codes were generated in the financial bankcard network to authorize and clear the transaction and may appear on the cardholder's monthly bill.

The purchase order messages form the actual purchase by the cardholder from the merchant. When the cardholder receives the merchant's response, the cardholder knows that either the payment is complete or that the transaction is waiting to be processed by the credit card financial network.

4.7.5 Authorization (AuthReq/AuthRes)

This process allows the merchant to verify that the cardholder has credit for the purchase and to obtain permission to charge the transaction to his or her credit card. In the authorization request, the merchant sends data about the purchase, signed and encrypted, to the acquirer. The PI from the cardholder is also forwarded in this request.

The data sent includes a hash of the order details as shown in Figure 4.24. If this matches the H(Order) present in the PI, the acquirer knows that the merchant and cardholder are in agreement about the ordered goods and purchase amount. The dual signature in the PI proves that it came from the cardholder. H(OIData) in the merchant request shows knowledge of OIData that is signed by the dual signature, showing

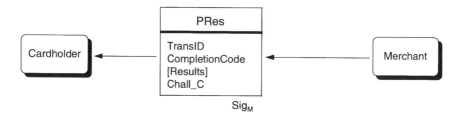

Figure 4.23 Merchant's purchase response message.

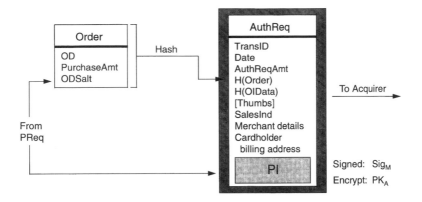

Figure 4.24 Constructing an authorization request for the purchase.

agreement on the order data without revealing it. Thumbs is an optional list of relevant certificates held by the merchant to prevent the acquirer sending them in the response. The cardholder billing address (obtained outside the SET protocol) and other merchant details such as business type are also expected.

Both authorization and capture can be performed in a single request, known as a sales transaction. SalesInd is used to indicate if the merchant wishes to do this.

Upon receiving AuthReq, the acquirer decrypts the message parts, verifies signatures, and checks for consistency between the purchase details sent by the merchant and those in the PI. If the merchant's request (AuthReqAmt) is not the same as the PurchaseAmt, it is checked that this difference is acceptable to policy. Next, the acquirer obtains the authorization through the existing financial network as shown in Figure 4.25.

Having received a good authorization from the card issuer, an authorization response (AuthRes) is returned to the merchant with the authorization code from the issuer. Illustrated in Figure 4.26, it also

Figure 4.25 Obtaining authorization for a purchase transaction.

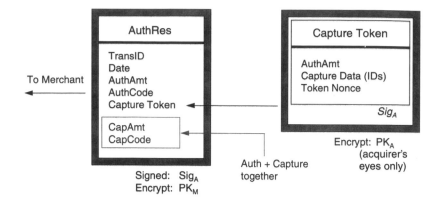

Figure 4.26 Authorization response with capture token.

contains a capture token, signed and encrypted, which is later used by the merchant to capture the payment. Only the acquirer can decrypt the token, keeping the capture data hidden from anyone else.

If capture was performed with the authorization (sales transaction), then the capture code and amount are returned instead of the capture token. Upon receiving a good authorization, a merchant can ship the goods purchased. A good authorization indicates that the card issuer has verified the card details and credit limit, and given the go-ahead for the purchase.

4.7.6 Capture of payment (CapReq/CapRes)
After processing an order, the merchant needs to request the payment previously authorized to be transferred to his account. The total payment for several authorizations can be captured in a single batch request, as shown in Figure 4.27. A merchant might accumulate many capture tokens (from authorization) throughout the day and then request reimbursement for these at the end of the day.

The contents of a capture request (CapReq) are shown in Figure 4.28. Many capture tokens from different transactions can be included in a single request for efficiency. For each token, the corresponding authorized amount and transaction ID are included. These should match the data encrypted within the capture token itself. CapID is a unique value used to identify this capture from others. The request is signed and encrypted by the merchant.

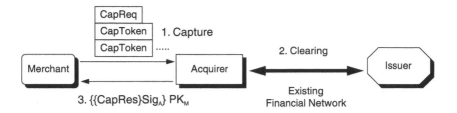

Figure 4.27 Capturing multiple authorized payments in a single request.

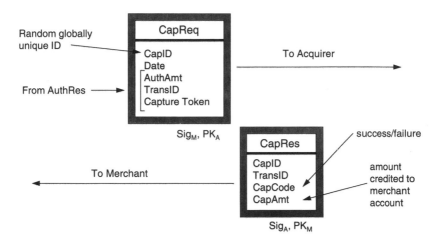

Figure 4.28 Capture request/response messages.

After verifying the capture request, the acquirer credits the merchant's account. Transaction fees may be deducted at this stage. The capture response (CapRes), signed and encrypted, contains a success indication, the settled amount, and a capture code from the financial network.

After a successful capture, the merchant has received the actual payment of money from the cardholder's purchase. If the merchant has not already sent the purchase response to the cardholder, this is now done.

4.7.7 Cardholder inquiry (InqReq/InqRes)

The inquiry messages allow a cardholder to check the status of a transaction. An inquiry can be sent any time after the purchase request, and cardholders can only inquire about their own purchases. The inquiry can be performed several times for a single transaction.

The message contents are shown in Figure 4.29. The inquiry request contains the transaction identifier and includes a new challenge variable. This should be unique to each invocation, since the inquiry may be sent repeatedly. The inquiry is signed to prove that the request comes from the correct cardholder.

The inquiry response returned by the merchant is very similar to PRes. It contains the transaction status and any result codes (authorization or capture) available. Having received an inquiry response, the cardholder can be sure as to how a specific purchase with an accredited merchant is proceeding.

4.7.7.1 Cardholder registration

All parties involved in a payment need key certificates to send SET messages. When cardholders want to start using SET to make network payments, they must obtain a public-key certificate from a certification authority (CA).

All cardholders need a signature certificate containing their public signature key so that messages signed by them can be verified. An encryption certificate, with a public-key exchange key, is optional since none of the SET payment messages sent to the cardholder is encrypted in the current version of SET.

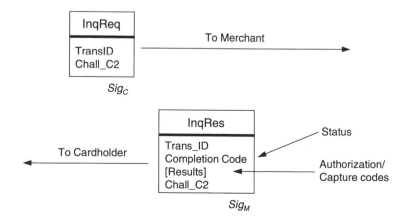

Figure 4.29   Inquiry request/response messages.

The method for obtaining a CA signed certificate is outlined in Figure 4.30. Whether the cardholder is obtaining one certificate or multiple certificates, the procedure is much the same.

Certificates have an expiry date, which usually matches the credit card expiry date. The procedure for renewing certificates is also very similar to that shown. Similar certificate registration and renewal processes exist for merchants and acquirers.

The registration process starts when the cardholder sends a request (CInitReq) to the CA asking for:

‣ CA's key exchange certificate. This will allow later messages sent to the CA to be encrypted with its public-key exchange key. Clearly, to verify this certificate, all users must have a copy of the root public key.

‣ An electronic registration form from the cardholder's financial institution (issuer).

The contents of CInitReq are shown in Figure 4.31. The request type indicates whether the cardholder seeks a signature certificate, an encryption certificate, or both. The BankID (BIN) is the first six numbers on the card and uniquely identifies the issuing bank. The Language field is used

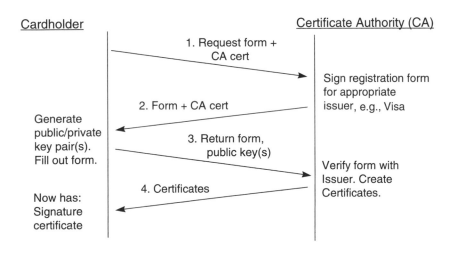

Figure 4.30 Cardholder registration.

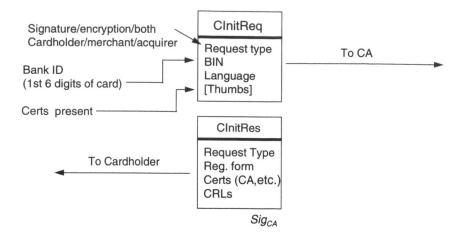

Figure 4.31 CInit request/response messages.

to request the language on the returned registration form. A thumbprint (Thumbs) of current certificates held is also sent.

The CA's response (CInitRes) holds the appropriate registration form, the CA's certificates and those needed to verify them, and a list of relevant revoked certificates (CRLs), all signed by the CA.

The cardholder now validates the certificates by traversing the trust chain and removes any certificates listed in the revocation list. The cardholder can now be confident that he or she has received a valid registration form from an accredited certificate authority. The registration form is filled out and includes the credit card number and expiry date. In order to send this sensitive data to the CA, it is encrypted directly with the CA's public RSA key–exchange key (SET extra-strong encryption).

The cardholder nonce (Nonce_CARD) will be combined with a CA-generated nonce (Nonce_CCA) at the CA to form PANNONCE. This nonce is used in the payment protocol (see Figure 4.31). H(CardData, PANNONCE) will also appear in the cardholder's certificates.

The cardholder signs the public keys that are to be certified and includes these with the registration form to construct the certificate request message (CertReq). The request is encrypted before sending it to the CA, as shown in Figure 4.32.

When the CA receives the certificate request, it authenticates the card with the issuing bank using an existing financial network. If the card

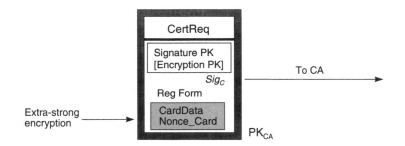

Figure 4.32 Certificate request message.

data is valid, it will generate and sign certificates for the cardholder's public keys. The contents of these certificates are discussed in Chapter 3.

The certificate response from the CA (CertRes) contains the new certificates and the strongly encrypted Nonce_CCA, as shown in Figure 4.33. The cardholder verifies the certificates and combines the decrypted CA nonce (Nonce_CCA) with the cardholder nonce (Nonce_CARD) to form PANNONCE.

$$PANNONCE = H(\text{Nonce\_Card XOR Nonce\_CCA})$$

It can then be verified that $H(\text{CardData, PANNONCE})$, which forms the globally unique cardholder ID, appears in the new certificates:

$$\text{Unique Cardholder ID} = H(\text{CardData, PANNONCE})$$

The cardholder now has the signature certificate required to make a purchase, and can start making credit card payments to SET merchants.

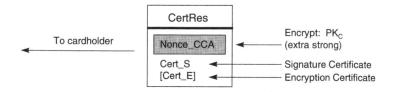

Figure 4.33 Certificate response message.

4.7.8 SET software components

From the time that the first versions of the SET standard became available in 1996, several technology companies began to develop software to support it. Initially, in order to provide guidance for developers, Visa and MasterCard contracted Terisa Systems to produce a reference implementation called SETREF. This software was freely available to companies to assist them in developing and testing their own applications. The reference implementation of SET was bound up with cryptographic libraries, which were export controlled. It failed to satisfy the needs of developer companies and after some months, the SETREF project was abandoned.

The first live SET transaction was performed in Denmark on December 31, 1996, in an IBM pilot scheme, but in reality, many of the infrastructural components that are needed for SET were not available at that time. Throughout 1997 tentative piloting activity began in a number of regions around the world.

The three major software components that need to be in place to carry out a SET transaction are first, the wallet—which resides in the user's workstation and operates in conjunction with the local Web browser. Second, the merchant server must have SET support added to process the purchase request dialogues. Finally, the acquiring bank or a related party must put in place a payment gateway that can handle SET transactions and also interact with the financial networks for authorizations and for completing the transactions.

Each of these three software components represents a considerable amount of complexity and since it is very unlikely that all three will come from the same vendor, there is great potential for interoperability problems. SETCo were mindful of these problems and have instituted a certification program that allows manufacturers to submit their products and be awarded a SET Mark indicating compliance with the standard. In the same vein, SETCo have sponsored so-called "interoperability festivals" which are periods of time in which companies may test particular software interfaces while operating with a SETCo-issued set of X.509 certificates. At the time of writing, more than 60 different products had either been awarded or were seeking SET Mark approval.

4.7.9 SET market acceptance

When SET was conceived in 1996, it was expected that it would have achieved widespread usage in a period of around two years. These projections turned out to be wildly optimistic. One of the first problems related to the complexity of the specification. The fact that SET is specified in three weighty volumes means that the software development and testing effort was considerable. Some minor changes to the standard were made as comments came in from developers and SET version 1.0 was not issued until May 1997. Interoperability testing was also a significant hurdle. Compliance testing was subcontracted to a single company and the cost levied on the software producers were quite high. All of this meant that the fundamental software components that make up a SET system were available later than planned and were significantly more expensive to produce.

The second barrier to rapid rollout was the need for a supporting certification authority hierarchy. Once again, the service provided by a CA involved the use of complex software. If the certification is to mean anything, strict security policies must be in force to safeguard the certificates and keys over their entire lifetime from issuance to revocation or expiry; and strict physical security measures need to be in place wherever the highly secret private keys are stored. SET requires each of the credit card brands not only to set up this infrastructure, but also to go through a strict certification procedure with the next level up in the hierarchy. This process must then be repeated for each card issuing and merchant acquiring bank as well as for payment gateway operators. Finally, all cardholders are required to go through a registration process in which they enable their credit card for SET operation and are issued with a certificate that must be loaded into their SET wallet. Experience in attempting to set up PKIs in other areas has proved to be a difficult, costly, and time-consuming process. SET has proved to be no exception to this rule.

A final barrier to SET acceptance lies in the difference between the way the banking industry has historically operated and the way the Internet is structured. In the past, when the banking industry wished to launch a new product they selected a geographic region, such as a town or province and commenced a pilot operation with their customers in that area. In that way, they could quickly achieve a high penetration of the product in that region and then monitor customer reaction. Since the concept of geographic region had almost no impact on Internet communication, this approach does not work very well. For example, merchants may put major effort into SET enabling their Web site and connecting to a payment gateway operated by their acquiring bank. The only customers that can make use of this Web site are either in their local region, served by the same bank, or ones from other regions where SET initiatives are under way. This led to a pattern in SET trials in which all of the software would be made to work for a small number of test transactions, only to be followed by a tiny trickle of real orders coming in through this route. At the time of writing, the major stakeholders in SET are experimenting with new initiatives to simplify SET deployment and somehow galvanize interest on behalf of cardholders and merchants in accelerating its deployment.

4.7.10 Server-side wallets

Since one of the major difficulties in deploying SET is in assembling a critical mass of cardholders that will download and use SET-enabled wallet software, some SET software companies have circumvented this by incorporating the wallet into the merchant software. Before this can work, the users must go to the merchant site and securely register, giving full credit card details which are stored for later use. When shopping on the site, users indicate that they wish to purchase and identify themselves using either a password or implicitly using a Web browser mechanism known as a *cookie*. The server software then composes a purchase request on the users' behalf and proceeds with the rest of the transaction using SET. If this option is used, then SET must be operated in a mode that does not require cardholder certificates.

A different variant of this is where a third party, such as a bank, stores the cardholder's details on a separate Web site. At the time of purchase, a merchant packages details of the purchase transaction and then passes control to this third-party Web site which then initiates the SET transaction on the users' behalf.

Both of these mechanisms get around the problem of users having to download wallet software. They also allow the user to make payments in situations in which downloading a wallet is not feasible, for example, on a public Internet kiosk. However, they do require a sign-up step on the part of each user and remove many of the benefits of having SET in the first place. They also introduce an additional danger of third-party Web sites needing to store large numbers of credit card details which, if compromised, could lead to large-scale fraud.

At the time of writing, Visa Europe has announced a system which it calls Three Domain SET (3-D SET) in which Visa will operate a server-side wallet holding customer details on behalf of their card-issuing banks. Details are a little sketchy, but the card-issuing banks will have some kind of role in authenticating their customers who wish to make Internet purchases, and ensuring the correctness of information stored on their behalf on the Visa wallet server. Merchants who engage in 3-D SET transactions with the Visa-run wallet will have much more protection against customer repudiation of these transactions. It remains to be seen what the market uptake of this system will be.

4.7.11 Using SET with smart cards

In Europe, most major banks have adopted a policy of a steady migration from magnetic stripe–based bank and payment cards toward those incorporating a chip or smart card. Nowhere is this more evident than in France, where the use of smart card–based payment terminals in stores is common. As a result, there is a large demand from the French and other European countries to leverage the security features of the smart card in a SET environment.

In 1998, after some earlier experiments with smart cards, a company called Cyber-COMM was formed consisting of the major French banks, card organizations, and smart card system providers to promote the use of chip cards in SET. They lobbied for and secured an extension to the SET standards [9]. This allows the insertion of cryptographic quantities generated by the smart card into SET messages in place of fields that were generated using certificates. They have also defined a specification for a smart-card reader system called MEERKAT that can be used with a user's workstation and suitable wallet software to produce SET dialogues containing smart card–generated fields. The payment gateway is also equipped with a secure hardware device, which is used to verify the smart card–generated quantities before the transaction is allowed to proceed into the financial network.

The Cyber-COMM solution was officially launched in April 2000 with several million customers targeted by 2002.

4.8 Summary

Credit cards have been enormously successful as a means of paying for retail Web-based transactions. There is a large base of users worldwide who have signed up for credit cards for conventional commerce, and are willing to use them for on-line purchases. There are a small number of major brands which have very wide acceptance worldwide and they are inherently multicurrency in their operation.

On the downside, however, when used in a "card-not-present" context, which is the default on the Internet, they are completely insecure and fraud can and does happen. At the beginning of this chapter, we first looked at the very simple way in which First Virtual avoided putting the credit card details on the network. Orbiscom and others have adopted a much more sophisticated way of doing the same thing while ensuring that what is used instead is valid for only a single highly constrained transaction.

We looked at the secure socket layer (SSL), which performs just two security functions. First, it offers some assurance that the operator of the Web site is a bona fide merchant, and, second, it encrypts the link so that an outside attacker cannot intercept the credit card details in transit. Arguably, these two risks are perhaps the least likely ones to give trouble in a typical credit card transaction. Nevertheless, since the deployment of SSL required very little work on the part of the merchant and none at all on the part of the consumer, it has been adopted by the vast majority of Web retailers. In the early days of the mass-Internet phenomenon, on-line merchants were desperate to get some kind of security in place. As e-commerce becomes more mature, greater focus is being put on the fraud rates that are being experienced and on how these can be lowered.

We looked at iKP as an example of a well-developed research payment system that was highly influential in the evolution of the major industry standard: Secure Electronic Transactions (SET). We have given this standard considerable attention since it guards against virtually all risks inherent in credit card payments and has huge support in the payment industry. Consumer uptake of this technology has been much slower than many people anticipated and we have examined some of the reasons why. The industry is now searching for ways of finding a middle ground between the simplicity of SSL and the rich functionality of SET.

References

[1] Kocker, P., A. Freier, and P. Karlton, *The SSL Protocol Version 3.0*, Netscape Communications Corp., March 1996, http://home.netscape.com/eng/ssl3/index.html.

[2] Dierks, T., and C. Allen, *The TLS Protocol Version 1.0*, IETF Request for Comments RFC-2246, January 1999, http://www.ietf.org/rfc.

[3] Bellare, M., et al., "iKP—A Family of Secure Electronic Payment Protocols," *Proc. 1st USENIX Workshop on Electronic Commerce*, New York, July 11–12, 1995, http://www.zurich.ibm.com/csc/infosec/past-projects/ecommerce/iKP.html.

[4] Bellare, M., et al., *Design, Implementation and Deployment of iKP—A Secure Account-Based Electronic Payment System*, IBM Research Report RZ 3137, July 1999, http://www.zurich.ibm.com/csc/infosec/past-projects/ecommerce/iKP.html.

[5] Eastlake, D., III, et al., *CyberCash Credit Card Protocol Version 0.8*, RFC 1898, February 1996, http://www.ietf.org/rfc.

[6] MasterCard and Visa Corporations, *Secure Electronic Transaction (SET) Specification—Book 1: Business Description Version 1.0*, May 1997, http://www.setco.org.

[7] MasterCard and Visa Corporations, *Secure Electronic Transaction (SET) Specification—Book 2: Programmer's Guide Version 1.0*, May 1997, http://www.setco.org.

[8] MasterCard and VISA Corporations, *Secure Electronic Transaction (SET) Specification—Book 3: Formal Protocol Definition Version 1.0*, May 1997, http://www.setco.org.

[9] *Common Chip Extension SET 1.0—Application for SETCo Approval, Version 1.0*, September 1999, http://www.setco.org/download/comchip_ext.doc.

Electronic checks and account transfers

Paper-based payments using a check, while still highly popular in the United States, have been falling out of favor in European countries. This process of decline has been encouraged by banks for two reasons. First, paper-based checks are expensive to process. They may involve the transport of the signed check all the way to the bank on which it is drawn before being able to determine that the payment can be made. The expense involved in the so-called *returned items* (bounced checks) means that the average cost per check is quite high. Second, the use of debit cards, in which each transaction involves an electronic verification of the availability of funds, has all the properties of a check-based payment without the attendant disadvantages.

It is clear, though, that there is a need for a check-like payment system in which funds are transferred from the payer's bank account to the payee's bank account at the time the transaction takes place. From the

127

banks' point of view, it would be desirable to use existing interbank funds transfer networks as much as possible. This chapter will examine a number of electronic check schemes and alternative check-like methods that allow value to be transferred between bank accounts during a purchase. Some of these payment systems are standalone in technology terms, while others make maximal use of the existing banking infrastructure.

5.1 Payment transfer between centralized accounts

When two parties hold bank accounts at two different financial institutions, a payment can be made by directly transferring money from the payer's account at one bank to the payee's account at another. Alternatively, an indirect payment may be made by giving an authorization to transfer funds from the payer account to the payee, such as with an electronic check. In each case a secure interface must be provided through the banks to the existing financial-clearing networks in order to settle payment.

When both the payer and payee hold accounts at the same centralized on-line financial institution, the transfer between accounts is much simpler. The payer securely connects to the bank, and informs it to move a certain amount from the payer's account into the payee's account. Since the bank only has to subtract an amount from one account and add the amount to another account, no financial-clearing networks are needed. If anyone is allowed to open and maintain an account, then user-to-user payments can be easily effected.

The centralized account model has become popular on the Internet, with over 20 different payment systems using this approach. Table 5.1

Table 5.1
Payment Systems Based on Centralized Account Model

Payment System	Web Site	Features
Amazon.com Payments	www.amazon.com	Amazon.com auction and small merchant payments
Beenz	www.beenz.com	Loyalty currency earned at participating Web sites

Table 5.1 (continued)

Payment System	Web Site	Features
BidPay	www.bidpay.com	Mails physical money order to payee
Billpoint	www.billpoint.com	eBay auction payments; international
C2it (Citibank)	www.c2it.com	Also AOL QuickCash. Payment bridge
CheckSpace	www.checkspace.com	Targeted at small businesses; check-like Web interface
Cybergold	www.cybergold.com	Earn currency by viewing advertisements
Ecount	www.ecount.com	Account identifier is also a valid debit card number
E-gold	www.e-gold.com	Account currency is ounces of real gold bullion
eMoneyMail	www.emoneymail.com	Payment bridge between traditional instruments
Flooz	www.flooz.com	Gift currency spendable at participating merchants
gMoney	www.gmoney.com	Group payment management
InternetCash	www.internetcash.com	Prepaid card; spendable at participating merchants
IPin	www.ipin.com	Aggregates payments and charges monthly
Mon-e	www.mon-e.com	Prepaid card; promotional account identifiers available
MoneyZap	www.moneyzap.com	Western Union user-to-user payment service
NETeller	www.neteller.com	Transfer to/from merchants; accepts PayPal payments
PayPal	www.paypal.com	4 million+ users; international payments possible
PocketPass	www.pocketpass.com	Prepaid telephone card, also spendable on-line
PrivateBuy	www.privatebuy.com	Anonymous debit card account
ProPay	www.propay.com	Payee's e-mail appears on payer's credit card statement
RocketCash	www.rocketcash.com	Parental control of spending; merchant spending only
Yahoo! PayDirect	paydirect.yahoo.com	Standalone but also integrated into Yahoo! services

lists some of the popular schemes including PayPal, Yahoo! PayDirect, InternetCash, and Cybergold. Each scheme is tailored to provide one or more different services.

For example, some schemes can be used only to pay for items bought at an on-line auction, such as the Billpoint payment service provided by eBay, the Internet auction company. Others are limited to paying on-line merchants participating in the scheme, such as InternetCash and Mon-e. Within this category some of the schemes aim to provide parental control of spending, such as RocketCash. Parents issue a certain amount of pocket money to their child's account and can limit the on-line stores where this money may be spent.

Schemes such as Cybergold and Beenz provide targeted advertising with users being rewarded with currency in the system for viewing advertisements or participating in special offers. Other systems allow any-one with an e-mail address to be paid, and are referred to as e-mail pay-ment systems. Examples include PayPal, Yahoo! PayDirect, Propay, and C2it (AOL QuickCash). Some of the user-to-user payment systems, such as gMoney, are geared toward managing and requesting group payments, such as payment from a group of users for their share of a group vacation.

Although each system is targeted at a specific market segment, they all use the same centralized account model. We will now examine meth-ods to securely fund the account, by depositing funds into it. Following this, we discuss how account holders are authenticated to the on-line account, and how they securely transfer money to another account holder within the same system. The payees need to be notified when they have received funds and we examine how this works for both a normal user and a merchant with a higher volume of transactions. For those schemes that allow it, we explain how money may be withdrawn from the on-line account system. Finally we outline the different business models in use, showing how the account maintainers can be remuner-ated for overseeing and ensuring the running of the system.

5.1.1 Funding the account

Each scheme usually offers several methods to deposit money into the centralized account. The account can usually be opened on-line through a secure Web interface, protected by SSL. SSL is described in detail in Chapter 4. The information requested is not as stringent as a real bank, and usually only includes the name, address, and contact details of the account owner. Depending on how the account is to be funded, existing physical bank account details may also be requested. These payment systems are not governed by national banking regulations and do not provide the facilities of a real certified bank. Since the assets are not as strictly insured as with a traditional bank, the funds that may be held in such an account are typically limited to $10,000 or less. In addition, there are restrictions on the amount of value that can be moved into or out of the account on a daily basis.

The most popular method of funding an on-line account is to use a payment card, either a credit card or a debit card. A payment is made to the party that maintains the centralized account, hereafter referred to as an on-line bank, using one of the existing payment methods for credit cards described in Chapter 4. In this scenario the bank acts as a credit card merchant, accepting the card payment and placing the funds into the user's on-line account. Due to the merchant fees normally associated with such payments, the bank may deduct a similar fee from the user to recuperate this overhead, so that the final amount lodged is likely to be slightly less than the full amount paid from the credit card. Initially, to encourage users to sign up for the system, such fees have been waived. Indeed, in some cases, such as with PayPal, users were paid up to $5 just for signing up, and another $5 for referring a friend who in turn signed up. The reasoning behind this is that it was a small price to pay to obtain a new user compared to other methods used to recruit and attract customers, such as commercial advertising.

Due to the lack of a unified system for verifying the name and address associated with a credit card issued outside the United States, those schemes that allow international credit cards to be used to fund an account may have extra security measures in place. For example, when dealing with international credit card holders, PayPal uses the following technique to authenticate the card owner. When the user signs up, PayPal sends two credit lodgments to the credit card account, each of different small random amounts between 1 cent and 99 cents. Each transaction will be labeled with two different unique PayPal merchant number identifiers, selected from a large pool of possible identifiers. These credits will normally settle into the credit card account within four business days. After this the user is required to query their credit card account statement, through their existing on-line banking system, to obtain the credit amounts and merchant identifiers. This information is then presented by the user to PayPal to prove that he or she is indeed the genuine card owner. If the information is valid, it shows that the user has access to the credit card account statement and is therefore likely to be the real card owner. Money can then be lodged to the PayPal account using the credit card.

Another popular method of funding an on-line account is to transfer funds from a regular bank account. When signing up, the real-world bank account details are given to the centralized account payment system. Upon the user's request, funds can then be transferred using existing financial networks from the user's existing bank account, to the on-line bank, where they will be deposited into the appropriate user's account. ACH debits are the most popular method of effecting this transfer, and other direct bank transfer methods are discussed in later sections of this chapter. Some systems use the term *e-check* to refer to debiting an existing bank account to fund the on-line account, although it is just an ACH account transfer, with no user digital signature involved. Electronic checks are discussed in detail in Section 5.2.1.

As with credit card lodgments, some schemes have extra security measures in place to authenticate the real-world bank account holder. For example, Yahoo! PayDirect will make two deposits to the bank account for random amounts between 1 cent and 99 cents. The user must then query his or her financial institution, usually through an on-line banking system, to ascertain the two amounts used. When the user repeats the correct amounts to the PayDirect system, the user has been authenticated as having access to the real-world bank account, and is allowed to fund their PayDirect account from it. Traditional nonelectronic means may also be used to fund the account, including posting a money order or a paper check to the offices of the on-line payment system.

A number of schemes allow their on-line accounts to be funded by buying a prepaid card in a physical store and using this to fund the account. Such prepaid value cards are already in widespread use in the telecommunications industry where they are used to buy value to spend on telephone calls. The prepaid card issuer creates a temporary account worth a specified amount, and identified by a large unguessable account identifier. Typically such account identifiers will consist of at least 12 characters, often more if only digits, rather than alphanumeric characters, are used. The value of the account is usually set to a multiple of ten, such as $10, $20, $50, or $100. The issuer maintains a database with the account identifier mapping to the exact account value. The account identifier is printed onto a physical disposable card and hidden from view.

This is done either by covering the card surface with an opaque material that can later be scratched off to reveal the account identifier, or by sealing it in some form of envelope. The cards are then distributed to physical stores where they can be bought by anyone wishing to fund an account with a particular payment system. The cards are specific to one payment scheme only.

The user reveals the account identifier on the prepaid card, and enters this on-line at the payment system's Web site. The communication is protected by SSL, and, once entered, the funds allocated for that account, according to the issuer database, are available for spending. The user is normally given the option of assigning his or her own, easier-to-remember, identifier to the account, such as an e-mail address or nickname, with a matching password or PIN. This information, or the original account identifier, can then be used to recognize the user each time he or she goes to spend funds from the account.

Rather than directly requiring a user to purchase a prepaid card, such a prepaid account identifier can be given away as part of a loyalty scheme when the user purchases other products. For example, Rocket-Cash account identifiers were given away with a popular soft drink, by concealing the account identifier underneath the bottle top.

One advantage of buying a prepaid card with cash in a physical store, is that a user's privacy is protected. The on-line account remains anonymous, as it is not tied to an existing identity through a payment card or physical bank account details. However, it is not as anonymous as electronic cash, described in Chapter 6, because although the user's identity is not known, all transactions made from the account are known by the on-line bank and can be linked to that account. If the user's identity is later revealed, perhaps by releasing a delivery address as one of the transactions, cooperation between the merchant with this information and the bank can reveal all the spending details of that user.

Prepaid cards are an alternative means of enabling on-line payments for those who do not have access to traditional payment cards or bank accounts. With Internet payments they have been deployed mainly by those account transfer systems which allow value only to be spent at participating merchants. Examples include InternetCash, RocketCash, and Mon-e. However, there is no reason why such prepaid cards could not be incorporated into any of the account transfer systems if desired.

With so many different independent account transfer systems, a typical user may hold accounts with several different systems. As competition increases for customers, some systems will allow funding from other related schemes. For example, a RocketCash account can be funded with monetary value from other centralized accounts, including Cybergold and Beenz. As the systems become more established and widespread, it is likely that exchange from one system to another will be possible. This may be facilitated by independent third parties who will take a commission on the transaction, in the same way that banks today will exchange one currency to another for a small fee.

5.1.2 Authenticated account transfer

To make a payment, account users are authenticated on-line to the central payment system Web site, where they enter the account identifier of the payee, and the payment amount. The value is subtracted from the payer account and credited to the payee account. Often there is a facility to specify the time and date of when the payment should be made. Figure 5.1 shows the steps involved in making an authenticated payment transfer from one account to another in the centralized account model.

The account holder is authenticated using an account identifier and a password, with all communications between the user and the bank protected using SSL. Since payments are effected through an SSL-enabled Web browser, any mobile device which allows secure Web browsing can be used to make a payment. Mobile payments are discussed further in Chapter 8. The account identifier must be unique within the payment system. For ease of use, many schemes use the user's unique e-mail address as the account identifier. Others allow a nickname to be chosen, or use the account number present on a prepaid card. The on-line bank

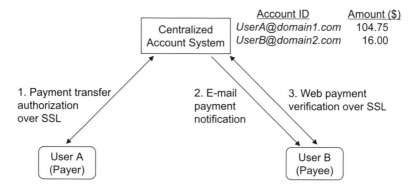

Figure 5.1 User-to-user payment in centralized account systems.

holds an SSL server certificate which is used, as part of the SSL proto-col, to authenticate it. Access to traditional on-line banking systems is protected in the same manner. SSL user certificates, in which a digital sig-nature is used to authenticate the account holder, are not yet used in these account transfer payment systems. As PKIs become established, and user certificates become more common, it is likely that such user certificates will be used to authenticate account holders.

For payment systems in which a payment card or checking account is linked to the on-line account, if sufficient funds are not present in the on-line account, monetary value may be automatically taken from these traditional payment accounts in order to meet a payment request.

In systems allowing user-to-user payments, the payees are notified by e-mail that they have received a specified payment. If the payees already hold an account with the given payment system, they may verify the payment by connecting to their account, securely over SSL, and viewing the balance and transaction history. Since the e-mail is not signed by the bank, it alone is not enough to verify that payment has actually been made, because such e-mail may be easily forged. An e-mail confirmation of every transaction is also sent to the payer.

If the payees do not hold an account with the payment system used, they must sign up to receive the actual payment. In doing so, the account system gains new customers, who in turn may make payments to further new customers, an example of viral marketing. If payees do not sign up within a certain time limit, the payment is cancelled and the money refunded to the payer.

In some cases a payer may not be entirely sure of a payee's e-mail address. Yahoo! PayDirect allows a payer-specified question to be sent to that e-mail address, and the answer returned to the payer. If the payer accepts the answer as proof of the correct identity, the money is sent; otherwise, the transaction is canceled.

Several schemes allow users not only to make payments to other users, but also to request payments from them. Such billing takes the form of an e-mail, sent by the system to the payer, requesting payment of the specified amount. Group billing is the process in which the e-mail is sent to several payers. A Web address, a uniform resource locator (URL), is included in the e-mail, which when clicked will bring the payer to the payment system login page. After authenticating to the system, the payer is presented with the payment details, so that he or she need only click a button to authorize payment. This facility can be used to bestow capabilities, similar to those given to credit card merchants, on normal users. Payment may be requested from a credit card holder, who, after signing up, moves funds from his or her credit card into the payee account through the payment system.

Since each transaction must be verified manually by the payee through examining recent transactions on-line with the payment system, such a system is not suitable, in this form, for processing more than a small number of payments per day. In order to allow a larger number of payments to be efficiently handled by commercial vendors, merchant Application Programming Interfaces (APIs) are made available to integrate the payment system with a merchant Web site. The basic idea is that a customer may select the payment system on the merchant Web site. The customer is then transferred from the merchant Web site to the payment system site, along with the transaction details, as shown in Figure 5.2. The user logs into the payment system and authorizes payment in the usual fashion, over an SSL connection. Once the payment is made, the merchant is informed and the user is transferred back to the merchant Web site to complete the transaction or receive the purchased goods.

The application scripts and programs used at the merchant Web site are similar to those used by credit card processor gateway APIs, such as those used by iTransact [1]. These also transfer a user from a merchant

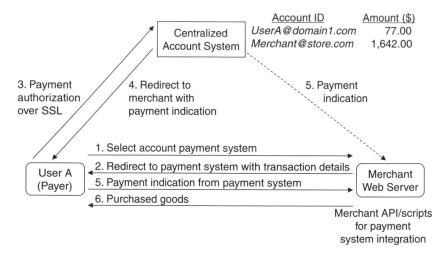

Figure 5.2 User to high-volume merchant payment in centralized account systems.

storefront to the credit card payment processor before transferring them back to the storefront with an indication of whether payment was successfully received. Such merchant APIs allow an account transfer system to be used by higher-volume commercial merchants. They are used by account transfer systems aimed at allowing traditional merchant payments, including InternetCash, Mon-e, RocketCash, Cybergold, and Beenz.

A number of schemes, including PayPal and Billpoint, allow the respective system to be integrated with popular auction sites so that a user selling an item by auction can automatically accept an account transfer payment from the winning bidder. For example, a PayPal business account allows automatic auction payment requests, and automatic emptying of payments into a bank account. However, the user name and password used at the auction site must be disclosed to the account transfer system in order for it to gain access and perform certain tasks automatically. Other features of the PayPal business account include regular mass payments destined for up to 10,000 users, and allow payments to be accepted through a merchant Web site.

5.1.3 Withdrawing funds from the system

Prepaid card systems, like the prepaid telephone cards, do not allow money to be taken out of the system, and the only option is to spend all value on-line. With other schemes monetary value remains in an on-line account until withdrawn back into traditional payment instruments. Funds can be credited to a payment card or lodged into a traditional bank account. Alternatively, some schemes will mail out a paper check to the account holder. Funds are usually insured, in some cases up to $100,000, for unauthorized withdrawals. As with the case of stolen credit cards, the user liability depends on how quickly it is reported that an incorrect transaction has occurred or that an account password has been lost or stolen. With a number of schemes, including C2it and eMoneyMail, monetary value is not held in an on-line account, but instead the system acts as a bridge for payment by facilitating transfer from one credit card or checking account to another.

5.1.4 Business models

The different account transfer schemes use a variety of different business models to earn a profit. As with a traditional bank, any money that is kept on deposit can be used to earn interest, and with a large number of accounts this amount can be substantial. Money will be available for the bank's use after an account has been funded, and during the period between a payer making a payment and the payee withdrawing the funds. Often payees will wait to receive several payments before making a withdrawal, or will keep funds in the account, in order to make a later payment themselves. PayPal allows users to earn money market rates on the account balance.

Transaction fees are usually imposed at some point within the system. For example, there may be a fee when using a credit card to fund an account, or when withdrawing funds from an account. This is particularly true when using international payment cards. For example, PayPal imposes a charge of 2.6% of the total amount plus 30 cents per transaction when funding with a credit card issued outside the United States. A merchant, or payee, may be assessed certain fees for receiving payments, as is the case with normal credit card payments. There is usually a charge for the extra facilities and convenience of providing higher volume business accounts with merchant APIs.

Revenue is also obtained through more traditional means such as banner advertising. In the case of Cybergold, advertisers are charged to have their product or offer promoted to Cybergold users who match a certain profile. As with many early-stage Internet startups, many of these payment systems have not yet become fully established and have yet to make a profit.

One drawback of the centralized account transfer model is that all participants must have an account with the same central payment system. Inevitably this will lead to users having to open accounts at several different systems. In the following sections we examine the efforts of the banking industry to allow account transfers between different traditional banks to be initiated from the Internet. Such initiatives will allow money to be transferred between parties with accounts at different banks.

5.2 FSTC payment initiatives

The Financial Services Technology Consortium (FSTC) [2] is a group of U.S. banks, research agencies, and government organizations, formed in 1993, that have come together to assist in enhancing the competitiveness of the U.S. financial service industry. There are more than 70 members, including Bank of America, Chase Manhattan Bank, CitiBank, and

Wells Fargo. Staff from the member organizations come together to undertake technology projects in areas of common interest.

In the area of electronic payments, the consortium has a number of projects that are of interest, some of which are ongoing, while others have been completed. The first was concerned with defining an electronic check and the new bank infrastructure that will be required to support not only electronic checks but also other forms of electronic commerce. A second project investigated how existing bank payment systems, such as ACH payments and wire transfers, could be securely initiated over the Internet. A more recent project considered how banks could act as trust brokers, by providing authentication services on behalf of their customers, for e-commerce transactions. Each of these three projects is now examined in turn in the following sections. A future project, entitled "Moving ATM to the Internet," plans to evaluate services which could be provided through banking ATMs once they are connected to the Internet. The overall strategy of the group is to accommodate new forms of payment and commerce by a process of managed evolution from the methods in use today. This also involves making maximum use of, and causing minimum disruption to, the infrastructure that already exists.

5.2.1 Electronic check concept

As with its paper counterpart, the electronic check will contain an instruction to the payer's bank to make a payment of a specified amount to an identified payee. The fact that the check is in electronic form and is being conveyed across computer networks should allow more flexibility in the handling of the check. New services can be provided, such as the ability to immediately verify funds availability. Security can be enhanced by allowing digital signature validation and check payments can more easily be integrated into electronic ordering and billing processes.

Figure 5.3 shows the overall concept. A payer would issue a check by assembling much the same information as is present on a paper check. Users are issued an X.509 certificate by the bank with which they have a checking account. The certificate is used by the payee to verify the payer's digital signature on the check. The bank can include account restrictions within the certificate, such as the maximum check value, currencies allowed, or a requirement for multiple signatures in the case of a corporate account.

It is envisioned that a central bank or government agency will act as the root certificate authority and issue certificates for participating banks.

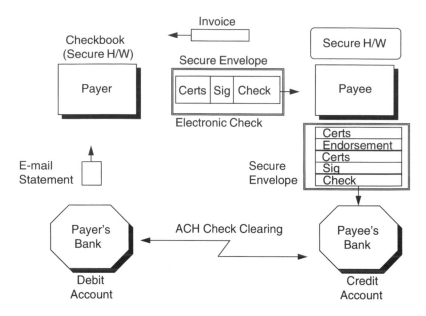

Figure 5.3 The FSTC electronic check concept.

One such global PKI was formed in 1999 when a group of eight inter-national financial institutions came together to construct Identrus.com (identity and trust). Since then, more than 35 financial institutions have joined the Identrus system, and each acts as a certificate authority under a single root CA. In this way a certificate trust hierarchy has been formed, as described in Chapter 3. ABAecom [3], a subsidiary of the American Banker's Association, acts as the root CA for another banking PKI, and has issued public-key certificates to over 200 banks.

By varying the information included in the check, one can produce a variety of different payment types in addition to a conventional check. For example, changing the currency field could produce a traveler's check, while applying a bank's digital signature will yield a certified check.

In the FSTC architecture [4, 5], all individuals capable of issuing elec-tronic checks will be in possession of an electronic checkbook device based on some form of secure hardware. The function of this device will be to securely store secret-key and certificate information as well as maintaining a register of what checks have been signed or endorsed recently. Figure 5.3 shows the check being transported to the payee in some kind of secure envelope. Since a number of widespread industry standards exist for providing secure encrypted enveloping, the exact form of the envelope has been left outside the scope of the architecture. It is envisioned that secure e-mail or an SSL Web session could be used to provide the confidentiality.

The payee endorses the check when it is received, again making use of a secure hardware device of some sort before forwarding it to the payee's bank. Once it has reached this point, the processing is identical to that undergone by any paper check today. This means that the banks involved clear the check using the normal ACH or electronic check presentment (ECP) methods.

The FSTC e-check technology was piloted in a market trial by the U.S. Treasury, who used it to make high-value payments over the Internet to more than 50 U.S. Department of Defense contractors. The first e-check payment, which was made as part of the trial, took place in June 1998, when an electronic check for $32,135 was e-mailed to GTE, a subsidiary of Verizon Communications, in payment for an Air Force information technology contract. E-checks can be sent both through e-mail and over the Web. During the trial a smart card, supplied by Information Resource Engineering (IRE), was used as the secure checkbook hardware device. The management of the FSTC e-check project was handed over to CommerceNet [6], a nonprofit e-commerce industry consortium, in October 1999.

5.2.2 Financial Services Markup Language (FSML)

In order to define the structure and contents of an electronic check, the FSTC designed the Financial Services Markup Language (FSML) [7]. It defines the possible contents of signed financial documents, including an electronic check. FSML is specified using the Standard Generalized Markup Language (SGML) [8], a complex markup language for specifying any type of data ranging from a musical score to the architecture of a space rocket. SGML was used as the specification language rather than XML [9], a simpler subset of SGML defined by the W3 Consortium, because at the time of the e-check project, the XML specification had not yet been finalized.

FSML defines a method to structure documents into different content blocks, which may then be signed by one or more parties. For example, FSML has a block to represent the contents of a check that would normally be handwritten, and this includes attributes such as the date, amount, currency, and the name of the person to whom the check is payable. Other blocks that are defined for e-checks include an account block for holding payer bank account information that would normally be printed on a physical check, an invoice block for describing the payment, an endorsement block containing information supplied by the payee, a signature block for holding a digital signature performed over other blocks, and a cert block for holding a signer's X.509 certificate.

An interesting feature of FSML is that it allows individual blocks to be signed, rather than having to sign the entire FSML document. Thus, a signer can chose one or more blocks that he or she wishes to sign. For example, a check endorser may or may not sign all the blocks that the payer signed. As a check passes from one party to another, additional blocks may be added and cryptographically attached to the check by signing the appropriate blocks. When certain blocks are removed from the document, the signatures still remain valid, although it may not be possible to see all the blocks that were originally signed. This is important for businesses that need to exchange data that they wish to keep private, such as invoice details, along with the payment. Although the invoice is signed as part of the entire e-check payment, it can be removed by the endorser, before sending the e-check for deposit to the bank.

A signature block contains the names of the other blocks that it signs, along with a hash of each of those blocks. Therefore, the e-check signature is actually a signed hash of the concatenated hashes of several blocks. One or more blocks can be removed, and the signature verifier will know that they exist but not what their contents are. Since the hash of each block is included in the signature, the contents of any block cannot be altered without being detected. In this way the e-check signature is similar to a dual signature, which is used to sign two message blocks in the SET credit card protocol described in Chapter 4.

The actual signatures can be generated using the popular available algorithms, including RSA and elliptic curve signatures with either MD5 or SHA hashes. Figure 5.4 shows a sample FSML electronic check, which contains a check block with payee information, a block containing payer bank account information, a payer signature of both the check and account blocks, and a block containing the payer's certificate. The check has not yet been endorsed with a payee signature.

In the U.S. Treasury pilot the typical size of a signed FSML e-check is 4,760 bytes, which increases to approximately 7,050 bytes when endorsed by the payee. The electronic checks are cleared and settled

```
<fsml-doc docname="echeck204" type="check">
<check>  <blkname>check1  <vers>1.0
<checkdata>  <checknum>187  <dateissued>20010719  <datevalid>20010719
<country>us  <amount>250.00  <currency>usd  <payto>John E. Smith
</checkdata>
<checkbook>2048  <legalnotice>This instrument subject to check law
</check>

<signature>
<blkname>sig7  <vers>1.5
<sigdata>
<blockref>check1  <hash alg="sha">vFnS/1Vm9QaRDFAgtijkE24cazk=
<blockref>acct-111111111-00000001
<hash alg="sha">fF51C8MwtSVgeCQP0mzDTBjy1Zg=  <nonce>9D9BC5AA75
<sigref>acct-11111111-00000001  <sigtype>check
<algorithm>sha/rsa  <location>us  </sigdata>
<sig>
Jinh43b1zYIydAELCmAo6j8nY/I=:KquV+Pas9mFrnDoD3wtQKVoWIpU56JK3WioPaNjXJ
7XcMnoISvEI3XB7WICVBN4TI2viUoWXB0XD1GJ3rXvb2XM3rC9EVX6MLNXCp2sxXVva23=
</signature>

<account>  <blkname>acct-111111111-00000001  <vers>1.5
<bankcode>111111111  <bankacct>00000001  <bankser>00000001
<expdate>20011231  <accttitle>Paul S. Echecker  <accttype>checking
<bankname>BankA  <bankaddr>123 BankA Blvd, New York NY
<bankphone>(212)555-1234  <bankfax>(212)555-1235
<bankemail>echeck@banka.com
<certissuer>/C=US/ST=MD/O=BANKA/OU=checking/
<certserial>1  </account>

<cert>  <blkname>cert-111111111-00000001  <vers>1.5
<certtype>x509v1  <certissuer>/C=US/ST=MD/O=BANKA/OU=checking/
<certserial>1
<certdata>
MZDFUUQEMMEa3LL45dAENR09GZSERBDORMTTG2fiiKKwSFZZjJ32JJMNFSX1QWFVSD7NVsE
SaFSjllw22ASDMjfs+/3JJELJE2WaRRsVoJJp7iK1wMNBSRfj9FASNfqww3/jo+RWIMvFJw
FKlSOAhRST3iIPK/BCqc77R3cJPL06CeeKQIUHIk1bb56d3VfEB51AxCDjfkslTUQxDjaMB
gNVBAoTBUJBTktBMREwDwYDVQQLEwhjaGVja21uZzAeFw05NzA0MTQw9Y5beVIZJcnMQun2
9GswiMxXKvU+8kNS6grKBn7p1SHPy9J9MQswCQYDVQQGEwJVUzELMAkGA1UECBMCjcBpgYH
KoZIzjgEATCGmgaje88WrsVX0lti2l111lsxXGJILMNQ22algWF6R2HK2DABprawyq3qsSWk
9+/g3JMLsBzbuMcgCKQIUx3MhjHN+yO=
</cert>
</fsml-doc>
```

Figure 5.4   Example FSML electronic check.

between banks using the ANSI X9.46 [10] and X9.37 [11] standards. The e-check, in FSML form, is transported in an X9.46 message instead of the traditional physical check image. While blocks are currently only defined for e-checks, FSML could be simply extended to cater for a range of signed payment instruments such as ACH payment authorizations, ATM network transaction authorizations, money orders, and gift certificates.

The FSML specification allows for extensions such as privately defined blocks, enabling FSML to be used to create and sign generic financial documents.

5.2.3 Electronic check functional flows

The ability to rapidly move the information in an electronic check from one party to another across computer networks means that the electronic check may be used in a variety of different payment scenarios. The FSTC has identified four distinct scenarios that are likely to be of importance.

The *deposit-and-clear* scenario is the first of these and mirrors the way in which most conventional paper checks are used.

Figure 5.5 shows the steps involved. The payer issues an electronic check signed in conjunction with the payer's checkbook device. This is sent to the payee, who endorses it, also using a secure hardware device before forwarding it to his or her bank. The bank will then clear the check with the payer's bank using ACH transfers. Steps 4 and 5 show the banks informing their customers of progress with "report" and "statement" steps. These are not key to the main message flow, and indeed could be paper reports posted out at regular intervals. One of the disadvantages of using the deposit-and-clear scenario is that all parties must have their networking and processing capabilities upgraded to deal with electronic checks, before a single payment can be made.

Figure 5.6 shows an alternative scenario referred to as *cash-and-transfer*. In this case, while the payee can accept checks electronically, his or her bank cannot. So in step 2, the payee cashes the check by presenting it to the payer's bank, specifying details of his or her bank account in the process. The payer's bank responds with a *Notify* message and then

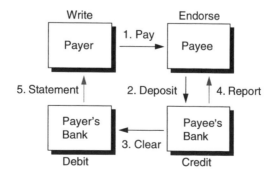

Figure 5.5   Functional flows in the deposit-and-clear scenario.

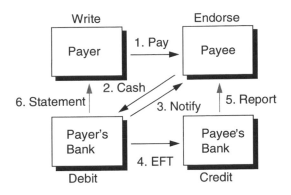

Figure 5.6 Functional flows in the cash-and-transfer scenario.

credits the payee's bank account using a conventional interbank electronic funds transfer (EFT).

The third scenario envisaged by the FSTC is referred to as the *lockbox* scenario. In this case, the electronic check is sent not to the payee, but to the payee's bank. The destination account may be either the payee's primary bank account or a special-purpose account referred to as a lockbox, which is maintained by a bank or other third party on behalf of the payee. The lockbox facility corresponds to a service offered by U.S. banks to corporate clients when dealing with conventional paper-based checks.

Figure 5.7 shows the payee's bank clearing this in step 2 and sending details to the payee in the form of an accounts receivable update. The transaction will ultimately appear in a regular statement sent to the payer.

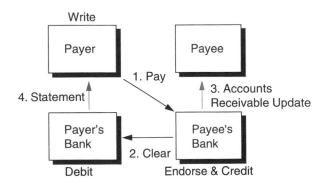

Figure 5.7 Functional flows in the lockbox scenario.

The final scenario is referred to as the *funds transfer* scenario. It is very similar to the *direct credit* banking facility that is in widespread use today. As shown in Figure 5.8, the payer generates an electronic check and forwards it directly to the payee's bank. The bank transfers the value to the payee's bank account, and debits that of the payer using conventional interbank EFT.

In this case, only the payer's bank needs to be equipped to process electronic checks, as all other flows are handled by existing bank-messaging systems.

These four scenarios have outlined how electronic checks can be used as a payment method in ways that fit well with existing banking procedures. Nevertheless, banks wishing to take full advantage of the electronic check must provide some new infrastructure to handle this new form of payment. Once again, the emphasis in the FSTC is on causing minimum disturbance to the systems that are already in use.

5.2.4 Check-handling infrastructure

The FSTC have investigated the changes that will be required in a bank's back office processing systems in order to process electronic checks as well as other existing forms of electronic payment. The initial results of this work were design considerations for an electronic payments infrastructure. Based on this architecture, a protocol for initiating payments over the Internet with the banking systems was designed. These areas are discussed in Section 5.2.5.

The starting point for this infrastructure is the existing set of interbank payment systems that are in place today. Figure 5.9 shows two banks, each equipped with systems for handling credit card transactions,

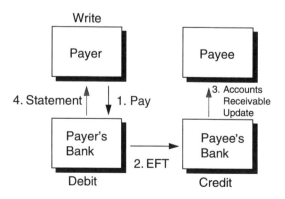

Figure 5.8 Functional flows in the funds transfer scenario.

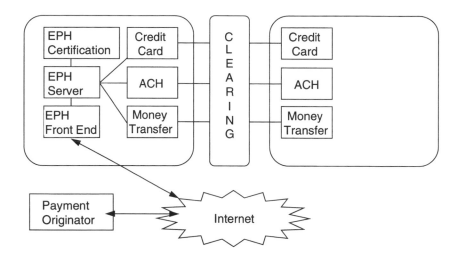

Figure 5.9 The interaction between the electronic payments handler (EPH) and existing payment systems.

ACH payments, and other forms of electronic money transfers. These systems connect to a variety of clearing networks to allow interbank transactions to take place. The FSTC group proposes that a new system, called the *electronic payments handler* (EPH), be added to those already in existence. This would be divided into a number of subsystems. The front end would interface to the Internet and communicate using its protocols. It would act as a secure line of defense for the EPH as a whole, being the only system that can be directly contacted by other machines on the public network. The core of the EPH system is the EPH server, which will allow many different forms of transactions to be made, including the processing of electronic checks. It would employ the services of the EPH Certification server, whose function is to issue certificates to customers of the bank and allow for their subsequent verification or revocation. The Certification server will also allow other banks' certificates to be verified, and the way the system is organized implies the existence of a banking certification hierarchy.

It is proposed that the EPH be introduced by banks in a phased manner, and Figure 5.9 shows the situation at phase 1. In this case, only the originator's bank is equipped with EPH subsystems and any communication with the other party's bank must take place through existing bank-clearing networks. In terms of the electronic check flows outlined earlier, this configuration would support the *cash-and-transfer* and *funds transfer* scenarios, but not the *deposit-and-clear* or *lockbox* situations.

In phase 2 of the deployment of the electronic commerce infrastructure, both banks involved in a transaction will be equipped with EPH systems, as shown in Figure 5.10. This configuration will allow all four electronic check flows to be carried out. The EPH systems at either bank can contact either party to the transaction to provide status information if required.

In order to encourage the adoption of such an electronic payments infrastructure, the FSTC have designed an EPH server and developed a secure protocol to allow Internet payers to initiate payments with it through the EPH front-end server. The project, known as the Bank Internet Payment System (BIPS), is now examined.

5.2.5 Bank Internet Payment System (BIPS)

Electronic checks provide an off-line method to effect a transfer from one bank account to another. Other direct payment methods effected through banks, such as credit transfers (giros), ACH payments, and wire transfer services, were discussed in Chapter 2. Due to the popularity of these alternative bank payment methods, especially for business-to-business (B2B) transactions, it would be useful to be able to initiate such payments over the Internet. BIPS enables payers to access these current bank payment mechanisms over an open network. Payers can send secure payment instructions over the Internet to a BIPS server at their

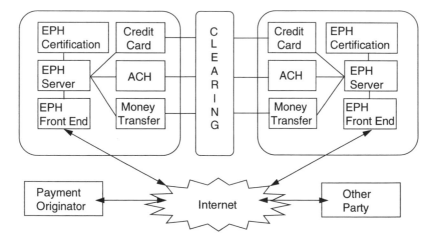

Figure 5.10 Phase 2 of EPH deployment.

bank, where the request is translated into a traditional bank payment transaction. The BIPS server acts as a gateway to multiple existing bank payment systems such as ACH, SWIFT, and wire transfer. The project was initiated in 1996, and the initial specification [12], an open protocol for sending payment instructions and a payment server architecture for processing those instructions, was released in 1998.

The scheme was designed to handle transactions ranging from high-value trade payments to low-value retail transactions. As part of the protocol, the most appropriate or cost-effective traditional bank payment mechanism can be selected, either by the payer or by the bank itself. Following the FSTC design philosophy of causing minimum disruption to existing infrastructure, BIPS uses existing standards and technologies and included new development only where there were gaps in the existing Internet protocols and bank systems. Only the payer's bank needs to be BIPS-enabled for payments to occur.

Figure 5.11 shows the BIPS architecture. A payer sends BIPS payment instructions to the payment server at the payer's bank, either through e-mail or by using the Web. The BIPS payment server interprets

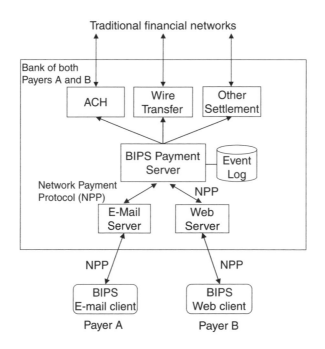

Figure 5.11 BIPS architecture.

and translates the instruction into bank payment transactions and sends these to the appropriate bank payment systems using traditional financial networks. The BIPS scheme relies on the existence of a PKI, where each BIPS participant is issued with an X.509 certificate, which is used for both creating signatures and encrypting sensitive material. Each BIPS instruction message is digitally signed by the sender, and includes the sender's certificate and a unique transaction identifier. A number of alternative algorithms are defined for implementing the digital signatures, including RSA with an MD5 digest. The signatures are encoded as ASCII characters using Base64 [13] encoding, in which each character represents 6 bits. At a high level the payment instruction is similar to an electronic check, in that it is digitally signed by the payer, but in this case it is sent directly to the payer's bank, instead of to a payee.

The BIPS protocol provides four different functions, in the form of request-response messages. The first is a feasibility request message which allows a prospective payer to negotiate an appropriate bank payment mechanism with his or her bank or to inquire if a specific payment mechanism is available and how long it would take to process before the payee receives the funds. The payment request message is used to send the actual payment instructions, and contains a number of fields including the type of payment, amount, execute date, and the identity and bank account details of both the payer and payee. For example, a payer might digitally sign an ACH debit authorization message, which is then sent as a payment request message. The status request allows a payer to inquire about the current status of an earlier payment instruction, and provides similar functionality to the inquiry messages of the SET payment card protocol. Finally, a stop request is used to attempt to cancel an earlier payment instruction, and its success will depend on the policies in place for the corresponding bank payment mechanism. For each request message the BIPS server replies with a signed response message, detailing the appropriate information or a success/failure indication.

The BIPS payment protocol, known as the Network Payment Protocol (NPP), is defined using the Extensible Markup Language (XML) [9]. XML provides a standard format for describing different types of data and messages, and for storing them in a text file. This allows message structures to be easily defined and manipulated. It is a simplified subset of the Standard Generalized Markup Language [8].

Each NPP message consists of a number of attribute fields, such as payment type, payer and payee details, and payment amount. To hide parts of an NPP message from certain individuals who may need to read only parts of the message, specific attributes can be symmetrically encrypted. DES in ECB mode is one of the symmetric algorithms suggested for this task. The overall privacy of an NPP message is outside the scope of the specification, but it can be encrypted using S/MIME for e-mail or SSL on the Web. An audit trail of all requests processed at a bank is available from the BIPS payment server log files at that bank.

Three initial prototypes have been constructed to validate the BIPS specification. The first, from Glenview State Bank, uses e-mail to transmit a payment instruction that in turn initiates an ACH payment. The second, from Mellon Bank, was designed to allow a payer to authorize payment of a utility bill through the Web, with the payment instruction again being translated into an ACH transaction at the bank. It is envisioned that one of the primary functions of BIPS will be as a bill payment scheme, although bill presentment capabilities are not included in the current specification. Finally, a third prototype from CitiBank provides a business-to-business bill payment solution.

5.2.6 Financial Agent Secure Transaction (FAST)

When two parties with no previous business relationship wish to participate in an e-commerce transaction, they usually need to authenticate each other or validate some information about each other such as the ability to pay. In Chapter 3 we showed how public-key certificates could be used to provide a framework for such authentication. However, both parties need to possess credentials, in this case a public-key certificate, from a common authority or from two different authorities within a common-trust hierarchy. Since PKIs are not yet widely deployed, it may often be the case that two unknown parties that want to transact cannot securely authenticate each other.

Although many customers and merchants may not have the means to authenticate each other, they do usually have existing relationships with financial institutions. In normal business transactions banks often act on behalf of parties unknown to each other. An example would be when a buyer in the United States does not know a supplier in Europe, but a local bank can vouch for each party as part of the trade agreement. An alternative approach to PKI-based authentication is to leverage the existing relationship that these parties have with their banks to provide validation services. Since financial institutions already strictly authenticate their own customers, they are well positioned to provide such a service.

The FSTC Financial Agent Secure Transaction (FAST) project aims to allow banks to provide an identity and attribute verification system on behalf of their customers. This alternative authentication service would allow two parties, previously unknown to each other, to conduct a transaction over the Internet when they have no authentication mechanism in common. The goal is to enable e-commerce transactions to have the same level of trust and confidence that are associated with financial transactions in the physical world.

FAST can provide a range of services from customer authentication to payment guarantee. Attributes which can be verified might include checking that a payer has a sufficient bank balance for the transaction, that the amount is within authorized limits, or that the customer has the authority to commit a company to a purchase.

Figure 5.12 shows the steps that occur in a FAST transaction. In the first two steps the two transacting parties negotiate which identities and properties to verify. As part of this process, a consumer merchant identifier (CMID) is created, and is used to uniquely identify the transaction to the financial institutions. In the third and fourth steps, both the consumer and merchant independently transmit the CMID along with additional transaction information, called the CMID/T, to their own banks. The additional transaction information is used to authenticate the sender to the bank and verify that they approve of the release of the requested

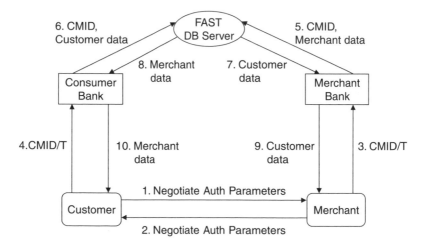

Figure 5.12 FAST message flow.

information. While protocol details were not yet fully specified at the time of writing, it is likely that all customer-bank communications will be protected by SSL, as with many existing on-line banking schemes. Each bank sends the necessary information to a FAST database server along with the CMID. The two sets of information with the same CMID are matched and the required new information passed back to the appropriate requesting bank. Each bank returns the results to their respective customer who initiated the transaction. Based on the returned results, the transaction can proceed or be aborted if certain criteria were not successfully met.

The purpose of the FAST server is to facilitate the secure exchange of consented customer information between banks. It is expected that banks would charge a transaction fee for providing this service. Phase one of the FAST project started in November 1999 and ran for six months. It defined the requirements and message flows without formally defining a protocol specification. A second phase is expected to commence in 2001 in which the FAST protocol messages will be defined and the feasibility of the system tested through pilots.

5.3 NACHA Internet payments

NACHA [14] is a nonprofit electronic-payments trade organization which develops operating rules and promotes the use of the ACH network. ACH payments were introduced in Chapter 2. NACHA represents the interests of over 14,000 financial institutions, and has a number of Internet payment projects. The Internet Council is the industry consortium of NACHA members who investigate, develop, and pilot electronic payment methods for open networks. Two NACHA Internet Council payment projects concerned with authenticated transfer between bank accounts are the Internet Secure ATM Payments (ISAP), which allows signed debit card transactions, and DirectPay, which aims to provide authenticated ACH credit transfers. The aims and activities of each are now examined in turn.

5.3.1 Internet Secure ATM Payments (ISAP)

Debit cards, also referred to as ATM cards, are gaining popularity as a means of effecting payment at a physical point-of-sale (POS) terminal. A user PIN is usually entered for authentication, and the transaction is authorized through an Electronic Funds Transfer (EFT) network, to which the POS terminal is connected. The issuing bank verifies on-line that the funds are available and debits the user's bank account. The repudiation rate for debit card transactions in the United States is less than 0.03%, which is significantly lower than that for credit card payments. The ISAP project is an NACHA Internet Council project which aims to allow ATM/debit cards to be used on the Internet.

An ISAP transaction is initiated when a user indicates to an ISAP-enabled merchant that he or she wishes to use a debit card for payment. The merchant returns payment data to the user, similar to the payment information that is assembled within a POS terminal in the physical world. SSL is used to secure the Internet connection between the user and the merchant. ISAP employs a user digital signature, instead of a PIN, to authenticate the card owner for an Internet purchase. The secret signing key is stored on a smart card chip that is embedded on the physical debit card. It is used to sign the payment information, along with the debit card account number. Clearly, for this to occur, the user's terminal must be equipped with a smart card reader and appropriate wallet software. The signed payment information is returned to the merchant who forwards it into the EFT network, via an optional merchant-payment processor.

Debit card authorizations from a POS are normally carried in an ISO 8583 message through the EFT network to the user's home bank. ISAP uses the regular ISO 8583 messages, but the additional digital signature is placed in one of the data element fields of the payment authorization request. When the user's bank receives the request, it verifies the digital signature, verifies that the funds are available, and returns an authorization response. The average time taken to authorize a transaction, from when it is submitted to the EFT network, until receiving back a response, is three seconds, the same as with a physical POS, even with the additional verification of the digital signature. During authorization the bank records that the funds have been spent. At the end of the day, the payments owed are cleared using the ACH network, as with traditional debit cards.

No digital certificates are used within ISAP, and this is partly due to the ISO 8583 message-size limitations. However, because the digital signature is only ever verified at the user's bank, which has a copy of the user's public key already, no certificate is required. An ISAP pilot was started in late 2000. Approximately 100 consumers were issued ATM smart cards by Commercial Capital Bank, allowing purchases to be made through an ISAP-enabled merchant site.

5.3.2 DirectPay

The NACHA DirectPay project [15] aims to allow ACH credits to be initiated by bank account holders over the Internet. For a number of years it has been possible to allow Internet users to make purchases directly from their U.S. checking/current bank account. The Internet merchant collects the user's account and bank information, and then performs an ACH debit against that account for the purchase amount. It has been left up to the merchant to authenticate the user presenting the information as being the valid account owner. Accordingly, since it is possible to steal this information as with credit card details, an account owner may unauthorize, or reverse the ACH debit transaction, for up to 60 days after it has occurred.

In contrast, an ACH credit is usually initiated directly by the account holder at his or her bank, and the funds are transferred over the ACH network directly to the merchant's account. Once the payment has been settled, the transaction is final and cannot be reversed. The aim of the DirectPay project is to define a method that allows ACH credits to be initiated by a user over the Internet. In this way, it is similar to the FSTC BIPS project, except that it is limited to ACH payments.

The DirectPay message flow is shown in Figure 5.13. In the first step the user sends his or her bank details to the merchant. The merchant is then able to make a secure connection to the bank, passing the transaction amount and merchant-bank account details. The merchant then redirects the user to his or her own bank. The bank leverages the existing

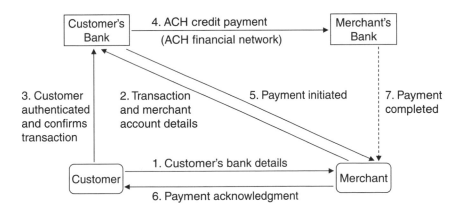

Figure 5.13 DirectPay message flow.

on-line banking authentication techniques to recognize a valid account holder, before presenting the transaction request details. The user confirms the payment, and an ACH credit is made across the traditional ACH financial network to the merchant's receiving bank. The user account information is never shared with the merchant, preventing it from being abused, unlike ACH debits or traditional credit card payments. The user's bank securely informs the merchant that the ACH payment has been made, and that the merchant can now safely deliver the purchased goods or service. Later the funds will arrive in the merchant's account and can be confirmed by the merchant's bank. While ACH payments usually incur a transaction fee, it is envisaged that for retail applications this charge will be absorbed by the merchant, rather than imposed on the consumer. At the time of this writing, the DirectPay project is in the initial planning stages.

While FSTC and NACHA have been formulating strategies for banks to deal with electronic checks and account transfers, the research community has also been formulating systems that would allow check-like payments across computer networks. Sections 5.4 and 5.5 describe two of these.

5.4   NetBill

NetBill is a payment system developed at Carnegie Mellon University [16, 17] that the developers claim is optimized for the selling and buying of low-priced information goods. While NetBill can allow repeated payments of small amounts (micropayments), it cannot provide the same efficiency or scalability of the payment systems designed specifically for making micropayments, which are examined in Chapter 7. The NetBill transaction protocol begins when a customer requests a quotation for a selected item and ends when a symmetric key is received for unwrapping the encrypted goods delivered during the goods delivery phase.

The participants in the system are shown in Figure 5.14 and consist of customers, merchants, and a NetBill server that maintains accounts for both customers and merchants. These accounts can be linked to conventional accounts in financial institutions. When a customer purchases goods, his or her NetBill account is debited by the appropriate amount and the merchant's account is credited with the value of the goods. A customer's NetBill account can be replenished by transferring funds from

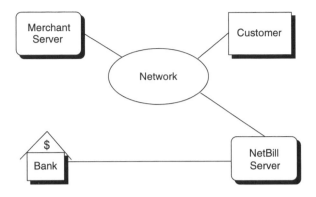

Figure 5.14   The NetBill concept.

his or her bank. Similarly, funds in a merchant's NetBill account are deposited into the merchant's bank account. NetBill guarantees that a customer pays for only the goods that the customer successfully receives. A NetBill transaction is similar to a check in that immediate transfers from one identified account to another take place at the time of purchase. The system does, however, lack the generality of a check in that one party must take on a merchant role for a payment to take place.

In April 1997 CyberCash, a payments company with expertise in processing Internet-based credit card payments, acquired exclusive rights to commercially use and sublicense the NetBill technology. However, NetBill has remained operational only as a trial system [18], where a fictitious currency, called Bibliobucks, is used within the prototype. Users can open a free account to obtain 1,000 bibliobucks that can be spent at a small number of merchants. The client checkbook functionality is packaged in electronic-wallet software known as the MoneyTool [19], which allows purchases to be made through the Web.

5.4.1   Protocol overview

NetBill provides transaction support through libraries integrated with different client-server pairs. The client library is called the *checkbook* and the server library is called the *till*. The checkbook and till libraries in turn communicate with the client and merchant applications, respectively. All network communication between the two is encrypted to protect against adversaries. The transaction protocol consists of a minimum of eight steps, shown in Figure 5.15.

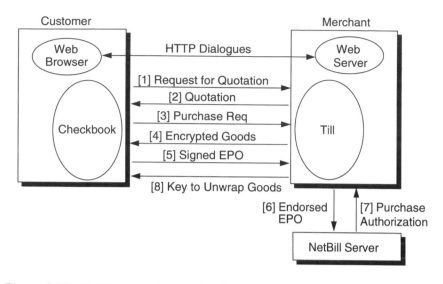

Figure 5.15 NetBill transaction protocol.

Before invoking the NetBill protocol, a user will locate the information required from a server (e.g., a Web server). The NetBill transaction begins when a customer requests a formal quotation from a merchant (Figure 5.15, step 1). There are provisions in the protocol to allow for negotiation of the standard listed price and for group/volume discounts and so forth.

The merchant, on receiving the request for a quotation, determines a price for the user and returns a quotation (step 2). If the customer accepts the price quoted, the customer instructs the checkbook to send a purchase request (step 3) to the merchant's till. Alternatively, the customer may configure his or her checkbook to send a purchase request automatically if the price is below a specified amount.

The till, on receiving the purchase request, fetches the goods from the merchant's application. It encrypts them with a one-time key and computes a cryptographic checksum on the result. The till then forwards the result to the customer's checkbook (step 4). The checkbook, on receiving the encrypted message, verifies the checksum. This gives the checkbook confidence that it has received the requested goods intact. Note at this point that the customer cannot decrypt the goods; neither has the customer been charged for them. The checkbook returns a signed electronic payment order (EPO) to the merchant's till (step 5).

At any time before the signed EPO is submitted, a customer may abort the transaction without danger of the transaction being completed against the cutomer's will. The submission of a signed EPO marks the "point of no return" for the customer. Upon receiving the EPO, the till endorses it and forwards the endorsed EPO to the NetBill server (step 6).

The NetBill server verifies that the price, checksums, and so forth are in order and debits the customer's account for the appropriate amount. It logs the transaction and saves a copy of the one-time key. It returns to the merchant a digitally signed message containing an approval or failure message (step 7). The merchant's application forwards the NetBill server's reply to the customer's checkbook, and if the purchase was successfully approved, the key to unwrap the goods is also released (step 8).

For transactions involving purchase of information goods, all NetBill transactions are atomic. In an ideal situation where only the above eight steps are involved, the NetBill server has to be contacted only once by the merchant. In the case of a dispute, a customer may contact the NetBill server directly. The intention of the designers was to keep the load on the NetBill server to a minimum, thus maintaining good response times.

5.4.2 Authentication procedure

In the course of a NetBill transaction, the parties involved identify themselves. The scheme used in NetBill is a modified version of the Kerberos scheme introduced in Chapter 3. The aim of the modifications is to retain the use of efficient symmetric encryption for the bulk of the traffic, but to decrease the Kerberos server dependency by allowing public keys to be used in certain parts of the protocol exchanges. The resulting scheme is called Public Key Kerberos [17, 20].

In traditional Kerberos, if A wishes to communicate with B, a ticket must first be procured (T_{AB}) from a special-purpose server as well as an encryption key (K_{AB}) that will be used to secure the dialogue with B. Although it contains K_{AB}, the ticket need not be kept secret, as it can only be decrypted by B. When A wishes to send a message to B, K_{AB} is applied to the data and, including the ticket, A sends the following:

$$T_{AB}, K_{AB} \text{ [Message]}$$

When B receives this, he can extract K_{AB} from the ticket and unwrap the message. The message has been kept secret from eavesdroppers, and A has been satisfactorily authenticated.

The NetBill scheme differs from this in that before the communication takes place, A gets the Ticket (T_{AB}) not from a special-purpose server but directly from B in the following manner. A invents a symmetric encryption key, $K_{Challenge}$, and sends it to B in the following message:

$$K_{OneTime}[A, B, TimeStamp, K_{Challenge}], PK_B[K_{OneTime}], Sig_A$$

It is assumed that both A and B have access to each other's public keys in certificate form. This allows B to validate Sig_A if he wishes to ensure that the source of the message is indeed A. B then uses his private key to reveal $K_{OneTime}$, and thus gets access to the main portion of the message that contains the $K_{Challenge}$. B now constructs a normal Kerberos ticket, T_{AB}, and associated K_{AB}, and returns these to A encrypted with $K_{Challenge}$:

$$K_{Challenge}[T_{AB}, K_{AB}]$$

A invented $K_{Challenge}$ in the first place, and it was shared only with the holder of SK_B (i.e., B). When this message successfully unwraps, A recovers T_{AB} and K_{AB} in plaintext and knows that they were generated by B.

In NetBill, before a transaction occurs, the customer contacts the merchant in the above manner and establishes T_{CM} to be used in subsequent dialogues. Similarly, Merchant servers will establish tickets T_{MN} with the NetBill server and the customer will maintain a T_{CN} for communication (via the merchant) with the NetBill server. The period of validity of the ticket is configurable, but would potentially span many transactions.

5.4.3 Transaction protocol

The NetBill transaction protocol can be divided into three distinct phases. In the first phase, a customer requests a merchant for a quote for one or more identified products. This requires a minimum of two message exchanges, or more if the price must be negotiated. In the second phase, which is the delivery phase, the merchant sends encrypted goods to the customer. In the final phase, the customer sends a signed authorization to the NetBill server via the merchant, allowing the purchase to be completed.

5.4.4 Price request phase

When a customer wishes to make a purchase, the following message is sent to the merchant:

$$T_{CM}, K_{CM}[\text{Credentials, PRD, Bid, RequestFlags, TID}]$$

The merchant extracts K_{CM} from the ticket and uses this to unwrap the request for quotation. The most important elements of this are the product request data (PRD), which describes the goods required, and the bid, which is the price being offered by the customer. Other elements include the customer's credentials [19], which specify any group memberships that may merit a discount; RequestFlags, which give more information on the nature of the purchase; and a unique transaction ID (TID).

On receipt of this message, the merchant will compute a quotation for the goods and send the following message back to the customer:

$$K_{CM}[\text{ProductID, Price, RequestFlags, TID}]$$

The inclusion of the transaction ID (TID) links the quotation back to the original request made by the customer. In the response, the Price and RequestFlags refer to the terms that the merchant is offering rather than those requested by the customer, and the ProductID is a textual description that will appear on the customer's statement if the transaction is completed.

5.4.5 Goods delivery phase

When the price negotiation is completed, the customer accepts the merchant's offer by sending the relevant transaction ID, which signals to the merchant that the goods can now be transferred across the network to the customer:

$$T_{CM}, K_{CM}[\text{TID}]$$

The merchant generates a random key, K_{Goods}, which it uses to encrypt the information being purchased, and then sends the blinded product to the customer:

$$K_{Goods}[\text{Goods}], K_{CM}[\text{SHA}[K_{Goods}[\text{Goods}]]], \text{EPOID}$$

The customer can verify the integrity of the goods by applying the secure hash algorithm (SHA) to the goods and checking that it matches that computed by the merchant. The customer will not, however, be able to decrypt the goods until the payment is made. The electronic payment order ID (EPOID) is a quantity that will be used to uniquely identify this transaction in the NetBill database. It contains fields that identify the merchant as well as timestamp information.

5.4.6 Payment phase

The customer signals a commitment to make the payment by constructing an electronic payment order (EPO). This consists of two parts, the first of which contains details about the transaction and is readable by both the merchant and the NetBill server. The second part contains payment instructions and can only be read by the NetBill server. Since the customer is now encrypting data for the NetBill server, it is assumed that the customer has already authenticated himself or herself and is in possession of an appropriate ticket, T_{CN}, and corresponding symmetric encryption key K_{CN}.

The transaction portion of the EPO includes the following fields:

▸ The customer's identity;

▸ The product ID and price specified in the merchant's quotation;

▸ The merchant's identity;

▸ A checksum of the encrypted goods.

The payment instruction portion of the EPO includes:

▸ A ticket proving the customer's true identity;

▸ The customer account number;

▸ A customer memo field.

To start the payment phase, the customer signs the EPO (by appending Sig_C) and sends it to the merchant:

$$T_{CM}, K_{CM}[EPO, Sig_C]$$

The merchant verifies the customer's signature, checks that the product ID, price, and goods checksum are in order before endorsing it and forwarding it to the NetBill server. The endorsement process involves concatenating the merchant's account number (MAcct), a memo field (MMemo), and the key used to encrypt the goods (K_{Goods}), and then signing the result with the merchant's private key to produce Sig_M. The quantity forwarded to the NetBill server is the following:

$$T_{MN}, K_{MN}[(EPO, Sig_C), MAcct, MMemo, K_{Goods}, Sig_M]$$

When the NetBill server receives the endorsed EPO, it unwraps the portion encrypted with K_{MN}, and performs checks on the customer's account. Assuming that the account is in good standing, it transfers the funds, and constructs a signed receipt as follows:

$$Receipt = [ResultCode, C, Price, ProductID, M, K_{Goods}, EPOID]\ Sig_N$$

The NetBill server includes some account status information with the receipt and sends the following to the merchant:

$$K_{MN}[Receipt], K_{CN}[EPOID, CAcct, Balance, Flags]$$

The merchant unwraps the receipt, keeps a copy, and reencrypts it using K_{CM} before forwarding the message to the customer:

$$K_{CM}[Receipt], K_{CN}[EPOID, CAcct, Balance, Flags]$$

The payment has now been made, and the customer can extract K_{Goods} from the receipt and unlock the goods that were delivered earlier. The fields CAcct, Balance, and Flags give all necessary information on the post-transaction status of their NetBill account.

5.4.7 NetBill characteristics

NetBill aims to provide a total payment system, from price negotiation to goods delivery. In the basic scheme, a NetBill transaction requires eight messages to be exchanged. There are many variations within NetBill that allow, for example, the customer to hide his or her identity from the merchant, for price negotiation to take place, for limited spending authority to be given to others, and for disputes of all kinds to be settled.

All transactions must involve the NetBill server before they can be completed. In communications terms, this is a substantial overhead, especially when the value of the goods is low. The protocol has been designed to ensure that communication between the NetBill server and the other entities involved is kept to a minimum. Despite this, the NetBill server is the obvious bottleneck in the scheme. The smooth running of the system is dependent on the continuous availability of this central server, and since there is no easy way to distribute the load, this will put an upper limit on the number of parties that may participate in the payment system, making it inherently unscalable.

5.5 NetCheque

A second check-like system that is also based on the use of Kerberos [21] is the NetCheque payment system [22–24] developed at the Information Sciences Institute of the University of Southern California. NetCheque is a distributed accounting service consisting of a hierarchy of NetCheque servers (banks) that are used to clear checks and settle interbank accounts. This hierarchy allows for scalability of the system. It also allows users to select the bank of their choice based upon criteria such as trust, proximity, reliability, and so forth. Figure 5.16 depicts such a hierarchy.

A NetCheque account is similar to a conventional bank account against which account holders can write electronic checks. An electronic check is like a conventional paper check in that it contains the customer's

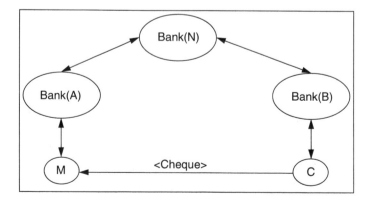

Figure 5.16 Hierarchy of NetCheque servers.

signature. Unlike a paper check, it has to also be endorsed by the merchant before the check is paid.

The NetCheque system makes use of Kerberos tickets [24] for creating electronic signatures and endorsing checks. Kerberos is based on symmetric-key cryptography and is thus more computationally efficient than schemes based on public-key algorithms. A NetCheque consists of the following fields:

- Amount of the check;

- Unit of currency;

- Date;

- Account number;

- Payee(s);

- Signature of the customer;

- Endorsement(s) by the merchant and bank(s).

The first five fields of the check are in cleartext and are readable by the bearer of the check. The last two fields are verifiable by the bank against which the check was drawn.

To write a check, a user generates the cleartext portion of the check. This user obtains a ticket from a Kerberos server that is used to authenticate him or her to his or her bank (B) and allows him to share a session key (K_{CB}) with the bank. The user then generates a checksum on the contents of the check and places it in an authenticator (Auth$_C$). He or she encrypts the authenticator with the session key that he or she shares with his bank and appends the ticket and the authenticator to the check:

$$\text{Sig}_C = [(\text{Auth}_C)K_{CB}, T_{CB}]$$

The ticket (T_{CB}) contains a copy of the session key (K_{CB}) and is encrypted with the *secret key* of the customer's bank (B). Figure 5.17 shows the exchange that takes place when a customer sends a signed check to a merchant.

The check can be sent to the merchant through electronic mail over an unsecure network, though in the interest of security it would be prudent to use an encrypted link. The latter requires that the customer

Figure 5.17 Signing a check.

obtain an additional Kerberos ticket for the merchant, which enables him to share a session key with the merchant and encrypt the link between them.

On receiving a payment, a merchant reads the cleartext part of the check and obtains a Kerberos ticket for the customer's bank (B) from a Kerberos server. The merchant generates an authenticator (Auth_M) endorsing the check in the customer's name and for deposit into the customer's account (see Figure 5.18). The customer appends the endorsement and the ticket to the end of the check. The merchant's signature (Sig_M) consists of:

$$\text{Sig}_M = \{(\text{Auth}_M)K_{MB},\ T_{MB}\}$$

The customer then forwards the endorsed check to the customer's bank (A) over a secure link. This can be done by obtaining a separate Kerberos ticket for the customer's own bank (A) and using the shared session key to encrypt the link.

If the merchant and the customer both use different banks, then the merchant's bank sends an indication to the merchant that the check has been deposited for collection. If the check has to be cleared through multiple banks, each bank attaches its own endorsement to the check, similar to that of the merchant. Once the check has been cleared by the customer's bank, the attached endorsements can be used to trace back the path to the merchant's account and eventually credit the customer's account for the same.

Figure 5.18 Endorsing a check.

5.6 Summary

The chapter started by examining the centralized account transfer schemes that have gained widespread popularity on the Internet. Such Internet bank accounts can be quickly funded with traditional payment instruments such as a credit card, and are user-friendly in that an e-mail address is used as the account identifier. Their success can be partly attributed to the ability to make a payment to anyone with an e-mail address, with the payee then having to sign up as a new customer to the system to actually access the money. However, it is also this lack of ability to transfer funds between the different systems which has led to the emergence of so many independent competing schemes. Each payee must have an account with the same system as the payer, inevitably leading to each individual requiring several different accounts.

In contrast, the banking organizations have considered a number of different ways to transfer monetary value between accounts at different banks from the Internet. When deployed, such solutions will be far more flexible and will be usable in far more scenarios than the current centralized Internet accounts. The banking schemes also differ quite markedly from the NetBill and NetCheque systems designed within the academic research community. The latter were designed for the domain of retail electronic-commerce applications in which one party acts as a merchant selling goods, while in contrast, the banking check-like schemes are much more general-purpose. The use of secure hardware within the FSTC electronic check solution and the NACHA ISAP project will limit their usefulness for on-line purchasing until such time as card-reader hardware becomes commonplace on networked workstations.

As with any payment scheme, a major factor in its success is consumer acceptance. Any system backed by big-name banking organizations or indeed the banking industry as a whole will easily build consumer trust. Schemes that have originated in universities are unlikely to be adopted unless they can be taken up by financial organizations that consumers know and trust.

References

[1] iTransact, Salt Lake City, Utah, http://www.itransact.com/.

[2] Financial Services Technology Consortium, 2001, http://www.fstc.org/.

[3]   ABAecom, http://www.abaecom.com/.

[4]   Financial Services Technology Consortium, *FSTC Electronic Check Project Details*, 2001, http://www.echeck.org/.

[5]   Anderson, M., "The Electronic Check Architecture," September 1998, http://www.echeck.org/library/index.html.

[6]   CommerceNet, http://www.commerce.net/.

[7]   Kravitz, J. (ed.), *FSML—Financial Services Markup Language, Version 1.5, Financial Services Technology Consortium*, Chicago, IL, July 1999.

[8]   Standard Generalized Markup Language, International Standards Organization (ISO) 8879, 1986.

[9]   Extensible Markup Language (XML) 1.0, 2nd ed., W3C Recommendation, October 2000, http://www.w3.org/.

[10] X9.46 Financial Image Interchange Architecture Overview, and System Design Specification, American National Standards Institute, 1997.

[11] X9.37 Specification for Electronic Check Exchange, American National Standards Institute, 1994.

[12] Bank Internet Payment System Specification, Version 1.0, Financial Services Technology Consortium, August 1998, http://www.fstc.org/projects/bips/index.html.

[13] Borenstein, N., "Multipurpose Internet Mail Extensions (MIME) Part One: Format of Internet Message Bodies," *IETF RFC 2045*, November 1996, http://www.ietf.org/.

[14] National Automated Clearing House Association (NACHA), http://www.nacha.org/.

[15] DirectPay Project, NACHA Internet Council, http://internetcouncil.nacha.org/.

[16] Sirbu, M., and J. D. Tygar, "NetBill: An Internet Commerce System Optimized for Network Delivered Services," *IEEE Personal Communications*, Vol. 2, No. 4, August 1995, pp. 34–39, http://www.ini.cmu.edu/NETBILL/.

[17] Cox, B., J. D. Tygar, and M. Sirbu, "NetBill Security and Transaction Protocol," *Proc. 1st Usenix Workshop of Electronic Commerce*, Berkeley, CA, 1995, pp. 1–12, http://www.ini.cmu.edu/NETBILL/.

[18] NetBill Trial Site, Carnegie Mellon University, http://www.netbill.com/.

[19] Kawakura, Y., et al., "Flexible and Scalable Credential Structures: NetBill Implementation and Experience," *Proc. 1999 International Workshop on Cryptographic Techniques and E-Commerce*, City University, Hong Kong, 1999, pp. 231–235.

[20] Sirbu, M., and J. Chuang, "Public-Key Based Ticket Granting Service in Kerberos," Internet Draft, Carnegie Mellon University/Information Networking Institute, May 1996, http://www.ini.cmu.edu/NETBILL/.

[21] Neuman, B. C., and T. Ts'o, "Kerberos: An Authentication Service for Computer Networks," *IEEE Communications*, Vol. 32, No. 9, September 1994, pp. 33–38. http://www.isi.edu/gost/info/kerberos/.

[22] Neuman, B. C., and G. Medvinsky, "Requirements for Network Payment: The NetCheque Perspective," *Proc. IEEE Compcon '95*, San Francisco, CA, March 1995, http://www.netcheque.org/.

[23] Neuman, B. C., and G. Medvinsky, "NetCheque, NetCash, and the Characteristics of Internet Payment Services," *MIT Workshop on Internet Economics 1995*, Massachusetts Institute of Technology (MIT), Cambridge, MA, March 1995, http://www.press.umich.edu/jep/works/ NeumNetPay.html.

[24] Neuman, B. C., "Proxy-Based Authentication and Accounting for Distributed Systems," *Proc. 13th International Conference on Distributed Computing Systems*, Pittsburgh, PA, May 1993, pp. 283–291, http://www.netcheque.org/.

Electronic cash payment systems

In Chapter 2, an analysis of current usage of conventional payment instruments showed that consumers make extensive use of cash. Depending on the country involved, somewhere between 75% and 95% of all transactions are paid in cash, even though the value of these transactions are for the most part quite low. It is difficult to pinpoint exactly what attributes of cash make it attractive, but they would undoubtedly include the following:

▸ *Acceptability:* Cash is almost universally acceptable as a form of payment, regardless of the transaction amount.

▸ *Guaranteed payment:* One of the reasons why it is so acceptable is that the physical handing over of the cash completes the transactions and there is no risk that the payment will not be honored at a later stage.

▸ *No transaction charges:* Cash can be handed from person to person, with no charges

171

levied. There is no authorization required and, consequently, no communications traffic or charges.

- *Anonymity:* Many other forms of payment involve a paper trail linking either or both parties with the transaction. Cash allows transactions to take place anonymously. In addition to being attractive to criminals, this also has appeal for perfectly honest consumers who are worried about the ability of large organizations to monitor their movements and lifestyle.

Attempts to create an electronic cash payment method have focused in on subsets of the above attributes, but to date no system has managed to capture all of the above. In Section 6.1, we examine the more influential systems that claim cash-like attributes.

6.1 Ecash

One of the first companies to launch an electronic cash payment scheme was DigiCash, which was based in Holland and the United States. The company was founded by David Chaum [1] who was one of the pioneers in the field of electronic cash, and has been called by some, "the father of digital cash."

Ecash [2] was developed by DigiCash to allow fully anonymous secure electronic cash to be used on the Internet. It provides the privacy of paper cash with the added security required for open networks. It is an on-line software solution allowing payment for information, hard goods, and even payout services, in which a client might receive back a payment as part of the service. Ecash is said to be fully anonymous because clients withdraw coins from a bank in such a way that the bank cannot know the serial numbers of those coins. The coins can be spent anonymously with a merchant, and even collusion between both the bank and merchant will fail to identify the spender. Strong security is provided in the system through extensive use of both symmetric and asymmetric (public key) cryptography.

In 1995 the Mark Twain Bank in St. Louis, Missouri, started issuing Ecash coins worth real monetary value in U.S. currency. The trial ran for about three years, when in November 1998 DigiCash filed for Chapter 11 bankruptcy protection. Since then DigiCash has been relaunched as eCash Technologies, Inc. [3].

6.1.1 The Ecash model

The participants within the system are clients, merchants, and banks, as shown in Figure 6.1. Clients and merchants have accounts at an Ecash bank. Clients can withdraw coins against their account and store them in their Ecash wallet software that resides on their computer. The Ecash wallet software is known as a *cyberwallet*. It stores and manages a client's coins, keeps records of all transactions, and makes the protocol steps appear as transparent as possible to the client. The withdrawal protocol prevents the bank from being able to see the serial numbers of the coins it is issuing.

A client can use the coins to later pay a merchant. At the time of purchase, the merchant must forward the coins to the minting bank to ensure that they have not already been spent. If the coins are valid, they will be deposited into the merchant's account. The merchant can then send the purchased goods or a receipt to the client. A merchant can also make payments to a client using the same procedure. This is useful for making refunds or providing payout services.

Currently, both client and merchant must have accounts at the same Ecash bank. Coins obtained from one bank will not be accepted by another. As Ecash becomes more widespread, it is likely that third parties might exchange coins from different banks or the banks might provide this exchange themselves. Interbank clearing may also become possible, although coins will still have to be forwarded to the minting bank for verification.

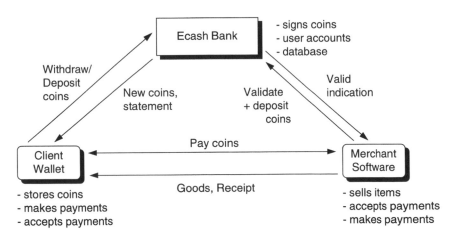

Figure 6.1 Entities and their functions within the Ecash system.

6.1.2   Ecash coins

The electronic coins used within the Ecash system are unique in that they are partly minted by the client before being signed by the bank. Each coin has a serial number that is generated by the client's cyberwallet software. The serial numbers are chosen randomly and are large enough so that there is very little chance that anyone else will ever generate the same serial numbers. For example, using a 100-digit serial number can guarantee this.

The serial number is blinded and sent to the bank to be signed. This is done using the *blind signature* protocol described in Chapter 3. The bank is unable to see the serial number on the coin it is signing. The method can be considered similar to putting the coin and a piece of carbon paper into an envelope. The envelope is sent to the bank where it is signed and returned to the client, as shown in Figure 6.2. The client opens the envelope and takes out the coin (unblinds it). The coin has now been signed. The carbon paper ensured that the bank's signature went through the envelope. The signature on the unblinded coin appears the same as any other normal digital signature. There is no way to tell from it that the coin was signed using the blind signature protocol.

6.1.3   Coin keys

However, there is a problem with this method. Since the bank cannot see what it is signing, how can a value be assigned to the coin? The value cannot be included with the serial number in the fields of the coin because the bank cannot see this. The client might assign a very high value and tell the bank that it is only a low-valued coin.

The problem can be solved by the bank using a different signature key for each coin denomination. The client informs the bank of the value it wants the blinded coin to be worth. The bank then signs the coin with the signature key representing this denomination and deducts that

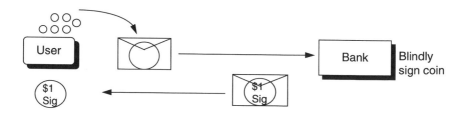

Figure 6.2   Blind signature analogy for withdrawing Ecash coins.

amount from the client's account. For example, the bank might have a one-cent signature, a 5-cent signature, a 10-cent signature, and so on. Figure 6.3 shows a coin worth 10 cents.

After the withdrawal process, a coin essentially consists of a serial number encrypted with the appropriate secret key of the bank. This acts as a signature:

$$\{Serial\#\}SK_{Bank's\ \$1\ Key}$$

To allow the signature to be quickly verified (decrypted) an indication of which public key to use (*keyversion*) is usually included with a coin. For convenience, the plaintext serial number is also included:

$$Coin = Serial\#, keyversion, \{Serial\#\}SK_{Bank's\ \$1\ Key}$$

Keyversion can be used to obtain other information about the coin, including its value, currency, and expiry date. This information is exchanged and stored during initial account setup with a bank, or again during withdrawal. The public keys needed to verify each different valued signature are also sent to the client at this time.

However, in the form described, where a coin can be any signed large number, forgery can occur. Using the inverse relation of RSA signatures, any party can generate a valid signed coin. For example, choose a large random number R and apply the bank's \$1 public key to this value to get another large number S:

$$S = \{R\}PK_{Bank's\ \$1\ Key}$$

Serial #

Signed:
Bank's \$0.10
signature

Figure 6.3   An Ecash coin worth 10 cents.

A forged coin will use this value S as the random serial number. The signature on S, which will also be a large number, can be shown to be equal to R:

$$\{S\}SK_{\text{Bank's \$1 Key}} = \{\{R\}PK_{\text{Bank's \$1 Key}}\}SK_{\text{Bank's \$1 Key}} = R$$

$$\text{Forged\_coin} = \{S, \text{keyversion}, R = \{S\}SK_{\text{Bank's \$1 Key}}\}$$

This works because encrypting with an RSA public key, followed by decrypting with the corresponding private key will yield the original value. This inverse relationship of RSA is described in Chapter 3.

The problem is that the serial numbers are completely random and there is no way to distinguish a genuine signed serial number from one created using the RSA inverse property with the above technique. This applies not only to Ecash coins but to any message that is directly signed without any modification using RSA. To prevent this attack the serial number, or message, must first be transformed into a related message by applying a one-way function H such as SHA. The transformed message is then signed:

$$S, \{H(S)\}SK_{\text{Bank's \$1 Key}}$$

For the forgery to now succeed the attacker must be able to reverse the one-way function to obtain the corresponding serial number, which is infeasible. One-way functions are described in Chapter 3.

In the Ecash system, security is further strengthened by using a redundancy-adding function in combination with a one-way hash function [4]. An Ecash coin is now defined as:

$$\text{Coin} = \text{Serial\#}, \text{keyversion}, \{f(\text{Serial\#})\}SK_{\text{Bank's \$1 Key}}$$

The redundancy function f() is defined as a recursive function. The input s, in this case the serial#, forms the rightmost block of the output. Subsequent blocks are formed by concatenating all the current rightmost blocks together in reverse order, and hashing the result, to form the next block s_t. The process continues until the total length of the combined blocks, the output length of f(s), is just below the size of the RSA signing modulus n, which is typically 1,024 bits:

$$f(s) = s_t, s_{t-1}, \ldots, s_1, s_0$$
$$s_0 = s$$
$$s_t = H(s_0, s_1, \ldots, s_{t-1})$$

6.1.4 Double-spending prevention

Like other forms of electronic cash, Ecash coins are just pieces of data that can be copied. To prevent copied coins from being spent repeatedly, this possible double spending must be prevented. Since the bank cannot see the serial numbers on the coins it issues, it cannot record these during a withdrawal. While providing full anonymity, this makes the bank's task of preventing double spending all the more difficult.

To ensure that a serial number is not spent twice, the minting bank must record every coin that is deposited back to that bank. A very large database of *all spent serial numbers* soon develops. A valid unspent coin must:

▸ Be signed, with any denominational signature, by the bank;

▸ Have an expiry date associated with it that is later than the present date;

▸ Not appear in the database of spent coins.

The third requirement can only be checked by the minting bank that maintains the database, and thus coins must be forwarded to it for on-line verification during a purchase, as shown in Figure 6.4.

When a valid coin is accepted, it then becomes spent and its serial number is entered into the database. An attempt to spend the coin again should fail. Like many electronic cash schemes, Ecash coins can only be spent once.

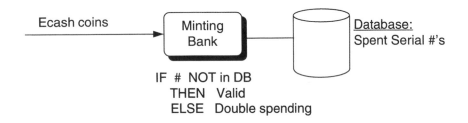

Figure 6.4 Preventing double spending of Ecash coins.

Clearly, the size of the Ecash database could become very large and unmanageable. By using expiry dates with coins, the serial numbers of those coins can be removed after the expiry date. Coins that have expired will not be accepted as legal tender. The wallet software can automatically ensure that coins are returned to the bank before they expire. The bank host machine needs to have an internal scalable structure to cope with the size of the database. To further handle the problem of scalability, multiple banks, each minting and managing their own currency with interbank clearing, could be used. Even still, if a large number of people start to use Ecash regularly, the system may begin to show unacceptable delays and signs of overloading.

6.1.5 Withdrawing coins

Figure 6.2 shows an analogy of the blind signature protocol used to withdraw coins. The cryptographic protocol used is now examined. Ecash uses the RSA public-key algorithm. As described in Chapter 3, a public key consists of a modulus m ($m = p \cdot q$) and a number e (the public encryption key), in the RSA scheme. The secret key is a number denoted by d. To create key pairs for different denominations, different values of e and d are generated for the same modulus m. For simplicity, we omit the serial encoding function, f(serial#) described earlier, from the following equations, although it can be assumed to have been applied wherever the serial# is used.

To withdraw a coin the following steps occur:

1. The user's wallet software chooses a blinding factor r at random.

2. The serial number of the coin, serial#, is blinded by multiplying it by the blinding factor raised to the power of the public exponent ($e2$) for the requested denomination:

$$\text{serial\#} \cdot r^{e2} \ (\text{mod}\, m)$$

Here, $e2$ is the public key for the 2-cent denomination key pair.

3. The bank signs the coin with its 2-cent secret signature key ($d2$):

$$(\text{serial\#} \cdot r^{e2})^{d2} \ (\text{mod}\, m) = \text{serial\#}^{d2} \cdot r^{e2 \cdot d2} \ (\text{mod}\, m)$$
$$= \text{serial\#}^{d2} \cdot r \qquad (\text{mod}\, m)$$

The bank cannot see the serial# since it does not know r. The signed blinded coin is returned to the user.

4. The user divides out the blinding factor:

$$\frac{serial\#^{d2} \cdot r}{r} \pmod m = serial\#^{d2} \pmod m$$

The signed coin is what remains. This appears as a normal RSA signature (encryption with a private key):

$$serial\#^{d2} = \{serial\#\}SK_{\text{Bank's 2-cent Key}}$$

It cannot be linked to the withdrawal. In this way, *full anonymity* may be maintained.

Many coins of different denominations, specified by the client, can be obtained in a single withdrawal request. The request must be signed with the client's secret key, and the whole request is protected by encrypting it with the bank's public key (PK_{Bank}). This key is distinct from the public coin keys. The withdrawal request contains the unsigned blinded coins and an indication of the denominations required. Figure 6.5 shows the effective withdrawal request without all of the implementation optimizations. A combination of both symmetric and asymmetric cryptography is used in the actual implementation for efficiency:

$$\{K_{Ses}\}PK_{Bank}, \{request, \{H(request)\}SK_{Client}\}K_{Ses}$$

For efficiency, the signature on a message consists of the request and a hash of the request encrypted with the signer's private key:

$$\{request\}Sig_X = \{request, \{H(request)\}SK_X\}$$

The symmetric algorithm that is currently used is Triple DES in CBC mode (see Chapter 3). The secure hash algorithm (SHA) is used to perform hashes.

After the bank has blindly signed the coins and debited the user's account, they are returned to the user. The withdrawal response is signed by the bank, as shown in Figure 6.5. The message is not encrypted because only the client who knows the blinding factor can unblind the coins and later spend them.

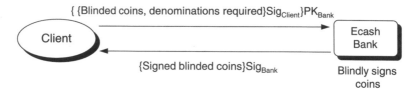

Figure 6.5 Messages used to withdraw Ecash coins.

6.1.6 An Ecash purchase

Once a client has Ecash coins stored in his cyberwallet software, he can spend these coins with a merchant. The client decides which item(s) to buy and places the order with the merchant. This might be done by submitting a form at a merchant's Web site. The initial shopping and ordering protocols are outside the scope of the Ecash protocols, but methods in which Ecash is integrated with the Web are discussed later.

Having received an order, the merchant sends a *payment request* to the client's cyberwallet. This message contains details about the order amount, the currency to be used, the current time, the merchant's bank, the merchant's account ID at that bank, and a description of the order:

$$payreq = \{currency, amount, timestamp, merchant\_bankID,$$
$$merchant\_accID, description\}$$

The request is sent in the clear, which might allow an eavesdropper to see what is being ordered and for how much.

The client's wallet presents the user with this information, asking if they wish to make the payment. The cyberwallet may also be configured to make payments automatically to specific merchants or for specific amounts. If the user decides to pay, coins valuing the requested amount are gathered from the wallet. The exact amount must be sent to the merchant because accepting change could compromise the user's anonymity (the merchant could record the serial numbers of the change and collude with the bank to reveal the user's identity). The cyberwallet will automatically assemble the correct amount and can withdraw new coins from the bank if more denominations are required.

6.1.7 Making the payment

The coins used in payment are encrypted with the bank's public key (PK_{Bank}) before they are sent to the merchant. This prevents them being stolen in transit and prevents the merchant being able to examine or tamper with them. The merchant forwards the coins to the bank to deposit them in the merchant's account. The payment message, sent to the merchant and later forwarded to the bank, consists of information about the payment and the encrypted coins:

$$payment = \{payment\_info, \{Coins\}PK_{Bank}\}$$

The payment information includes details about the bank, amount, currency, number of coins, current time, and merchant IDs, among other things:

$$payment\_info = \{bankID, amount, currency, ncoins, timestamp,$$
$$merchant\_IDs,$$
$$H(description), H(payer\_code)\}$$

The payment information is forwarded to the bank, along with the encrypted coins, during the merchant's deposit. A hash of the order description is included with the payment information. Since the merchant already knows the order, the merchant can compare this value with a hash of the merchant copy of the order, to verify that the client agrees on exactly what is being purchased. When the payment information is forwarded to the bank, the bank cannot know what is being purchased since only a hash of the order description is included.

6.1.8 Proving payment

Payer_code is a secret generated by the client. A hash of it, $H(payer\_code)$ is included in the payment information so that the client can later prove to the bank, after the merchant has deposited the coins, that the client made the payment. The bank will record that the merchant deposited a payment containing $H(payer\_code)$. If the client reveals payer_code, the bank can be certain that the creator of payer_code (that is, the client) made the payment.

However, for this to work, the bank needs to be assured that *payment_info* was not tampered with between the time it left the client and the time it was deposited by the merchant into the bank. If it could be altered, the value of $H(payer\_code)$ could be changed. To prevent this, a hash of the payment_info is included with the coins before they are encrypted:

$$\{\text{Coins, } H(\text{Payment\_info})\} \, PK_{Bank}$$

When the bank receives the payment, it will generate its own hash of the payment_info. If this matches the value encrypted with PK_{Bank}, which only the bank can decrypt, then it can be assured that the message was not altered. The full payment message is now:

$$\text{payment} = \{\text{payment\_info}, \{\text{Coins}, H(\text{payment\_info})\} PK_{Bank}\}$$

The payers (clients) remain anonymous, unless they decide later to prove the payment. The payees (merchants) are not anonymous as they must deposit the coins and they are identified in the payment information constructed by the clients.

6.1.9 Payment deposit
Upon receiving the payment message, the merchant forwards it to the bank as part of a deposit request:

$$\text{deposit} = \{ \, \{\text{payment}\} Sig_{Merchant} \, \} PK_{Bank}$$

The deposit may optionally be signed by the merchant and encrypted with the bank's public key. The bank checks that the coins have not been spent (double spending) and credits the merchant's account. An indication of success is returned to the merchant:

$$\text{deposit\_ack} = \{\text{result, amount}\} Sig_{Bank}$$

A similar deposit message format can be used by a client to return unspent coins to a bank.

Having received a good payment, the merchant may return the purchased item or a receipt to the client. If the merchant fails to do so, the client can prove that the payment was made and accepted by revealing the payer_code.

6.1.10 Integration with the Web
Figure 6.6 shows how Ecash is normally integrated with the Web at present. The client runs the cyberwallet software and a Web browser side by side. When an order is selected from a merchant's Web page, the merchant's Ecash software is automatically started by means of a common

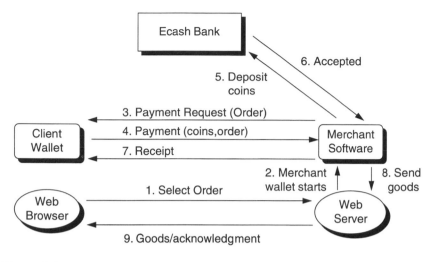

Figure 6.6   Using Ecash with the World Wide Web.

gateway interface (CGI) script [5]. The CGI simply provides a means of running a program from a Web server and allowing it to pass back results through that server. The merchant software proceeds with the Ecash purchase as before. If the payment was successful, the item or purchase indication may be returned through the Web to the client's browser as shown (steps 8 and 9). This method has the advantage that it can be easily integrated with most Web browsers and servers.

6.1.11   Ecash in the mail

Ecash payments may also be made using electronic mail. The merchant still contacts the bank, through e-mail, to deposit the coins and prevent double spending before delivering the goods. The coins are protected in the same way as with the on-line protocol.

6.1.12   Transferring Ecash

User-to-user transfer of Ecash is possible, although the amount transferred still has to be forwarded to the bank for verification. The exchange uses the same protocols as with an Ecash purchase, as shown in Figure 6.7. The coins are forwarded through the payee to the bank where they are deposited. New coins worth the same amount are then returned to the payee. This is all done transparently by the software so that it appears that the new coins were received directly from the payer.

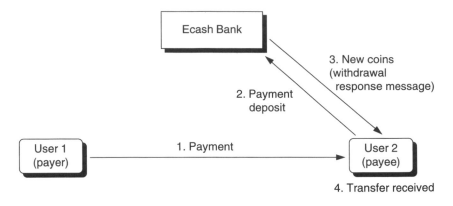

Figure 6.7   User-to-user transfer of Ecash.

Currently, as with merchant payments, both users must have accounts at the same Ecash bank in order to perform a user-to-user transfer.

6.1.13   Lost coins

If the network fails or the computer crashes during a payment transaction, coins might be lost. There is a mechanism available to recover the value of these lost coins. The client whose coins have been lost notifies the minting bank of this occurrence. The bank then sends the exact messages from the last n withdrawals to the client. Currently $n = 16$, so that all the signed blinded coins from the last 16 withdrawals are sent, as shown in Figure 6.8.

The client must still have the blinding factor used for these withdrawals; otherwise, the coins cannot be unblinded. The client's wallet will unblind all the coins and then deposit them into the client's account at the bank. It is necessary to deposit the coins because it will not be known which coins from the last 16 withdrawals have already been spent and which have not. The bank will check each coin deposited to see if it has already been spent or not. This is the normal verification to prevent double spending. The client's account will be credited the unspent amount. The value of any lost coins will have been recovered and the client can now withdraw new coins to spend.

6.1.14   Ecash and crime

There is a concern that fully anonymous electronic cash, like paper cash, will help to hide the identity of criminals. There are fears that it could be

Figure 6.8 Recovering lost Ecash coins.

used for money laundering, tax evasion, bribes, black markets, and other such crimes.

With Ecash, only the payer (client) is anonymous. The payee (merchant) who receives a payment must deposit it into a bank account to validate the coins. The bank can monitor the deposits of suspected criminals. However, it would still be possible for a criminal to accept payments under the guise of a legal business. As described in Section 6.1.9, it is also possible for a payer to prove to a bank that the payer made a payment. Thus, with the cooperation of the client who made the payment, the payee can be identified as accepting that payment.

While the person who receives a payment can be monitored, new coins that have been withdrawn are completely anonymous. The cryptographer Bruce Schneier described how to commit the "perfect crime" [6] and obtain such anonymous coins:

- An anonymous kidnapper takes a hostage.

- The kidnapper then prepares a large number of blinded coins. These are sent anonymously to the bank as a ransom demand.

- The bank signs the coins due to the hostage situation.

- The kidnapper demands that the signed blinded coins be published in a public place such as a newspaper or on television. This will prevent the pickup being traced. Nobody else can unblind the coins.

- The kidnapper can safely take the blinded coins from the newspaper or television and save them on computer. The coins are then unblinded and the kidnapper now has a fortune in anonymous digital cash.

6.1.15 Magic Money

Magic Money [7] is another implementation of fully anonymous digital cash using blind signatures. It has many similarities with the Ecash system and was designed for experimental purposes by a group of cryptographic enthusiasts, known as cypherpunks, on the Internet. The source code is available in C and there is an example client program that can automatically accept and pay out Magic Money currency.

6.1.16 Remarks

Ecash provides secure, fully anonymous electronic cash for open networks. The Ecash software has been integrated with both the Web and e-mail. While payments as low as one cent are possible using Ecash, the computationally intensive cryptography, multiple messages, and database lookups prevent it from being used for efficient repeated micropayments. Also, the scalability of the system is perhaps limited by the cost of maintaining and searching a large database of all spent serial numbers during a purchase.

6.2 Project CAFE

The research that led to the Ecash product has continued. CAFE (Conditional Access for Europe) was a project funded under the European Community's ESPRIT program [8, 9]. It began in 1992 and lasted for a duration of three years. The aim of the project was to develop a general system to administer rights to users (e.g., access to confidential data, entry to buildings, and so forth). The most significant outcome of the project was the development of an advanced electronic payment system. The CAFE protocols are based on the idea of untraceable electronic cash proposed by David Chaum [10] and the concept of checks with counters as described in [11]. CAFE is thus a hybrid scheme in the sense that it offers all the benefits of anonymous electronic cash but at the same time lets the user sign checks up to a specified amount. Unlike other electronic payment schemes, the CAFE protocols allow for security of all parties involved in the system. Strong state-of-the-art cryptographic techniques are employed to protect all payment transactions, thus guaranteeing the security of the financial institutions. The use of tamper-resistant devices and observers ensures the security of the users of the system.

6.2.1 Goals of CAFE

CAFE is designed to be a universal, prepaid, off-line payment system with multiparty security. The following are the salient features of the system:

> • *Multiparty security:* Most existing systems provide *one-sided security* (i.e., the security of the financial institutions or money issuers from attack by fraudulent users). The designers of CAFE have found this to be inadequate to address the needs of users of electronic payment systems and designed the CAFE protocols around the idea of multiparty security. The security of each entity in the system is guaranteed without the need to trust a third party. This implies that each party must be able to trust the device that they are using. Also, procedures and algorithms used in the protocol must be open and available for inspection by all.

> • *Off-line payments:* There is no need for a payee (merchant) to contact a central database, usually maintained by an electronic currency issuer, at the time of purchase. This reduces the costs of maintaining/establishing a communications channel between the two.

> • *Detection of double spending:* The CAFE protocols rely on tamper-resistant devices to provide the basic security of the system. If, however, under extreme circumstances the tamper resistance of a device is broken, then double spending can take place. The cryptographic protocols are designed such that double spending of electronic currency will be detected with a very high probability. This detection is achieved at a cost of maintaining a database of recently spent payment slips by the financial institutions.

> • *Untraceable payments:* Under normal circumstances, payments cannot be linked to a user even if there is collaboration between the merchants and the banks. The identity of a user is, however, revealed if the user double spends a payment slip. As with current banking procedures, the identity of the payee is not protected.

2.2 Architecture

The CAFE architecture is similar to most other payment systems in that there are three main participants in the protocols. They are the custom-ers, merchants, and financial institutions. We elaborate on the role of each briefly:

- *Payer:* A payer (customer) is equipped with a tamper-resistant device such as a smart card or an electronic wallet, which is used to store electronic currency and make payments.

- *Payee:* A payee (merchant) will receive electronic payments from customers in exchange for goods or services. The payee will deposit the payment with the payee's bank (at a later stage) for clearance.

- *Bank:* A bank's role can be divided further into an *issuer/acquirer* of electronic currency. The issuer loads electronic money into a cus-tomer's account and ensures that the correct amount is debited from the customer's account. The acquirer accepts deposits from merchants and clears them through existing interbank clearing channels.

Figure 6.9 shows an overview of the protocol exchanges that take place between the various entities in the system.

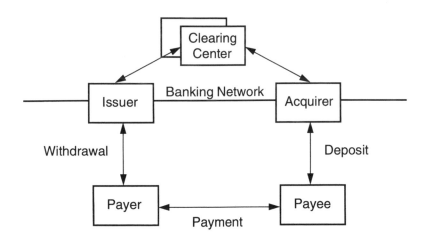

Figure 6.9 CAFE architecture.

6.2.3 CAFE devices

There are a number of tamper resistant secure electronic devices used in the CAFE system. These devices are used to store electronic money by the user, perform cryptographic operations, and make payments to merchants.

- *Smart card:* This is the simplest of the devices used in the protocol. It is similar to a credit card and has an embedded microprocessor powered by an external source. All the information is stored on the chip, which also performs the cryptographic computations. It is referred to as the α (alpha) system.

- *Wallets:* A wallet consists of two parts that work in conjunction with each other. One part is known as an *observer* (see Chapter 3) and protects the bank's interests, and the other part is known as the *purse* and protects the user's interests. The purse includes a keyboard and a display. This further protects the user as he or she can enter his or her PIN on the purse and does not have to trust any third-party device. Furthermore, all communications between the wallet and the outside world are done exclusively through the purse, guaranteeing that the observer cannot divulge any secret information to the bank without the user's knowledge.

  1. *Two-button wallet* (α^+): The two-button wallet, as its name suggests, consists of a two-button keyboard and a digital display. The observer module is implemented as a smart card that also performs all the transactions. The purse monitors, verifies, and relays all communication from the smart card via an infrared interface to the payment terminal. The α^+ system is fully compatible with the α system.

  2. *Full wallet:* The full wallet (see Figure 6.10) has a full numeric keyboard and a display larger than that used in the α^+ device. The full keyboard allows the user to also enter amounts and PINs. The observer is implemented as a built-in smart card microprocessor. Unlike the smart card in the α system, the observer exclusively protects the interests of the bank. The wallet uses an adapted version of the protocols in the α system and ensures better privacy for the user. The full-wallet system is called the Γ (gamma) system and is compatible with the α and α^+

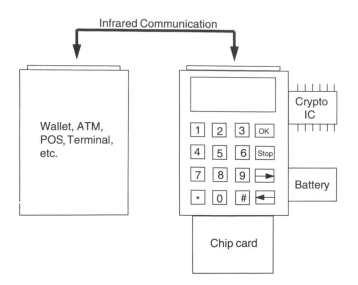

Figure 6.10   A full CAFE wallet.

systems. In addition, it has a slot into which an α smart card can be inserted and money can be transferred.

6.2.4 Role of observers

Observers, or guardians as they are also known in CAFE, are devices implanted into a smart card to protect the interests of the financial institutions. They ensure the correctness of all transactions performed by the user. A user will not be able to successfully complete a payment transaction without the cooperation of an observer. Also, genuine merchants will not accept payments that have not been authorized by a certified observer. An observer approves each payment in a manner similar to creating a digital signature. The form of this approval is such that one cannot obtain either the identity of the observer or the user from it.

6.2.5 Protocol overview

CAFE employs two types of security mechanisms to protect the system against attack. The first line of defense is the use of secure tamper-resistant devices to store cryptographic keys and to perform all cryptographic transactions. Protection against double spending is only guaranteed as long as the tamper resistance is not compromised. CAFE has a cryptographic fallback mechanism that allows the financial institutions to detect double spending of electronic currency (after it has been spent) and blacklist suspected users. The banks distribute these lists to all the merchants in the system.

6.2.6 Off-line coins

The CAFE system uses the idea of off-line coins first proposed in [12] as a fallback mechanism. At a very simple level, a CAFE off-line coin is one where the identity of the payer is encoded into the coin number, which is constructed from two parts. When the coin is used in a payment transaction, the payer must reveal one part of the coin. If the same coin is used again, the user will have to reveal the second part of the coin. The coin is constructed in such a way that revealing a single part of the coin will not identify the payer, but if the coin is double spent, then the identity of the payer is revealed.

The following analogy will help to explain how the system works. The identity (I) of the user is encrypted with a one-time random number (P). The coin consists of two parts. The first part contains the encrypted identity $I \oplus P$, while the other part contains the key P. Each part is further encrypted with a commitment (encryption) scheme to produce $C(I \oplus P)$ and $C(P)$. In one payment transaction, the payer will have to open one of the commitments, which will be either $I \oplus P$ or P, which does not reveal the identity of the payer. However, if the other part is opened, then the identity of the payer will be found out. To detect such double spending, a bank maintains a database of all recently deposited coins and searches for corresponding pairs before clearing payment transactions. More efficient versions of the scheme are used in the actual system.

The concept of untraceable off-line coins was proposed in [13] and is used as a starting point in the design of the α and Γ protocols. A *payment slip* in CAFE refers to a "*k*-spendable instrument" consisting of k parts, where each part can be spent once during a payment transaction. All signatures except signatures on payment slips are Schnorr signatures [14]. The Schnorr scheme proposes an efficient way to create digital signatures and minimizes the work to be done by the smart card. This is important since the 8-bit processor smart cards currently used in CAFE are rather limited. The scheme requires about 12 modular multiplications for a single signature generation and most of the work can be done in the background (i.e., during the idle time of the processor).

6.2.7 The α protocol

The α (alpha) protocol refers to the set of protocols used by the smart card. There are a number of primitives, ranging from withdrawal of electronic currency to recovery of the value in lost cards.

6.2.7.1 Withdrawal

A payer usually only needs to communicate with the bank through a withdrawal session, which results in a number of blank electronic payment slips being loaded into the payer's smart card. The bank keeps track of the balance in the card by means of a counter in the observer part of the smart card. The balance is updated during a withdrawal request and the corresponding amount deducted from the user's bank account. A withdrawal session consists of the following steps:

- The user's smart card sends the identity of the user's bank and information about the user's bank's public-key certificate to the terminal. This allows the terminal to connect to the correct bank and verify/update the bank's public-key certificate stored in the smart card.

- The card and bank then mutually authenticate each other through the terminal. The card generates a random number and sends it to the bank. The bank signs this with its secret key and returns the signature. The card verifies the signature using the public key of the bank. The card in turn authenticates itself to the bank by signing a random quantity sent by the bank. In addition, it also sends a snapshot of its currency table (counters). The bank verifies the signature.

- In order to ensure that the bank can identify double spending of payment slips, a public key (PK_{Id}) derived from the user's secret key (SK_{User}) is incorporated into the payment slips. To protect the identity of the user, the card blinds this value.

A payment slip consists of:

1. PK_{Blind}, which is a blinded version of PK_{Id}. This value also serves as a slip identifier.

2. Two auxiliary one-time public keys PK_1 and PK_2, which are not known to the bank.

Figure 6.11 shows the overall process of obtaining a blank payment slip from a bank. The user generates a payment slip and forwards the hash H(Payslip) of it to the bank. The bank creates a digital signature (Sig_{Bank}) on the forwarded hash. The signature binds the payment slip to the two one-time public keys, PK_1 and PK_2. The user needs to only store the bank's signature on the card as all the other values can be regenerated by the user at the payment stage. This allows for efficient storage of payment slips.

6.2.7.2   Payment

The payment transaction consists of the user filling in an amount into a blank payment slip together with the name of the payee, signed with the user's secret key. Figure 6.12 shows the steps involved in a payment transaction.

The protocol details are as follows:

▸ A customer inserts his or her card into a merchant's (payment) terminal. The terminal tells the card the identity of the payee, the date, the amount to be deducted from the currency table, and so forth. This information is encoded by the card into the payment slip (M).

▸ The card regenerates the next payment slip to be used. This consists of generating the secret quantities and the one-time public keys. This is the most time-consuming part of the protocol and is usually done in the background while the payment parameters are being negotiated by the user and the merchant.

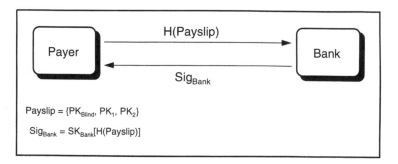

Figure 6.11 Generation of payment slips.

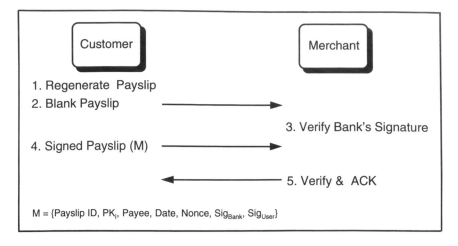

Figure 6.12 Payment transaction.

- The card sends the blank payment slip to the merchant, consisting of the bank's signature and the public keys needed to use the slip (PK_i, where $i = 1$ or 2 depending on whether the slip is being used the first or second time). The payment slip is marked as being spent by the card even though the payment has not been completed yet.

- The terminal verifies the signature of the bank on the blank payment slip.

- The card prepares a message corresponding to the contents of the payment slip. It contains the following fields:

  1. The public keys of the payment slip PK_{Blind} (slip identity) and PK_i;

  2. Merchant ID;

  3. Date;

  4. Amount;

  5. Random string to ensure uniqueness of the message.

The message is signed with the secret key of the user (SK_{User}) and the random strings used to generate the payment slip. This results in a digital signature Sig_{User}.

> • The terminal verifies that the payment has the proper form. It does this in conjunction with the blank payment slip sent previously.

When the payment has been finalized, the terminal sends an acknowledgment to the card. The card updates its counters.

6.2.7.3 Deposit
Upon accepting a payment slip, the payee forwards it to the acquirer (at a later date) who in turn clears it through the existing financial clearing system. The acquirer:

> • Verifies the contents of the payment slip and validates the bank's signature;

> • Verifies that the payment slip has not been deposited previously;

> • Looks for a matching pair PK_i in its database to verify that the corresponding part of the payment slip has not been spent previously.

If the first two conditions are fulfilled, the payee is entitled to be credited for the amount of the payment. A payee is responsible for checking all received payment slips against their local copies of the blacklist during a payment protocol. If a blacklisted slip is detected, the payee aborts the transaction. If a payee fails to check received payment slips against the blacklist, then the payee will have to accept responsibility for them as the clearing center will reject them. When the clearing center detects double spending, the payment slip will immediately be added to the blacklist.

6.2.8 The Γ protocol
The Γ (gamma) protocols are a modular extension of the α system. The Γ wallet consists of a purse that is capable of performing public-key cryptography. All communications between the observer and the outside world take place via the purse. This provides additional security for the user as the purse will blind/neutralize any communications that may disclose secret information about the user to the outside world. The Γ wallet is able to hold more payment slips than the α smart card. There is an onboard power supply which enables the wallet to compute intensive precomputations in the background. Users are also able to transfer a value from their Γ wallet to their α smart card. This feature is useful if the users do not want to carry their wallets around with them or only want to carry a small amount on their persons.

6.2.9 Additional features

The basic CAFE system has the following additional features:

> • *Multiple currencies:* The CAFE wallets have several "pockets" for different currencies. Like cash, the user may either exchange currency at the bank (lowering the amount in one pocket and increasing it in another) or pay in nonlocal currency if the merchant accepts it.

> • *Fault and loss tolerance:* If a user loses his or her wallet, the bank can recover the money from a backup and the deposit transcripts. This is done by regular backups during a withdrawal transaction. If a user wants to recover lost money, he or she reveals the identity of the payment slips stored after the last withdrawal. This enables the bank to track these payment slips.

6.2.10 Remarks

CAFE is an advanced payment mechanism that makes use of secure tamper-resistant devices such as smart cards and strong cryptographic protocols. It provides untraceable electronic payments and guarantees the security of all parties concerned. This feature is an important selling point for most consumers who are currently skeptical about the use of other payment systems that only provide for the security of the financial organizations.

6.3 NetCash

NetCash [15–17] is an identified on-line electronic cash system for open networks, developed at the Information Sciences Institute of the University of Southern California. It consists of distributed currency servers that mint electronic coins and issue these coins to users of the system, accepting electronic checks in payment for them. The system is *on-line* in that each coin must be verified as being valid and unspent by forwarding it to the minting currency server for verification during a purchase. Although the digital cash is *identified*, with each coin having a unique serial number, there is an exchange mechanism to provide *limited anonymity*. Anyone with valid coins can exchange them anonymously with a currency server for new ones.

NetCash is a macropayment system suitable for selling hard goods, information, or other network services. Users can both make and accept payments. It is a software-only solution, requiring no special hardware; both asymmetric and symmetric cryptography are used to provide the network security of the system and to limit fraud. All parties must have their own public/private key pair (PK_x, SK_x). The use of multiple currency servers allows the system to *scale*, that is, to handle the addition of users and usage without causing performance to significantly drop.

6.3.1 Framework/model

The NetCash system consists of buyers, merchants, and currency servers, as shown in Figure 6.13. Since there are multiple currency servers, a user might choose one that is geographically close and trustworthy. A currency server provides the following four services to its clients (buyers or merchants):

- Verifying coins, to prevent double spending;

- Issuing coins in return for payment by electronic check;

- Buying back coins, giving an electronic check in return;

- Exchanging valid coins for new ones, which thus provides some anonymity.

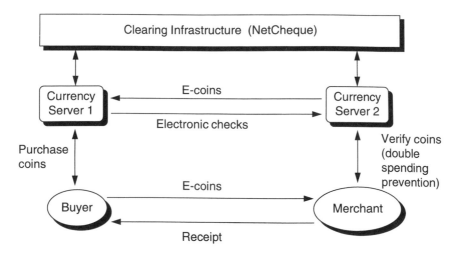

Figure 6.13 The NetCash system.

NetCheque [18–20] (see Chapter 5) is proposed to provide the electronic check infrastructure required to bring monetary value into and out of the NetCash system. Not only can clients buy and sell NetCash coins in exchange for electronic checks, but NetCash servers can use electronic checks to settle debts between themselves.

When a buyer is making a purchase from a merchant, both parties may use different currency servers. The buyer may have bought coins from one currency server (CS1), but the merchant may want to verify these coins through the merchant's local currency server (CS2). Coins can only be ultimately verified by the currency server who minted them. CS2 will have to forward the coins received from the merchant to CS1 to be verified. In return for valid coins, CS1 will generate an electronic check for CS2. In turn, CS2 can either issue new coins to the merchant or send an electronic check in exchange for the valid coins minted by CS1. All the checks can be cleared through the NetCheque accounting and clearing infrastructure. While NetCheque is the clearing mechanism proposed, it is conceivable that any other similar electronic check scheme or clearing infrastructure could be used.

If CS2 indicates to the merchant that the coins were valid, a receipt and/or the purchased goods can be returned to the buyer. The structure of a NetCash coin and the protocols involved in making a basic purchase are now examined in turn.

6.3.2 NetCash coins

An *electronic coin* is a piece of data representing monetary value within an electronic cash system. NetCash uses *identified electronic cash*, in which each coin is minted by a currency server and has a serial number unique to that server. A NetCash coin, as shown in Figure 6.14, has the form:

$$Coin = \{CS\_name, CS\_addr, Expiry, Serial\#, Value\}SK_{CS}$$

{Currency Server
Network addr.
Expiry date
Serial #
Value}SK$_{CS}$

Example:
{CS1, bank.com, 26-July-98, 12345678, $1} SK$_{CS1}$

Figure 6.14   Structure and example contents of a NetCash coin.

Each coin is encrypted with the minting server's secret key (SK_{CS}). This forms a digital signature to show that it is authentic. In an actual implementation, to improve efficiency, the digital signature might be formed by taking a hash of the coin's fields and encrypting the result with the server's secret key. This would be more efficient than encrypting all the fields as above. The purpose of each field is now briefly explained:

CS_name: The name of the minting currency server. If CS_addr is invalid, this could be used to look up the current network address of the server in a public directory.

CS_addr: The network address of the minting currency server.

Expiry: The date on which a coin becomes invalid and will no longer be accepted as valid currency. The purpose of this is to limit the amount of serial numbers that must be remembered by a currency server to prevent double spending.

Serial#:   A unique identifier of the coin to the minting currency server.

Value: The amount the coin is worth.

6.3.3 Double-spending prevention

Since an electronic coin is just a piece of data, it is easy to copy it and try to spend it repeatedly. To prevent double spending, a currency server maintains a list of the serial numbers of every coin minted by it *in current circulation.*

During a purchase, the payee will verify that the coins haven't been double spent by returning them to the minting server, as shown in Figure 6.15. The currency server checks that a coin's serial number is

Figure 6.15 Preventing double spending in the NetCash system.

present in its database. If it is, the coin is valid. The serial number must then be removed from the database and the coin will be replaced with a new coin with a different serial number (or an electronic check). The new serial number will be recorded in the database and the coin will be returned to the payee.

A coin can be valid for one purchase only. If it were left in circulation, there would be no way of distinguishing it from one that had already been spent. If a coin's serial number does not appear in the database, then it has either been spent before and removed, or it may have expired. Serial numbers that have expired may be removed from the database to limit its size and to allow serial numbers to be reused.

6.3.4 Coin transfer

Monetary value can be exchanged between individuals but, as with a basic purchase, the minting server will need to be contacted to prevent double spending. Where the individuals trust each other not to doubly spend the coins, coins could be transferred directly. Eventually, all coins will have to be returned to the minting server to be verified before they expire.

6.3.5 Certificate of insurance

Within NetCash, only currency servers are required to have a certificate, known as a *certificate of insurance*. It has two functions:

- ‣ A means of distributing the server's public key (PK_{CS}) securely, signed and verified by a trusted third party. This key is used to verify the signature on a coin and to encrypt messages sent to the server.

- ‣ It proves that a third party, called the Federal Insurance Corporation (FIC), is providing insurance for a currency server to produce and manage NetCash coins. It indicates that coins minted by this server can be accepted as legal tender.

A NetCash certificate of insurance has the form:

$$Cert = \{Cert\_ID, CS\_name, PK_{CS}, Issue\_date, Expiry\}Sig_{FIC}$$

The purpose of each field is as follows:

Cert_ID: A globally unique identifier of the certificate.

CS_name: The name of the minting currency server.

PK_{CS}:   The public key of the currency server.

Issue_date: The date from which the certificate is valid.

Expiry: The date the certificate expires and is no longer valid.

The certificate is digitally signed with the secret key of the FIC, which acts as a central certification authority (CA). Any buyers or merchants who contact a currency server directly need to obtain that server's certificate. The protocols for distributing certificates to buyers and merchants, and for initially obtaining a server certificate from the FIC are not defined for the NetCash system. Clearly, if the scheme is to be piloted, solutions for these problems will have to be found and implemented.

6.3.6 Basic purchase

To make a purchase using NetCash, a potential buyer first obtains coins from a currency server, buying them with an electronic check. While not discussed by the designers of the system, it is conceivable that an alternate mechanism, such as a credit card scheme, could be used to buy coins. Some of the purchased coins are then sent to the merchant in payment for an item. To protect against double spending, the merchant will verify the coins, either directly with the minting server or indirectly through a server of the merchant's choice. In exchange for valid coins, the merchant can receive new coins, minted by the server that the merchant contacted, or an electronic check. A signed receipt from the merchant, and possibly the purchased item, may then be sent to the buyer.

The steps involved in a basic purchase are shown in Figure 6.16 and are now explained in more detail.

6.3.7 Obtaining coins

The user sends an electronic check, along with a randomly generated one-time symmetric session key, encrypted with the server's public key to the server:

$$\{\text{E-check}, K_{\text{Buyer}}\}PK_{\text{CS1}}$$

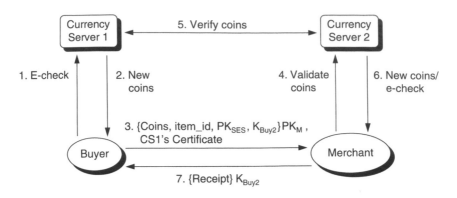

Figure 6.16   Making a purchase with NetCash.

The message can only be decrypted and read by CS1. The check should be such that it can only be spent once, so that replaying the message will achieve nothing. The server will return new coins to the buyer, encrypted with the session key K_{Buyer}:

$$\{\text{New coins}\}K_{Buyer}$$

The exchange with the server can be generalized so that either a check or coins can be exchanged with the server for either new coins or a check. Obviously, a check is never exchanged for another check. The generalized request becomes:

$$\{\text{Instrument}, K_X, \text{transaction}\}PK_{CS}$$

where *Instrument* is either an electronic check or coins, K_X is a session key generated by sender X (buyer or merchant), and *transaction* indicates whether new coins or a check are wanted in exchange. A successful reply is simply the desired instrument (coins or check), protected by the session key:

$$\{\text{Instrument}\}K_X$$

These messages can be used to anonymously exchange coins with a server as detailed in Section 6.3.10.

6.3.8 Paying a merchant

The buyer sends a purchase request to the merchant, encrypted with the merchant's public key (PK_M):

$$\{Coins, item\_id, PK_{Ses}, K_{Buy2}\}PK_M, CS1\text{'s certificate}$$

The buyer must securely obtain PK_M before the purchase can take place. The designers suggest that this be done by sending the buyer's public key (PK_{Buyer}) to the merchant. The merchant can then safely send his or her public key (PK_M) to the buyer, encrypted with that buyer's public key (PK_{Buyer}):

$$\{PK_M\}PK_{Buyer}$$

This is not entirely safe since an attacker could intercept PK_{Buyer} and return a false merchant public key:

$$\{PK_{Attack}\}PK_{Buyer}$$

Payments can then be intercepted since they will be encrypted with the attacker's public key. A more secure means of distributing public keys, such as by using certificates, could be used to defeat this attack.

The fields of the purchase request have the following purposes:

Coins: The purchase amount in NetCash coins.

item_id: A means of identifying the item the buyer wishes to purchase.

PK_{Ses}: A freshly generated public-key session key. After a successful purchase, this may be used to encrypt the purchased goods or to uniquely identify the buyer. If the buyer does not wish to remain anonymous to the merchant this could be the buyer's normal public key, PK_{Buyer}.

K_{Buy2}: A freshly generated symmetric session key. This is used to encrypt the response, and should be different than K_{Buyer} (used to obtain coins from the server).

The method of selecting goods and price negotiation are outside the scope of NetCash.

6.3.9 Verifying coins

The merchant verifies the signature on the coins using the server's certificate, which was included in the request. To verify that the coins have not been double spent, the merchant forwards them, in this case indirectly, to the minting server (CS1) through the merchant's preferred server (CS2). An exchange request is used:

$$\{\text{Coins}, K_M, \text{transaction}\}PK_{CS2}$$

K_M is a symmetric session key generated by the merchant. CS2 in turn forwards the coins to CS1 for verification, accepting an electronic check in return (for valid coins). New coins minted by CS2, or a check, are then sent to the merchant, depending on which was requested in the transaction:

$$\{\text{New coins/check}\}K_M$$

Finally an encrypted receipt, signed by the merchant, is returned to the buyer:

$$\{\text{receipt}\}K_{Buy2}$$

where

$$\text{receipt} \quad = \quad \{\text{amount, transaction\_id, date}\}Sig_M$$

The signature on the receipt can be verified using the merchant's public key (PK_M). The delivery of the purchased item or service is outside the NetCash protocols. However, transaction_id, the receipt, and PK_{Ses} can be used for authentication and encryption when the item is delivered.

6.3.10 Providing limited anonymity

When a user buys coins from a currency server, the server could record the serial numbers on the coins it issues and to whom they were given. If the server later receives the coins back from a merchant, a record of the user's spending habits may be built. Since users can select which server they deal with, they might choose one that they trust not to keep such records. Even still, it would be more reassuring if there was a mechanism to guarantee some anonymity.

The *anonymous coin exchange* mechanism can be used to provide this limited anonymity. As shown in Figure 6.17, anyone can exchange valid coins anonymously with the minting server for new coins. The currency server will only know the network address of where the request is coming from. However, if all individuals are equipped with personal machines, a network address may be a good indication of where a transaction originated. In this scenario, the transaction could be forwarded through another host, called a *proxy*, to conceal the originating network address. K_x is a temporary session key that does not identify the owner.

When coins are exchanged in this way, it might be the buyer or the merchant (as part of coin verification) who performs the exchange. At best, the currency server could maintain records matching the serial numbers of the old coins against the new ones. When the coins are eventually redeemed for a check, the server will know who initially bought the coins and who eventually traded them in, but not who held any intermediary coins. This prevents the server from keeping accurate spending profiles, provided the merchant doesn't collude with the server. However, by spending with a merchant who is known to always exchange coins for an identified check, anonymity may be limited.

Clearly, the anonymity provided is far less than some fully anonymous digital cash systems, such as Ecash, described in Section 6.1.

6.3.11 Merchant anonymity

A merchant may remain anonymous to a currency server by using the anonymous exchange protocol to obtain new coins from the coins presented by a buyer. The buyer remains anonymous to the merchant, although the merchant will know the network address from which the

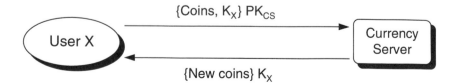

Figure 6.17 Exchanging coins anonymously with a currency server.

buyer's requests originate. The merchant can be anonymous to the buyer provided the merchant generates and distributes a temporary public-key pair instead of using PK_M for every purchase. This is perhaps not very practical since public keys take far longer to generate than symmetric ones, and this will delay the purchase. A receipt from an anonymous merchant is also of limited value.

6.3.12 Preventing anonymity

By refusing to exchange coins for new ones, and instead issuing named checks, a currency server can prevent its users from being anonymous. The server can know to whom it issues coins and from whom those coins are received back. Buyers and merchants may still remain anonymous to each other using the protocols described earlier.

6.3.13 Clearing

To reconcile balances (in the form of checks) between currency servers, it is proposed that each server have an account with a NetCheque accounting server (AS), as shown in Figure 6.18. When a currency server CS1 verifies coins with the minting currency server CS2 on behalf of a user, the currency server will always accept an electronic check in exchange for the coins. This ensures that a server only issues its own coins to users. At the end of the day, a currency server can present all checks collected that day from other servers or buyers to their accounting server,

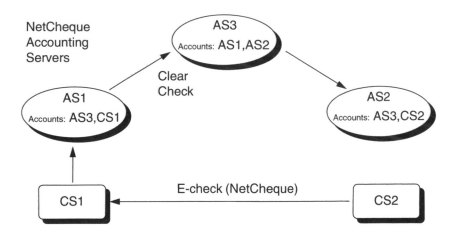

Figure 6.18 Using NetCash to reconcile balances between servers.

which will clear it through the NetCheque infrastructure. NetCheque is described in Chapter 5.

6.3.14 Extensions
Two main extensions are proposed. The first aims to prevent merchant fraud by guaranteeing the buyer a valid receipt or a refund. Normally, there is no mechanism to prevent a merchant from accepting a buyer's money and then never delivering the goods or a receipt. The second proposal covers *off-line operation*, in which a currency server does not have to be contacted at the time of purchase. Both extensions are now examined.

6.3.15 Preventing merchant fraud
To prevent merchant fraud, a coin is extended to have both user- and merchant-specific parts, valid only during specified time windows:

$$\text{Coin} \quad = \quad \{C_M, C_{Buy}, C_X\}$$

The basic idea is that the first part of the coin, C_M, can only be spent by the merchant. If the merchant spends this and does not honor the purchase, the buyer can obtain proof from the bank that the merchant was paid by using the second part of the coin, C_{Buy}. C_X, the third part, is a precaution that allows the coin to be spent by anyone if C_M and C_{Buy} are never used within their valid time windows.

Each of the three parts contains all the information present in a regular NetCash coin, such as the same serial number and value fields. These fields are identical in all three parts. However, the expiry field will be modified in each such that C_M is valid during the first time frame, C_{Buy} during the second, and C_X after that:

$C_M = \{CS\_name, CS\_addr, Serial\#, Value, Merchant\_info, time\_frame1\}SK_{CS}$
$C_{Buy} = \{CS\_name, CS\_addr, Serial\#, Value, Buyer\_info, time\_frame2\}SK_{CS}$
$C_X = \{CS\_name, CS\_addr, Serial\#, Value, time\_frame3\}SK_{CS}$

C_M will contain information pertaining to a specific merchant, including PK_M. C_M will only be accepted as legal tender by the currency server if the holder can prove knowledge of SK_M (which only the merchant should know) and the current time is within the validity window specified within the coin. The exact method used to prove knowledge of SK_M is not given in the NetCash specification. For example, though, knowledge of SK_M could be proved by encrypting a secret with PK_M and asking the merchant to decrypt it:

$$SK_M (PK_M (Secret)) = Secret$$

Similarly, C_{Buy} will contain buyer-specific information, such as PK_{Buyer}, which can be used to authenticate the buyer if she tries to spend the coin during the second time window, when it is valid. The third part of a new coin, C_X, which is valid during a third time window, will not have any additional information or keys embedded in it. The time windows of the three coin parts do not overlap.

Figure 6.19 shows how a buyer can obtain and spend an extended coin to prevent merchant fraud. The buyer obtains the coin from a currency server in much the same way as before, except that dates for the coin's time windows (date$_M$, date$_{Buy}$) and the merchant's public key (PK_M) are included. The buyer must know who the merchant is, and have the merchant's public key, before the extended coins can be obtained. Another disadvantage is that the currency server will have to mint and sign all three parts of the coin when the buyer initially requests it.

C_M is valid during the first time window and is sent in payment to the merchant using the same protocol as for the basic purchase. The merchant validates the coin with the minting currency server as before, accepting new coins or a check in exchange. The merchant should then return a signed receipt to the buyer.

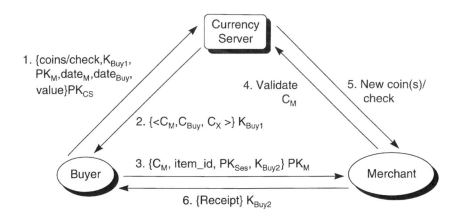

Figure 6.19 Preventing merchant fraud by using extended NetCash coins.

If no receipt or purchased goods are returned, the buyer will send C_{Buy} to the currency server during the second time window, as shown in Figure 6.20. The currency server checks whether C_M was spent during the first time window. If it was, the server returns a receipt that includes the merchant's identity, the merchant's public key, and the value of the spent coin, all signed by the server:

$$\{Merchant\_id, PK_M, amount, date\}Sig_{CS}$$

The receipt proves that the merchant received and spent the buyer's money. It could also include the buyer's identity. If C_M was never spent, then the server will refund the value of the coin by returning a new coin. If neither C_M nor C_{Buy} is spent during their respective validity periods, C_X can be spent as a normal coin in the third time window.

6.3.16 Off-line protocols

The extended coin with time windows, described in Section 6.3.15, can be used in an off-line protocol. The buyer must know the merchant in advance and obtains the coin as shown in steps 1 and 2 of Figure 6.19. At any later time during the time window of C_M, the coin can be spent at the merchant. The merchant knows that the coin cannot already have been spent since it is specific to the merchant and can only be spent by the merchant within the first time window. However, the merchant must check that a buyer did not already pay him or her using the same coin. Any time later within the first time window, the merchant can redeem the coin with the currency server without fear of it already having been spent.

The actual length of the time windows is not discussed in the Net-Cash specification. If it is a very large value, then the buyer will have to wait a considerable amount of time before C_X can be spent if C_M and C_{Buy} are not used. Alternatively, if the time window is small, the merchant will have to verify the coins quickly and the benefits of an off-line system

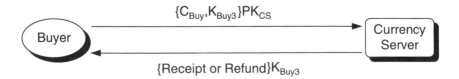

Figure 6.20 Obtaining a purchase receipt or refund during the second time.

will be lost. A time window length that balances out the opposing effects of these two scenarios should be chosen.

The designers also suggest that the basic NetCash protocol could be used with tamper-resistant smart cards. An observer within the smart card prevents a buyer double spending coins and eliminates the need for on-line verification of coins with a server. Smart cards and observers are discussed in Chapter 3.

Finally, it has been suggested that other off-line electronic cash schemes, such as those by Chaum [21], could be integrated with the Net-Cash framework. Chaum's scheme identifies an individual who double spends coins after the crime has occurred.

6.3.17 Remarks

NetCash provides a secure and reasonably scalable identified electronic cash system. Limited anonymity is possible and can be controlled. Use of strong cryptography and particularly public-key cryptography may make it computation-intensive and cause delays. Another drawback is that coins of different denominations may have to be obtained from a currency server to make an exact payment during a purchase.

6.4 Mondex

As was the case with checks, the approach taken by researchers to electronic cash and the approach taken by the banking industry are quite different. The trend in banking has been toward the use of more sophisticated payment cards to effect payment in the retail context. A number of schemes have been tested [22] that involve preloading a chip card with value that could then be spent at retail outlets. These schemes are generally referred to as *prepayment cards,* and one of the more successful of them is the Mondex electronic cash card.

The concept of the Mondex card was developed at NatWest, a major U.K. banking organization, in 1990. The technology was developed with a number of manufacturers involved in the production of secure hardware, including Hitachi Corporation, and this led to a trial in 1992 involving 6,000 staff at a NatWest office complex in London. This limited trial was followed in July 1995 by a major public trial in Swindon, a town of some 190,000 inhabitants near London. In July 1996, a separate company, Mondex International, was formed to promote the technology through a series of trials in many different locations around the world.

The Mondex payment scheme relies on the use of a contact chip card, the core of which contains a chip based on a modified Hitachi H8/310 microcontroller. This is an 8-bit microprocessor with on-chip RAM, ROM, and EEPROM as well as a serial communications controller to allow it to converse with the outside world. The control program for the Mondex payment scheme is implemented in the ROM of this microcontroller and allows value to be transferred from one Mondex chip to another using a proprietary (and secret) chip-to-chip protocol.

To facilitate this value transfer, a number of Mondex support devices are available. The card is initially loaded by contacting a bank using either a Mondex automated teller machine (ATM) or using a specially adapted telephone. These access devices do not need to know how the chip-to-chip protocol works, but rather they incorporate an *interface device* (IFD) that contains a control processor that mediates in the dialogue between the card and the bank. At the bank, a form of money safe called a *Mondex value box* is installed. This is a hardware device that can hold large numbers of Mondex cards and acts as a store of value for dialogues with the issued card population. Transfers to and from the *value box* are monitored by a software system referred to as the *value control and management system*, and the movements will then be reflected in the bank accounts of the cardholders.

Figure 6.21 shows this process taking place. A Mondex card is inserted into an ATM (or adapted telephone) whereupon chip-to-chip dialogues take place between the IFD and the card under the control of the ATM device. The Mondex IFD then establishes a dialogue with the bank. Once the cardholder's account number has been established, and the card identity verified, value is transferred from the cards in the bank's value box by chip-to-chip protocol to the destination chip residing in the card. The value control and management system will inform the bank's accounting systems to debit the cardholder's bank account for the amount.

Spending is a similar process, where retailers are equipped with a device called a *value transfer terminal*. Once again, this contains an IFD device that facilitates the transfer from the customer card to the retailer card. There is no need for an on-line dialogue with the bank to verify the transfer. At a later stage, the retailer may contact the bank, transfer

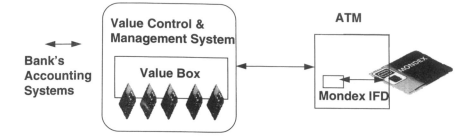

Figure 6.21   Loading a Mondex card with value.

the value to the bank's value box, and simultaneously have the amount credited to the retailer's account.

A wide range of other devices are available to assist in using the card. A keyring-sized reader can be used by cardholders to read how much money is stored in the card. A more elaborate device about the size of a pocket calculator allows individuals to move cash from one card to another. This device could of course be used to sell goods in a store but, being handheld, would be unsuited to over-the-counter transactions. Hardware is available to allow vending machines to be converted to accept the card, and a PC card device can allow Mondex cards to be attached to a workstation, and used for payment or money transfer across a network such as the Internet.

Little is publicly known about the security features [23] used in the protocol, but public-key technology of some kind is used to apply a form of signature to the messages moving from chip to chip. The card maintains a *purse narrative* that remembers the last 10 transactions in which the card took part and the retailer's hardware keeps records of the last 300 transactions [24]. This limits the anonymity of the system, which may be seen as a disadvantage by some card users. A strategy is in place that involves the Mondex card issuers periodically capturing transaction information in order to build a statistical sample of the transactions taking place. This measure is used in an attempt to detect fraud within the system at an early stage.

If a card is lost, the value stored in it cannot be recovered. The card, however, can be *locked* such that value cannot be transferred without entering a personal ID number (PIN) via a card interface device. If the card is subsequently found, a card ID can be read by the bank, allowing them to discover the owner.

Each card has two different security schemes available to it, one that is active and one that is dormant. Periodically, cards are instructed to activate the dormant system. As time goes on, new or renewed cards carry the dormant system as the new active system and carry a new dormant system. In this way, the Mondex security system can be constantly renewed without the need to change any of the interface devices.

As a protection against the use of the card by money launderers, each Mondex card has a position in a hierarchical *purse class* structure. This structure imposes rules on what other classes of card it can exchange value with and the associated maximum transaction value. Card issuers can ensure that high-value cards can only exchange value directly with the banking industry, ensuring that all such transactions produce an audit trail.

6.5   EMV cash cards and CEPS

The Mondex scheme is not the only system to be advanced using smart cards to effect cash payments. Since 1994, EMV, a consortium consisting of Europay (a group of European card-issuing banks) together with the two major international credit card companies (MasterCard and Visa) have been working on common specifications for integrated circuit cards (ICCs), terminals to read the cards, and card applications. In June 1996, a three-volume specification was issued defining the physical and electrical characteristics of the cards [25] and terminals, the architecture for a multiapplication card reader terminal [26], and an application specification for handling credit/debit transactions [27]. No common specification was arrived at for an electronic purse application, but the specifications have meant that a population of card reader terminals can be deployed that can accommodate a number of different purse schemes independently.

Europay International was the first to launch a stored-value card, called the *CLIP Card*, which makes possible a reloadable card that is capable of handling multiple currencies. This application was demonstrated in Seville, Spain, in June 1996, and at the time of writing a number of European countries had announced intentions to launch CLIP-based payment schemes.

The major credit card companies, Visa and MasterCard, have been active in the smart card area for some time. For a number of years, Visa has operated several different (and incompatible) smart card–based cash schemes under the common brand of VisaCash. MasterCard had plans for its own scheme using an EMV-compatible card and launching it worldwide under the brand name of MasterCash. All of this changed in 1997 when MasterCard acquired a controlling interest in Mondex and shelved plans for its own scheme. The EMV standards were updated in December 2000, and Visa placed its weight behind a new scheme called CEPS (described in Section 6.5.2) that is compatible with this new specification.

6.5.1 EMV2000

EMVCo, LLC was formed in February 1999 by Europay International, MasterCard International, and Visa International. Its primary role is to manage, maintain, and promote the EMV Integrated Circuit Card (ICC) specifications for payment systems. The primary aim of the consortium is to achieve global interoperability between card and terminal processes of different operators and manufacturers. In December 2000, EMVCo announced the availability of the EMV2000 Integrated Circuit Card Specification for Payment Systems (version 4.0). EMV2000 is an enhanced version of the EMV'96 specifications.

The EMV2000 specifications consist of four parts. Volume 1 [28] defines the functionality required by the ICCs and the terminals for correct operation and interoperability. In particular, the specification defines the electromechanical characteristics, the interface, and transmission protocols for the exchange of information between the ICC and a terminal. In addition, it describes the structure of the file system within the card. Volume 2 [29] describes the security functionality of the devices in the system and management of cryptographic keys. The third volume [30] specifies the procedures necessary to effect payment such as the mapping of data elements onto data objects and the structure and coding of messages between the devices. The last volume [31] deals with the terminal requirements that are necessary to support the acceptance of an ICC.

6.5.2 Common Electronic Purse Specification (CEPS)

The Common Electronic Purse Specification (CEPS) has been jointly developed by CEPSCO Española A.I.E., EURO Kartensysteme (Germany), Europay International, and Visa International. The CEPS specifications, which define the business [32], functional [33], and technical [34] requirements, were released in March 1999. Together they define the requirements for a globally interoperable electronic purse system and require compatibility with the EMV specifications for smart cards. The need for interoperability is driven by the increasing movement of card-holders across national boundaries and the need for efficient payment for goods and services. In Europe, the adoption of the Euro is pushing the need for interoperability across markets. In October 1999, CEPSCO, LLC was formed to oversee the development and administration of CEPS. It is responsible for the management of the ongoing standardization activities, establishing certification processes, and for promoting CEPS as a global open electronic purse standard. In July 2000, Groupement des Cartes Bancaires and Proton World International joined CEPSCO, LLC. Figure 6.22 shows the main entities involved in the CEPS system:

Merchant Acquirer—The main function of the Merchant Acquirer is to clear and settle point-of-sale (POS) transactions. The acquirer is also responsible for the integrity of the POS device and the Purchase Secure Application Module (PSAM) contained within it. The PSAM is a secure hardware device for storing and processing data used to authenticate a transaction.

Load Acquirer—The Load Acquirer manages the authorization requests for load and currency-exchange transactions. The Load Acquirer consists of a load device and a load acquirer host. It is the responsibility of the load acquirer host to initiate card authentication requests to the Card Issuer and funds authorization requests to the Funds Issuer. The Load Acquirer keeps a log of all transactions processed by its systems. A load device can be anything from a present-day ATM to devices attached to a PC in the home.

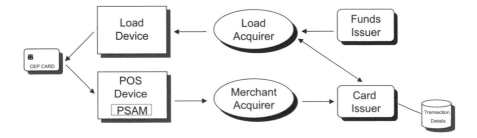

Figure 6.22   CEPS entities.

Card Issuer—The Card Issuer is responsible for the issuance of CEP cards and has a relationship with one or more CEP Scheme Providers. The Card Issuer is liable for all value loaded onto the CEP card.

Funds Issuer—The Funds Issuer is the entity that authorizes funds to be loaded onto a CEP card for an unlinked load. There are two ways in which funds can be loaded onto the CEP card, namely, linked and unlinked loads. In the case of a linked load funds are not moved between financial institutions. During an unlinked load funds have to be transferred from the Funds Issuer to the Card Issuer's funds pool. This requires additional cryptographic message exchanges over and above a linked load transaction.

In some cases the transactions may not flow directly from the Merchant or Load Acquirer to the Card Issuer and will have to be processed by intermediate nodes in the network. These nodes are known as processors.

The CEPS system supports a transaction set which consists of the following commands:

Load—A load transaction is an on-line transaction, which allows for funds to be added to the CEP card. A card issuer can issue cards that can support linked loads, unlinked loads, or both. In the case of a linked load, the cardholder has an account with the card issuer, and funds are moved from the cardholder's account to the funds pool controlled by the issuer. In an unlinked load the funds movement is not under the direct control of the Card Issuer. All the entities involved in a load transaction must authenticate each other before allowing a funds transfer to take place. CEPS also supports multiple currencies in different "slots" within the card. The actual number of slots available is issuer specific.

Purchase—A purchase transaction is an off-line transaction initiated at a POS device. It allows the cardholder to pay for goods or services against electronic value held on the card. We describe the steps involved in a purchase transaction in more detail in Section 6.5.2.1.

Incremental Purchase—POS devices such as telephones or Internet kiosks require that they be fed tokens/funds (small valued payments) at regular intervals to provide continuous service to the cardholder. A transaction is performed for the initial amount and the CEP card remains within the POS device for additional transactions, which are sent to the CEP card at regular intervals.

Purchase Reversal—A purchase transaction may be reversed, prior to the removal of the CEP card from the POS device.

Cancel Last Purchase—This command is an off-line transaction. It allows the cardholder to be recredited with the value of the last transaction if and only if the transaction to be canceled is the last transaction completed by the card. It is not mandatory for a POS device to support this command.

Currency Exchange—The currency exchange transaction is used to convert the value in one currency in a CEP card slot to another currency. It requires interaction between the CEP card, the Load Acquirer, and the Card Issuer. The resulting value may be added to a new or existing slot.

6.5.2.1 Purchase transaction

On inserting the CEP card into the POS device, the card and the PSAM in the POS device perform a mutual authentication using a combination of public and symmetric key cryptography. The value of the electronic purse in the card is adjusted and the PSAM computes MACs to validate the transaction. The transaction details are stored on the POS device, and are periodically collected by the Merchant Acquirer from the POS device. The Merchant Acquirer sends the POS transactions to the Card Issuer and a settlement takes place.

The purchase transaction is an off-line transaction initiated by the POS device once the CEP card has been inserted into the device. The POS device sends an Initialize for Purchase command to the card (step 1). The message contains a number of parameters such as the Currency to be Used, the Location of the POS Device, Timestamp, and others. Figure 6.23 shows the sequence of message flows between the two entities.

Next, the POS device and the CEP card exchange public-key certificates to mutually authenticate the CEP card and the PSAM device (step 2). This results in each device now possessing the other's public key. The hierarchy of public keys used must be at least three levels deep. Such a hierarchy consists of a CA public key as the root contained within the PSAM, an issuer public key, and a card public key held within the CEP card. Optionally there can be a four-level hierarchy, which has a regional public key, which also resides on the card. Once the amount for the purchase has been manually approved by the cardholder, the POS device

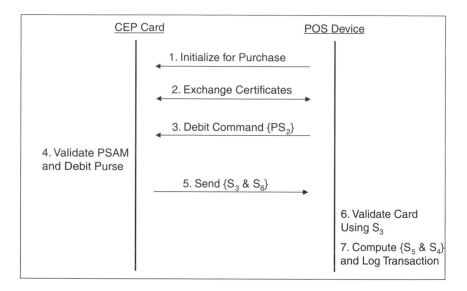

Figure 6.23   CEPS purchase transaction.

sends a debit command to the card (step 3). The command contains a signature {PS$_2$} generated by the PSAM using its private key. There are a
number of data fields within the signature of which the most important is
the Amount to be Debited and the Session Key. This is in turn encrypted
with the public key of the CEP card. The card uses its private key and the
PSAM's public key in turn to recover the data including the Session Key
in the digital signature (step 4). The card then creates a MAC S$_3$ by signing a number of fields such as the Updated Balance with the Session Key
(step 5). The card also generates another MAC S$_6$, which is intended for
the Card Issuer and sends it to the POS device. The PSAM authenticates
the S$_3$ MAC from the card, which allows it to validate the transaction
(step 6). An S$_5$ MAC must be created by the PSAM for each record that
is logged onto the POS device. The PSAM also generates an S$_4$ MAC that
is used to protect the count and the amount of transactions in a batch
until the merchant acquirer collects them from the POS device (step 7).

6.5.2.2   CEPS micropayments
CEPS supports an efficient micropayment scheme called an incremental
purchase transaction. A micropayment is a small-valued transaction that
is used for paying for low-valued goods or services. In the context of the

CEPS system one could envisage using a CEP card for payment for phone calls or Internet access from a public terminal. Chapter 7 presents a comprehensive description of the various micropayment schemes in operation.

A purchase transaction is performed as before and an initial amount is debited from the card. However, the card remains inserted within the POS device and further incremental purchase transaction requests are now sent to the card. The cardholder does not need to authorize the subsequent steps of the incremental purchase transaction. The cardholder has the option to abort the transaction at any stage if he or she wishes to do so.

The message exchanges are the same as Figure 6.23 with the last step (step 7) replaced with step 7 in Figure 6.24. The amount of the next purchase is determined and sent to the card. If the CEP card requires mutual authentication of the two devices during all subsequent incremental transaction steps, then the debit command sent to the card contains an S_2 MAC computed by the PSAM using the generated Session Key. The most important parameter to be authenticated is the Amount to be Debited field. The CEP card decrements the value of the incremental purchase from the purse and as before creates the S_3 and S_6 message authentication codes. The remaining steps are as outlined in Section 6.5.2.1. If this is not the last purchase transaction, we loop back to step 7 and resume processing. A single record is generated for the whole transaction.

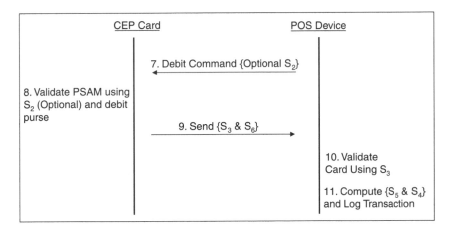

Figure 6.24   Incremental purchase.

6.5.3 Remarks

There are a large number of electronic purse schemes in operation at present with a huge population of smart cards in circulation worldwide, many of which are proprietary and noninteroperable. Interoperability is an essential feature that needs to be addressed as this will help in the acceptance of the technology on a worldwide scale. The Common Electronic Purse Specification is a step toward such domestic and crossborder interoperability. It is hoped that the first rollout of CEPS-based systems will occur in 2001, with many CEPS-compliant systems becoming operational by mid-2002.

6.6   SmartAxis

The previous sections discussed in detail a number of cash-like electronic payment schemes (e.g., Ecash, NetCash, Mondex). However, each of these systems is characterized by the use of proprietary protocols. In addition, the merchant base associated with such systems is usually quite small and has resulted in few end-users making serious use of the system. SmartAxis is an innovative service launched in March 1999 that has been developed with the specific aim of providing interoperability and brokering between various cash-like payment solutions regardless of the underlying payment technology.

SmartAxis provides multicurrency, multischeme smart card–based digital cash payment service, which enables the efficient sale of network services and "digital goods" across the Internet. SmartAxis supports the various electronic cash schemes without modification to the existing payment protocol. This allows for merchants to accept payment from all the payment schemes supported by the system. At the time of this writing, the SmartAxis system supports the Mondex and Proton schemes.

The SmartAxis system is comprised of Buyers, Merchants, and Payment Servers, of which the Payment Server can be located at either the SmartAxis operations center or at a value collector's (e.g., bank) premises. Figure 6.25 shows the overall transaction process. A customer uses a browser to surf a merchant's Web site (Catalog Server) and when the customer decides on a product, the customer chooses a brand of electronic cash from a simple menu on the site. On clicking the "Pay" button, the Catalog Server sends an Internet Payment Ticket (IPT) to the customer's access device. The Payment Ticket consists of a number of fields, for example: Price, Currency, Electronic Cash Scheme, Product

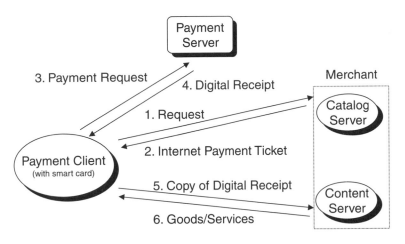

Figure 6.25 SmartAxis payment transaction.

Description, Expiry Date, and Location of the Payment Server. Upon receipt of the IPT, the customer's access device launches the SmartAxis Payment Client software. The Payment Client is a separate window that shows the customer the details of the transaction. The consumer pays for the selected goods by inserting his or her electronic purse card into the card reader and clicking on the "Buy" button on the Internet Payment Client window. The Payment Client ensures that the cardholder has sufficient funds to complete the transaction and forwards a Payment Request (PR) which includes the IPT to the Payment Server. A Payment Server is dedicated to a particular electronic cash scheme and currency. The Payment Server checks the validity of the Payment Request using the merchant's public key and issues a signed Digital Receipt (DR) to the client. The client forwards a copy of the DR to the Content Server, whose location is identified within the DR. The Content Server checks the authenticity of the DR using the Payment Server's public key and delivers the goods. The SmartAxis system maintains and runs a CA that issues public-key pairs to the entities in the system.

In addition to customers and merchants, the SmartAxis system also has Value Collectors. A Value Collector receives electronic purse funds from a Payment Server and uses the services of banks to remit funds through the SmartAxis network to the merchants. There are also Merchant Service Providers (MSPs) who are primarily an Internet hosting service. MSPs can host merchant sites and facilitate payment via the SmartAxis system without the merchants having to integrate the Smart-

Axis software into their own servers. When the consumer makes a payment, instead of the money going directly into the merchant's account, it is transferred to the Value Collector, who deposits it into a holding account. Once a certain agreed level of sales has been reached or after a specified time period, the money will be paid to the merchant. There are two options by which this can be done. The first option is where the money (less commission payable to each party) is sent from the holding account directly into the merchant's bank account. The second option is where the money is sent from the holding account to the MSP who then pays the merchants.

The SmartAxis system brings together the various payment systems in existence and allows merchants to accept electronic cash from a number of electronic payment schemes. The system has some of the attributes of cash such as spontaneous payment and hopes to build a global payment network with a large merchant base.

6.7 Remarks

If usage patterns in electronic payments are to follow those in conventional commerce, there is no doubt that a cash-like method of payment will be in demand. It is difficult to isolate the exact reasons why users are attracted to cash, but anonymity is certainly among them. The Ecash and CAFE systems introduced early in this chapter have provided this using innovative cryptographic techniques. The NetCash system relaxes the requirement for anonymity, which makes the system considerably simpler.

Despite the fact that Ecash is in use in a number of areas throughout the world, the banking industry has yet to rally behind it in great numbers. This may be because the idea of total anonymity of the payment instrument causes some unease among the banking community. Mondex, however, while initially claiming to provide anonymity, subsequently proved to be maintaining a limited audit trail of the transactions that took place. The technical details of how EMV-based electronic purses work are not available in the public domain, but at least in the case of VisaCash, a disposable version of the card is available and this implies the possibility of anonymity. At the moment, however, since card readers are not typically part of a network workstation, these devices cannot be used for payments across a network. In recent years we have seen efforts by industry to standardize the various purse schemes in operation such as the CEPS initiative and the introduction of brokering services such as SmartAxis to expand the merchant base available to consumers. However, we seem to be still some ways away before we can see a mass uptake of electronic cash schemes by the general public.

References

[1]   Chaum, D., "Achieving Electronic Privacy," *Scientific American*, Vol. 267, No. 2, August. 1992, pp. 76–81, http://www.chaum.com/articles/ Achieving_Electronic_Privacy.htm.

[2]   Wayner, P., "Digital Cash," *Byte*, Vol. 19, No. 10, October 1994, p. 126.

[3]   eCash Technologies Inc., http://www.ecashtechnologies.com/.

[4]   Schoenmakers, B., "Security Aspects of the Ecash Payment System," *State of the Art in Applied Cryptography, Course on Computer Security and Industrial Cryptography (COSIC '97)*, Lecture Notes in Computer Science, Vol. 1528, Berlin: Springer-Verlag, 1998, pp. 338–352.

[5]   Sanders, T., et al., "The CGI Specification," 1995, http://hoohoo.ncsa.uiuc.edu/cgi/interface.html.

[6]   Schneier, B., *Applied Cryptography: Protocols, Algorithms, and Source Code in C*, 2nd ed., New York: John Wiley and Sons, Inc., 1996, p. 145.

[7]   Product Cypher, *Magic Money Digital Cash System*, 1994, ftp://ftp.funet.fi/pub/crypt/ecash/.

[8]   Boly, J. P., et al., "The ESPRIT Project CAFE," *Computer Security—ESORICS '94, Proc. 3rd European Symp. Research Computer Security*, Lecture Notes in Computer Science, Vol. 875, Berlin: Springer-Verlag, 1994, pp. 217–230.

[9]   Bosselaers, A., et al., "Functionality of the Basic Protocols," *Technical Report, ESPRIT Project 7023 (CAFE), Deliverable IHS8341*, October 1995.

[10] Chaum, D., "Blind Signatures for Untraceable Payments," *Advances in Cryptology: Proc. CRYPTO '82*, New York: Plenum, 1983, pp. 199–203.

[11] Bos, J., and D. Chaum, "Smart Cash: A Practical Electronic Payment System," *Technical Report, CWI-Report: CS49035*, August 1990.

[12] Chaum, D., and T. Pedersen, "Wallet Databases with Observers," *Advances in Cryptology—CRYPTO '92, Proc. 12th Annual Intl. Cryptology Conference*, Lecture Notes in Computer Science, Vol. 740, Berlin: Springer-Verlag, 1993, pp. 89–105.

[13] Brands, S., "Untraceable Off-Line Cash in Wallets with Observers,"
      *Advances in Cryptology—CRYPTO '93, Proc. 13th Annual Int. Cryptology
      Conference*, Lecture Notes in Computer Science, Vol. 773, Berlin:
      Springer-Verlag, 1994, pp. 302–318.

[14] Schnorr, C., "Efficient Identification and Signatures for Smart Cards,"
      Advances in Cryptology—CRYPTO '89 Proc., Lecture Notes in Computer
      Science, Vol. 435, Berlin: Springer-Verlag, 1990, pp. 239–292.

[15] Medvinsky, G., and B. Clifford Neuman, "NetCash: A Design for Practical
      Electronic Currency on the Internet," *Proc. 1st ACM Conference Computer and
      Communications Security*, November 1993, http://gost.isi.edu/info/netcash/.

[16] Medvinsky, G., and B. Clifford Neuman, "Electronic Currency for the
      Internet," *Electronic Markets*, Vol. 3, No. 9/10, October 1993, pp. 23–24,
      http://gost.isi.edu/info/netcash/.

[17] Clifford Neuman, B., and G. Medvinsky, "NetCheque, NetCash, and the
      Characteristics of Internet Payment Services," *MIT Workshop on Internet
      Economics 1995*, Massachusetts Institute of Technology (MIT), Cambridge,
      MA, March 1995, http://www.press.umich.edu/jep/works/
      NeumNetPay.html.

[18] Clifford Neuman, B., and G. Medvinsky, "Requirements for Network
      Payment: The NetCheque Perspective," *Proc. IEEE Compcon '95*, San
      Francisco, CA, March 1995, http://www.isi.edu/gost/info/netcheque/
      documentation.html.

[19] "The Check Is in the E-Mail," *University of Southern California Chronicle*,
      November 1994, http://www.isi.edu/people/bcn/newsclips/
      usc-chronicle-941107/netcheque-usc-chronicle-941107.html.

[20] Clifford Neuman, B., "Proxy-Based Authentication and Accounting for
      Distributed Systems," *Proc. 13th Int. Conference on Distributed Computing
      Systems*, Pittsburgh, PA, May 1993, pp. 283–291, http://www.isi.edu/gost/
      info/netcheque/documentation.html.

[21] Chaum, D., A. Fiat, and M. Naor, "Untraceable Electronic Cash," *Advances
      in Cryptology—CRYPTO '88 Proc.*, Lecture Notes in Computer Science,
      Vol. 403, Berlin: Springer-Verlag, 1990, pp. 319–327.

[22] Harrop, P., *Prepayment Cards: The Electronic Purse Becomes Big Business*, A
      Financial Times Management Report, *Financial Times Business Information*,
      London, 1991.

[23] Jones, T., "The Future of Money as It Affects the Payment Systems in
      the U.S. and Abroad," Submission to the U.S. House of Representatives,
      June 1996.

[24] Gilham, R., *Letter to Mr. Simon Davies of Privacy International in response to
      complaint on Mondex anonymity claims*, Area Trading Standards Officer,

Bromley, U.K., June 1996, http://www.privacy.org/pi/activities/mondex/mondex_response.html.

[25] Europay International S.A., MasterCard International Incorporated, and Visa International Service Association, *EMV '96: Integrated Circuit Card Specification for Payment Systems*, June 1996, http://www.emvco.com/.

[26] Europay International S.A., MasterCard International Incorporated, and Visa International Service Association, *EMV '96: Integrated Circuit Card Terminal Specification for Payment Systems*, June 1996, http://www.emvco.com/.

[27] Europay International S.A., MasterCard International Incorporated, and Visa International Service Association, *EMV '96: Integrated Circuit Card Application Specification for Payment Systems*, June 1996, http://www.emvco.com/.

[28] *EMV2000 Integrated Circuit Card Specification for Payment Systems, Book 1—Application Independent ICC to Terminal Interface Requirements, Version 4.0*, December 2000, http://www.emvco.com/.

[29] *EMV2000 Integrated Circuit Card Specification for Payment Systems, Book 2—Security and Key Management, Version 4.0*, December 2000, http://www.emvco.com/.

[30] *EMV2000 Integrated Circuit Card Specification for Payment Systems, Book 3—Application Specification, Version 4.0*, December 2000, http://www.emvco.com/.

[31] *EMV2000 Integrated Circuit Card Specification for Payment Systems, Book 4—Cardholder, Attendant, and Acquirer interface Requirements, Version 4.0*, December 2000, http://www.emvco.com/.

[32] *Common Electronic Purse Specifications—Business Requirements Version 7.0*, March 2000, http://www.cepsco.com/.

[33] *Common Electronic Purse Specifications—Functional Requirements Version 6.3*, September 1999, http://www.cepsco.com/.

[34] *Common Electronic Purse Specifications—Technical Specifications Version 2.2*, May 2000, http://www.cepsco.com/.

.

Micropayment systems

Of the conventional payment instruments of cash, check, and card, the one most suited to low-value transactions is cash. Versatile as it is, it is limited in that no transaction can involve less than the value of the smallest coin (e.g., a penny). There are entire classes of goods and services where this poses a problem. Some examples include obtaining a quotation of the current price of a share on the stock market or making a single query of a database service. In conventional commerce, the solution to this has been to use a subscription mode of payment, where the buyer pays in advance and can avail of the product or service for a fixed period. While this ensures that the content provider can be paid for services rendered, it seals off what is in many cases a large customer base of people who may only wish to use a service very occasionally. It also restricts the ability of people to try out a service.

It is clear that the subscription model does not adequately solve the problem and that there is a need for a payment system that can efficiently transfer very small

227

amounts, perhaps less than a penny, in a single transaction. This implies that communications traffic, which in itself costs money, must be kept to an absolute minimum. A system in which the costs of conveying the payment are greater than the payment itself is unlikely to succeed. In many of the payment systems covered in previous chapters, a merchant validated each payment by having a real-time dialogue with a server on the network representing the payment systems provider, either to check that funds are available, or to complete the payment. This represents a very high per-transaction overhead and must be eliminated in the design of a micropayment system.

The low value per transaction also means that the profit made on each transaction must also be small. For a server to be viable under these conditions, it must be able to process transactions at a high rate. This gives rise to a further requirement that micropayment systems must be able to make the payment verification inexpensively. If a server is taking appreciable time to do public-key encryption or decryption, then its throughput, measured in transactions, cannot be very great. Consequently, a successful micropayment system must not involve computationally expensive cryptographic techniques.

The electronic payment methods outlined in earlier chapters have involved systems that mirror the properties of conventional payment instruments already in existence. Micropayments, however, have not been available in conventional commerce, and their introduction opens up many new areas of business. One can envisage network users paying to consult an on-line encyclopedia, purchasing a single song from an album, ordering just the business pages from a selection of daily newspapers, and so forth. The remainder of this chapter will outline the most influential systems available in this new field of electronic commerce.

7.1 Millicent

Millicent [1, 2] is a decentralized micropayment scheme that was developed at Digital Equipment Corporation (now Compaq) which is designed to allow payments as low as one-tenth of a cent ($0.001) to be made. A Millicent payment can be efficiently validated at a vendor's site without the need to contact a third party. This distributed approach, without any additional communication, expensive public key encryption, or off-line processing, allows it to scale effectively for repeated small payments.

The Millicent system uses a form of electronic currency called *Scrip*. Scrip can be thought of as the loose change you carry around in your pocket. It is fast and efficient to verify that it is valid, and if one loses a small piece of change by accident, it is not of great concern. Scrip is *vendor-specific* in that it has value at one particular vendor only. The security of the protocol is designed to make the cost of committing a fraud more than the value of a purchase. By using fast symmetric encryption the protocol can be both lightweight and secure.

7.1.1 The Millicent model

Figure 7.1 shows the three main entities in the Millicent system: *brokers, vendors,* and *customers.*

7.1.1.1 Brokers

A Millicent broker mediates between vendors and customers to simplify the tasks they perform.

Aggregating Micropayments   Typically, it might take a customer several weeks or months to make enough micropayments at a specific vendor to cover the cost of a standard macropayment financial transaction to that vendor. Thus it would not be efficient for customers to buy *vendor scrip* (scrip that can be spent at a specific vendor only) from every vendor from which they wish to buy. However, it is likely that a customer will make enough micropayments in total at different vendors to cover the cost of a

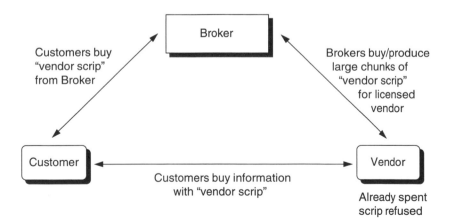

Figure 7.1   The Millicent model.

macropayment transaction. A *macropayment* is a transaction capable of handling payments worth several dollars or more, such as those systems described in previous chapters.

One of the functions of the broker is to provide all the different vendor scrip needs of a customer in return for a single macropayment. In other words, the broker sells vendor scrip to customers. The aggregation of the different vendor scrips justifies a macropayment transaction to purchase these pieces of scrip. A single vendor selling his or her own scrip would not normally justify this.

Replacing Subscription Services   In a subscription service, a vendor usually maintains account information for customers who have paid to use the service for a set length of time. Customers have to maintain account information for each different vendor. Vendors have to create, maintain, and bill accounts for possibly a large number of users. The Millicent broker frees both the customer and vendor from these tasks, replacing a subscription service with a pay-per-access micropayment system.

Selling Vendor Scrip   Brokers handle the real money in the Millicent system. They maintain accounts of customers and vendors. Customers buy vendor scrip for a specific vendor from their broker. The broker will have an agreement with each vendor whose scrip the broker sells. There are two main ways in which a broker gets the vendor scrip:

Scrip warehouse: The broker buys many pieces of vendor scrip from the vendor. The scrip is stored and then sold piece by piece to different customers.

Licensed scrip production: The actual broker generates the vendor scrip on behalf of that vendor. This is more efficient because:

- The broker doesn't need to store a large number of scrip pieces.

- The vendor does less computation since the vendor doesn't have to generate the scrip himself or herself.

- The license, which can be granted and sent across the network, is smaller to transmit than large chunks of scrip.

The license will allow the broker to only generate a specific amount of vendor scrip. The license should be enforceable through normal business practices. Brokers will typically be financial institutions or network service providers. They are assumed to be trusted by the other entities.

7.1.1.2 Vendors

Millicent vendors are merchants selling low-value services or information. A vendor accepts his or her own vendor scrip as payment from customers. The vendor can validate his or her own vendor scrip locally and prevent any double spending. The merchant sells vendor scrip at discount or a scrip-producing license to a broker. This discount or selling commission is how the broker profits from the scheme.

7.1.1.3 Customers

Users buy *broker scrip* with real money from their chosen broker, as shown in Figure 7.2. Broker scrip has value at that broker only. A macropayment scheme such as SET or Ecash could be used to initially buy the broker scrip. Using this broker scrip, the customer buys vendor scrip for specific vendors. The vendor scrip can then be used to make purchases.

7.1.2 Purchasing with Millicent

Initially, the customer buys some broker scrip using one of the macropayment systems, as shown in Figure 7.2. Typically, enough broker scrip to last a week might be bought, although more can be obtained at any time.

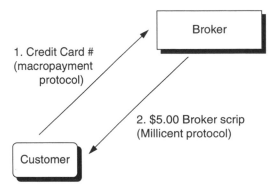

Start of week:

1. Credit Card #
(macropayment
protocol)

Broker

2. $5.00 Broker scrip
(Millicent protocol)

Customer

Vendor

Figure 7.2 Buying broker scrip.

When a customer first encounters a new vendor, he or she must buy vendor scrip from the broker to spend at that vendor's site. Figure 7.3 shows a customer buying 20 cents of vendor scrip using the $5 of broker scrip purchased earlier. Both the new vendor scrip and the change in broker scrip are returned. The same process will take place when a customer needs more vendor scrip, perhaps at the start of a new day.

The vendor scrip is sent to the merchant with a purchase request. The vendor will return a new piece of vendor scrip as change along with the purchased content. Remember, scrip is vendor-specific, and can be spent only at a particular merchant.

Figure 7.4 shows the customer buying from the *same vendor* again using the change. The customer already has valid vendor scrip for the vendor, so there is no need to contact the broker. Again, the scrip and purchase request are sent to the vendor who returns the item and the correct change. In this example the customer has bought an article costing 4 cents.

Repeated payments at a specific vendor are highly efficient in regard to network connections. If the customer already has valid scrip for that vendor, only a single network connection is required. Compare this with the number of network connections required in a secure macropayment scheme such as SET or Ecash. This increased communications efficiency is provided at the cost of slightly relaxing the security, as discussed later.

New day or new vendor:

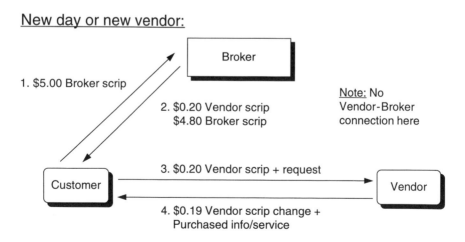

Figure 7.3   Purchasing from a vendor.

Uses current change:

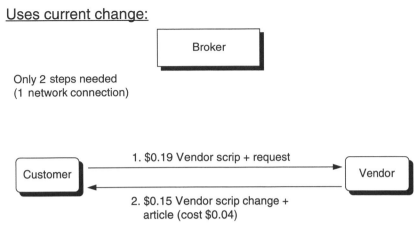

Figure 7.4 Further purchases from the same vendor.

7.1.3 Scrip

Scrip is a piece of data used to represent microcurrency within the Millicent system. Scrip has the following properties:

- A piece of scrip represents a prepaid value, much like prepaid phone cards, fare cards, or coupons.

- Scrip can represent any denomination of currency. Expected values range from one-tenth of a cent up to about $5, although there is no defined upper- or lower-bound limits.

- The security of scrip is based on the assumption that it is only used to represent small amounts of money.

- It is vendor-specific and thus has value at one vendor only.

- It can be spent only once. Double spending will be detected locally by the vendor at the time of purchase.

- It can be spent only by its owner. A shared secret is used to prevent stolen scrip being spent, as discussed in Section 7.1.11.

- Scrip cannot be tampered with or its value changed.

- It is computationally expensive to counterfeit scrip. The cost of doing so outweighs the value of the scrip itself.

- Scrip makes no use of public-key cryptography. It can be efficiently produced, validated, and protected using a one-way hash function and limited symmetric cryptography.

- Scrip cannot provide full anonymity. It has visible serial numbers that could be recorded and traced. Some limited anonymity could be maintained by buying broker scrip using an anonymous macropayment system.

7.1.4 Scrip structure

Figure 7.5 shows the data fields that make up a piece of scrip. The purpose of each is now briefly examined:

Vendor: Identifies the vendor at which this scrip has value.

Value: Specifies how much the scrip is worth.

ID#:   A unique identifier of the scrip, much like a serial number. It is used to prevent double spending of the scrip.

Cust_ID#:   An identifier used to calculate a shared secret (customer_secret) that is used to protect the scrip and any scrip issued as change. Cust_ID# need not have any connection to the real identity of the customer, but it must be unique to every customer. Scrip issued as change will have the same Cust_ID# as the original scrip used to make the payment.

Expiry: The date on which the scrip becomes invalid. Used to limit the ID#s that must be remembered by a vendor to prevent double spending.

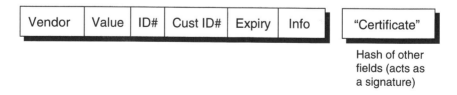

Figure 7.5 Scrip data fields.

Info: Optional details describing the customer to a vendor. They might include the customer's age or country of residence. Such information could assist the vendor in making a sales decision on such matters as selling adult material and the levying of sales tax. The exact fields used, if any, will depend on an agreement between the brokers and vendors.

Certificate: The certificate field prevents the scrip being altered in any way and proves that it is authentic (but not already double spent). In this sense, it acts as a digital signature, although it is not created or validated using asymmetric key cryptography.

7.1.5 Scrip certificate generation

When a piece of scrip is generated the certificate field is created as a signature or "certificate of authenticity" for that scrip. The certificate is really a stamp of approval that cannot be forged and that prevents any of the scrip's fields from being altered.

It is created by hashing the other fields of the scrip with a secret, as shown in Figure 7.6. Only the vendor (or trusted broker) who mints the scrip will know this secret, which is called a *master scrip secret*. The vendor will maintain a list of many different master scrip secrets, numbered from 1 to *N*, for the purpose of minting scrip. Which master scrip secret is used with a particular piece of scrip depends on some part of the scrip's ID#. As a simplified example, if the last digit in the ID# was 6, then master scrip secret 6 might be used.

Since the certificate is the product of a one-way hash function, such as MD5, it prevents the scrip's fields from being altered successfully. Any change will result in a recomputed certificate not matching the original one. Only the party who knows the master scrip secret can generate scrip. Thus the scrip certificate prevents both tampering and counterfeiting.

7.1.6 Scrip validation

At the time of purchase, a vendor must be sure that the scrip the vendor is accepting is valid. It must be:

- Authentic scrip produced by the vendor or licensed broker;
- Not already spent (double spending).

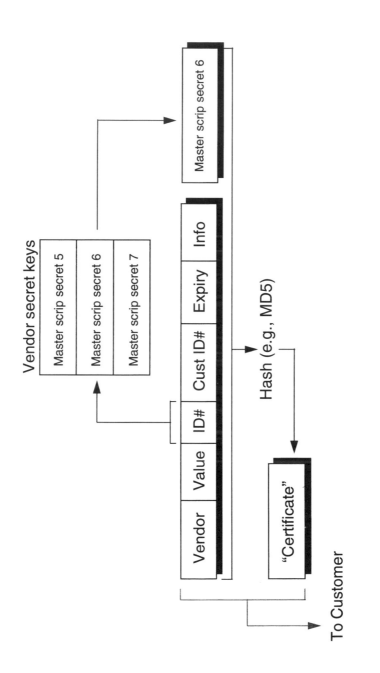

Figure 7.6 Scrip certificate generation.

The merchant recalculates the certificate and compares it with the scrip certificate from the customer. This is shown in Figure 7.7. Both certificates will match if the scrip has not been tampered with.

7.1.7 Preventing double spending

To prevent double spending, the vendor checks that the ID# has not already been spent. The vendor maintains bit vectors (data structures where one bit is used to represent each ID#) corresponding to the issued serial numbers (ID#s) to keep track of spent scrip. Vectors covering ranges that have been fully spent or expired can be discarded. This will allow the vendor to keep the database of valid scrip ID#s in memory, which will speed up transactions.

7.1.8 Computation costs

Table 7.1 shows the computations required in a Millicent purchase. Compared to macropayment systems examined in earlier chapters, accepting a Millicent micropayment is cheap and efficient.

7.1.9 Sending scrip over a network: the Millicent protocols

When sending scrip over a network, different levels of efficiency, security, and privacy may be required. For example, on an internal network within an organization, there may be little need for privacy or security. However, on the public network these may be more important.

There are three main Millicent protocols that provide different levels of these requirements. Table 7.2 compares their characteristics. Each is now examined in turn.

7.1.10 Scrip in the clear

In the simplest protocol, the customer sends the scrip unprotected across the network to the vendor. The vendor will also return the purchased content and change in the clear. No network security is provided in this protocol. An attacker can intercept the scrip or the change and use it himself or herself. Remember, the stolen scrip can only be spent at one particular vendor.

7.1.11 Encrypted network connection

To prevent scrip being stolen, and to prevent an eavesdropper gaining any information from the transaction, the network connection can be

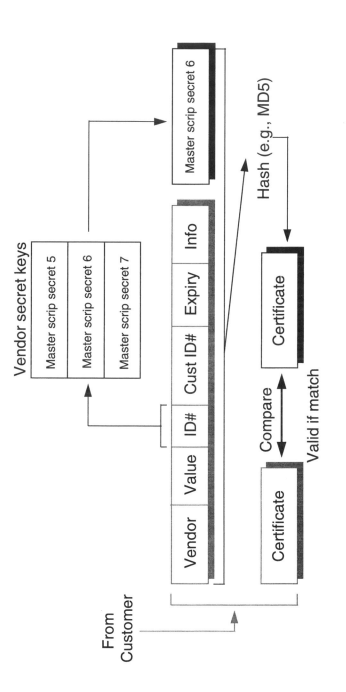

Figure 7.7   Validating scrip at the time of purchase.

Table 7.1
Computational Costs of Accepting Scrip

Action	Cost
Recalculate certificate	One hash function
Prevent double spending	One local ID# database lookup (in memory)
Making purchase across network	One network connection

Table 7.2
Characteristics of the Three Millicent Protocols

Millicent Protocol	Efficiency Ranking	Secure	Private
Scrip in the clear	1	No	No
Encrypted connection	3	Yes	Yes
Request signatures	2	Yes	No

encrypted. This can be done using a shared symmetric key, called the *customer_secret*, between the customer and vendor. The customer_secret is used to secure the communications channel using an efficient symmetric algorithm such as Rijndael, RC6, or DES. Figure 7.8 shows a purchase using the customer_secret to encrypt the network connection. The protocol is both secure and private.

Scrip cannot be stolen and an eavesdropper cannot see the purchase or scrip details. Vendor_ID and Cust_ID# are sent in the clear in both messages so that the recipient can calculate customer_secret. Section 7.1.11.1 describes how the customer_secret is generated. The original scrip certificate is included in the response to show that it is the correct response to the request.

7.1.11.1 The customer_secret

Figure 7.9 shows how the customer_secret is generated when the scrip is created. It is formed by hashing the customer identifier with another secret, called the *master_customer_secret*. Only the vendor (or trusted broker) will know this secret. As with the master_scrip_secret, the vendor

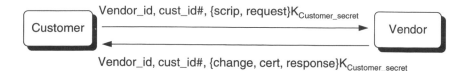

Figure 7.8   Purchase using encrypted network connection.

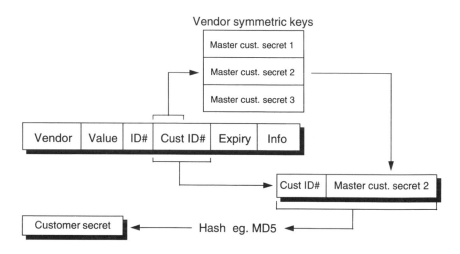

Figure 7.9   Generating a customer_secret.

maintains a list of many different master_customer_secrets, numbered from 1 to *N*. Part of the Cust_ID# is used to select the master_customer_secret.

The vendor can recalculate the customer_secret at any time from the piece of scrip. The customer must also obtain the customer_secret. It is returned to the customer when the vendor scrip is purchased from a broker, as shown in Figure 7.10. To protect the customer_secret as it passes from broker to customer, the transaction could be performed using a secure non-Millicent protocol. Alternatively, a secure Millicent transaction could be used, where a customer_secret exists for the broker scrip being used by the customer. The customer_secret would be used to encrypt the connection in much the same way as in Figure 7.8. The customer_secret for the broker scrip must be obtained using a secure protocol outside the Millicent system.

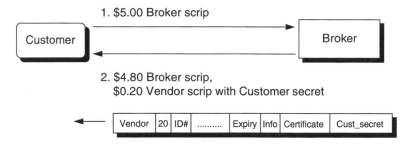

Figure 7.10 Buying vendor scrip.

Table 7.3 summarizes the purpose and usage of the three different types of shared secret used in Millicent.

7.1.12 Request signatures

A fully encrypted network connection might be more than is required, especially if privacy is not important. A third Millicent protocol removes the encryption but maintains a level of security that prevents scrip being stolen.

The customer_secret is used to generate a *request signature* instead of being used for encryption. It is similar to the certificate field of a piece of scrip in that it is a hash of other fields. The request signature is generated by hashing the scrip, customer_secret, and request together, as shown in

Table 7.3
Secrets Used in Producing, Validating, and Spending Scrip

Secret	Shared by	Purpose
Master_scrip_secret	Vendor, minting broker	Prevents tampering and counterfeiting of scrip. Used to authenticate scrip.
Customer_secret	Customer, vendor, minting broker	Proves ownership of the scrip. May be required to spend the scrip.
Master_customer_secret	Vendor, minting broker	Derives the customer_secret from customer information in the scrip.

Figure 7.11. It is created by the customer and sent along with the scrip and request to the vendor. This is shown in Figure 7.12.

The vendor verifies the request signature by recomputing it, as shown in Figure 7.13. Remember, the vendor can compute the customer_secret using the scrip and a master_customer_secret (Figure 7.9). If the request has been tampered with, then the two request signatures will not match and the vendor will refuse to process the transaction.

For a valid request, the vendor returns the purchase reply, change in scrip, and a reply signature. The reply signature is generated in the same way as the request signature, using the same customer_secret. The change cannot be stolen by an attacker because it cannot be spent without knowledge of the customer_secret. This is because without the customer_secret, a valid request signature cannot be calculated, and the merchant will refuse the transaction.

Thus, while an eavesdropper can see all parts of the transaction (no privacy), the purchase request cannot be altered and the scrip cannot be stolen. Security has been provided more efficiently than using encryption, but at the cost of losing the privacy.

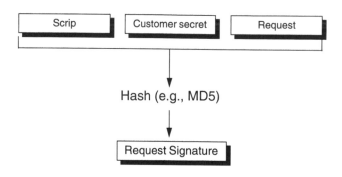

Figure 7.11   Generating a request signature.

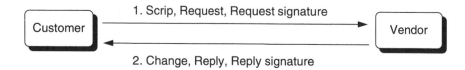
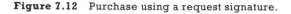

Figure 7.12   Purchase using a request signature.

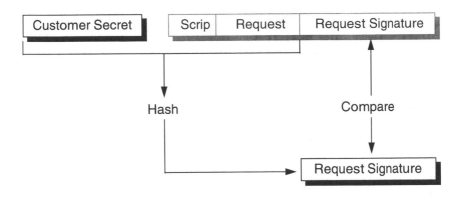

Figure 7.13   Vendor verifies the request signature.

7.1.13 Performance

It is desirable that both vendors and brokers can process a large number of transactions a second in order to make small micropayments viable. Initial tests of a Millicent implementation on a Digital AlphaStation 400 4/233 [1] produced the following results:

- 14,000 pieces of scrip can be produced per second;

- 8,000 payments can be validated per second, with change scrip being produced;

- 1,000 Millicent requests per second can be received from the network and validated.

The bottleneck appears to be in handling the network connection, which in this case was TCP, the transport protocol used on the Internet. Thus, Millicent is capable of handling the maximum number of micropayment purchases that can be received from the network per second.

7.1.14 Millicent with the Web

Millicent is well suited for paying for Web content. The Millicent protocol can be implemented as an extension to the Web's HTTP protocol. A software implementation consists of a user wallet, a vendor server, and a broker server.

Since Millicent supports small micropayments, users may not be so tempted to steal or copy content worth only a cent. The designers feel that users will consider it foolish to steal if the price is already so low.

7.1.15 Extensions

Millicent can securely handle transactions from one-tenth of a cent up to a few dollars. This makes it suitable for micropayments, such as paying for information content, database searching, or access to a service. However, it could also be used with a broad range of other applications that may or may not involve payments, both on the Internet and private networks. These might include:

- *Authentication to distributed services:* Scrip could be used to provide Kerberos-like authentication (see Chapter 3) for access to network services. At the start of the day, a user obtains authentication scrip from a broker. This authentication scrip is then used to buy scrip for access to particular network services. Access is dynamically provided based on a user having scrip for that system.

- *Metering usage:* Millicent could be used with accounting and metering applications inside private networks. The organization will act as a broker, with employees as the customers. The vendors will be the servers to which the employees have access.

- *Usage-based charges:* Millicent could be used for per-connection charges for such services as e-mail, file transfer, Internet telephony, teleconferencing, and other on-line services. However, it would not be efficient enough for charging per packet for these services.

- *Discount coupons:* Further fields could be added to scrip to provide discounts for certain content. For example, having bought the first half of an article, the change scrip could contain a discount for buying the second half of the article, provided it was bought the same day with that scrip.

- *Preventing subscription sharing:* By using scrip to access a prepaid subscription service, sharing of that subscription account can be prevented. The scrip acts as an access capability to the service, with the scrip change giving access the next time. However, trying to gain access with an already used piece of scrip (such as shared scrip would be) will fail.

7.1.16 Summary

The Millicent protocol was first published in 1995 [1, 2], and in the following years a number of Millicent pilot experiments took place around the world. However, it wasn't until June 1999 that the first commercial application of Millicent went live in Japan. This first deployment based on real currency, the Japanese yen, is a cooperation between Compaq and KDD Communications. Japanese users are able to buy Millicent scrip using a credit card, and are able to make purchases as small as 0.1 yen (less than $0.001). At the time of writing, there are plans to make Millicent commercially available in North America and Europe, although deployment schedules are likely to depend on the success of the Japanese venture.

Millicent is an efficient, lightweight, flexible micropayment system. It can support multiple brokers and vendors and can be extended for use with many applications.

One drawback of the scheme is that both the broker and vendor must be trusted to issue the correct change, as there is no way to prove that change scrip is owed. Similarly the user cannot independently verify the validity of a piece of scrip, since the user cannot regenerate the scrip certificate. For the small amounts involved, vendors are unlikely to try to defraud customers, especially since the anomaly will be revealed when the user later returns to spend the change. Lightweight hash functions are used to achieve this relaxed level of security, which is suited to low-value micropayments, and Millicent significantly reduces the computational and communications overhead, compared to macropayment systems, for multiple accesses to the same vendor within a short time.

7.2 SubScrip

SubScrip [3] is a simple micropayment protocol designed for efficient *pay-per-view* payments on the Internet. It was developed at the University of Newcastle, Australia, and is a *prepaid system* with no need for user identification.

In essence, it works by creating temporary prepaid accounts for users at a specific vendor. The user makes micropayment purchases from the vendor against this account. Since the account is temporary and prepaid, it does not carry the normal overhead associated with subscription services. The system does not require its own billing or banking hierarchy.

Instead, any existing macropayment scheme, such as a credit card scheme, can be used to make the initial payment to a vendor to set up the prepaid account.

As with Millicent, the level of security is relaxed due to the low value of the transactions. The designers aimed to make the expense necessary for a successful attack much higher than the financial gain possible. In its basic form, no encryption is used at all.

7.2.1 Basic SubScrip

SubScrip uses techniques similar to some of Millicent's features to achieve a very low transaction cost. As with Millicent, a micropayment can be verified locally by a vendor without the need for any on-line clearance with a third party. Similarly, there is an initial overhead associated with making a payment to a new vendor. Both systems are optimal for repeated payments to the same vendor over a short time period.

7.2.2 Establishing a temporary account

However, unlike Millicent, SubScrip does not use a broker to mediate between users and merchants. Instead, an existing macropayment scheme takes over this role. A user chooses a macropayment scheme that a vendor can accept. The user makes a payment large enough to cover the macropayment transaction costs to that vendor, as shown in Figure 7.14. This payment will typically be of a few dollars and is used to set up a *temporary account* at the merchant.

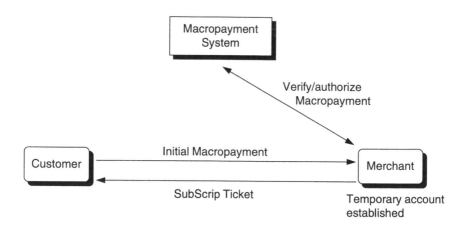

Figure 7.14 Establishing a SubScrip account with a vendor.

In order to make micropayment purchases against the temporary account, the user needs some type of account identifier. Within the SubScrip system, this account identifier is called a *SubScrip ticket*. The merchant returns a SubScrip ticket to the user to access the new account.

7.2.3 Providing anonymity

A SubScrip merchant need not know the identity of a user with whom he or she is dealing. The anonymity provided will depend on the anonymity of the macropayment system used to initially pay a vendor. If a nonanonymous system is used, the merchant can link the name to the temporary account set up, and track all payments made against that account. With an anonymous system, the merchant will only know the network address from which the customer's requests are coming. Both the customer and merchant will have to agree on the same macropayment protocol to use.

7.2.4 A SubScrip ticket

A SubScrip tickct is the special account identifier used to authenticate the account owner to the account maintained at a vendor site in order to make a micropayment purchase. It is valid only at one particular merchant. As shown in Figure 7.15, it consists of the following fields:

Acc_ID: An account identifier that uniquely identifies the account at a vendor. It is chosen so that it is hard for an attacker to guess a valid account identifier. A large random number can be used.

Val: The amount of money remaining in the account at the vendor.

Exp: The date on which the account will expire. This limits the number of accounts that must be maintained by a vendor.

Figure 7.15 A SubScrip ticket.

The merchant maintains a database of valid account IDs with the amount and expiry date of each account. Knowledge of the account ID is the only way to gain access to the account. The SubScrip ticket does not actually have value itself and is therefore not an electronic coin. However, without it, the prepaid value at the merchant cannot be accessed. The problem of lost or stolen tickets is discussed in Section 7.2.9.

SubScrip value is *transferable* to another user. This is done by giving that user the valid ticket for the account balance at a specific vendor.

7.2.5 A SubScrip purchase

To make a purchase, the user sends the SubScrip ticket to the vendor, who verifies that it is valid by checking the database, as shown in Figure 7.16. The micropayment amount is deducted from the account balance. A new random account identifier and a matching ticket with the new balance are then generated for the account and returned to the user along with the purchased information or service. The user stores the new ticket, along with the address of the merchant, for further purchases.

It is not possible for users to commit fraud by altering the value or expiry fields on their SubScrip ticket. This is because these fields are included in the ticket for the user's information only. The database of accounts maintained by the merchant will always have the real account balances and expiry dates.

7.2.6 Security and privacy

The SubScrip tickets are sent in the clear, with no encryption used during a purchase. An eavesdropper can see exactly what is purchased and for how much in a transaction. The amount remaining in the user's account at the vendor can also be clearly seen from the new ticket returned. No privacy can be provided by the protocol in this form.

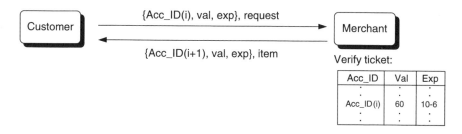

Figure 7.16 Purchasing with a SubScrip ticket.

It is possible for an eavesdropper to obtain a valid account ID as a new ticket is returned to the customer as change. A stolen ticket could be spent by an attacker, and when the user next tried to spend it, it would already be invalid. An active attacker could also intercept a valid ticket being sent to the merchant as a purchase request. Once a valid ticket reaches the merchant, it is invalidated, and the attacker would have to prevent this ticket or a retransmission of it reaching its destination to successfully steal it.

The SubScrip designers accept the possibility of fraud in these ways. They feel that since a SubScrip ticket is only valid at one particular merchant, the amounts involved do not warrant the possibility of large-scale fraud. They consider the lightweight limited security to be adequate for normal pay-per-view micropayments.

7.2.7 Protected SubScrip
To provide increased security, at the cost of lowering the computational efficiency, a protected SubScrip protocol using public-key cryptography is proposed.

When a customer first buys a temporary SubScrip account at a merchant, the customer's public key, PK_C, is also forwarded. The merchant stores this public key with the account ID in the account database. Whenever the merchant sends a new ticket for this account to the customer, it is encrypted with that customer's public key, as shown in Figure 7.17.

The ticket is not encrypted as it is sent from the customer to the merchant. The designers feel that it is unlikely that an attacker will go to the trouble of preventing the ticket reaching its destination (where it will be invalidated) in order to steal it.

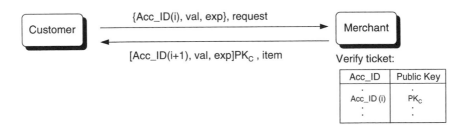

Figure 7.17 A protected SubScript purchase.

7.2.8 Refunding SubScrip

Another proposed extension is to allow customers to convert unspent tickets back to real money. This would be done by sending the ticket to the vendor, who would pay the remaining account balance to the user using an existing macropayment system. A system in which any user can accept payments, such as electronic cash systems or by using credit card chargebacks, will have to be used for this purpose. The cost of the macropayment transaction may have to be covered by the merchant by charging a fee for this service.

7.2.9 Lost tickets

A user might lose a ticket through an unsuccessful transmission or a software failure. An implementation of the merchant software might record the delivery addresses of users. Lost account IDs could then be recovered by sending the delivery address and approximate time of last access to regain the account.

In conclusion, SubScrip provides a lightweight, efficient, account-based micropayment system with limited security. It reduces the overhead required to maintain a complete subscription database and allows for some anonymity.

7.3 PayWord

PayWord [4] is a credit-based micropayment scheme designed by Ron Rivest (MIT Laboratory for Computer Science, Massachusetts) and Adi Shamir (Weizmann Institute of Science, Rehovot, Israel). The scheme aims to reduce the number of public-key operations required per payment by using hash functions, which are faster. Table 7.4 gives performance measurements comparing the number of asymmetric (public key), symmetric, and hash functions, that can be performed per second on a typical workstation. The measurements were taken on a 850-MHz Intel Celeron processor under Windows 2000, using Crypto++ [5], to provide a C++ implementation of all the algorithms. The operations performed per second are based on a 64-byte input message size. Fast hash functions and symmetric-key cryptography are more suitable for micropayments, where speed is important, than the slower public-key cryptography used in many macropayment schemes.

PayWord uses *chains of hash values* to represent user credit within the system. Each hash value, called a *PayWord*, can be sent to a merchant as

Table 7.4

Comparison of Computational Speed of Cryptographic Operations
on a Typical Workstation

Operation	Number per Second
PK signature generation (RSA 1024)	95
PK signature verification (RSA 1024)	3,300
3DES (Triple DES)	75,000
IDEA	185,000
DES	210,000
Rijndael	495,000
RC6	530,000
RC5	645,000
SHA hash	800,000
MD5 hash	1,650,000

payment. A PayWord chain is vendor-specific and the user digitally signs a *commitment* to honor payments for that chain.

Brokers mediate between users and vendors and maintain accounts for both. They vouch for users by issuing a *PayWord certificate* allowing that user to generate PayWords. They redeem spent PayWord chains from vendors, transferring the amount spent from the user's account to the vendor. It is not necessary for both a vendor and user to have an account at the same broker.

As with other micropayment schemes, security is relaxed to increase efficiency. While it is possible for some users to overspend, parties that continue to abuse the system can be detected and removed.

7.3.1 PayWord user certificates

Since PayWord is a credit-based scheme, vendors need some assurance that users will honor their PayWord payments. A *PayWord certificate* authorizes a user to generate PayWord chains, and guarantees that a specific broker will redeem them. Brokers and vendors do not need PayWord certificates in the PayWord scheme.

Users obtain a certificate when they initially set up an account with a broker, as shown in Figure 7.18. A macropayment scheme or credit card payment could be used to pay money into the account. The certificate

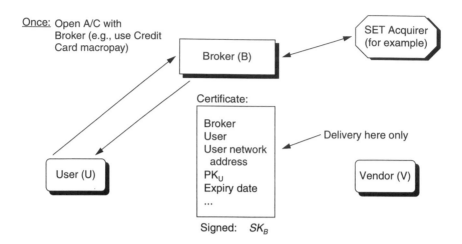

Figure 7.18 Obtaining a PayWord user certificate.

will typically have to be renewed every month. This limits fraud by ensuring that users who have overdrawn accounts will not be issued with a new certificate, which would allow them to continue generating PayWords.

A PayWord certificate is of the form:

$$C_U \;=\; \{B,\, U,\, A_U,\, PK_U,\, E,\, I_U\}\, SK_B$$

The certificate is signed by the broker (B). The certificate fields have the following meaning:

B   Identifies the broker who issued the certificate. PayWords accepted from the user (U) will only be redeemable at this broker.

U   Identifies the user who is authorized by this certificate to generate PayWord chains.

A_U The user's delivery address. This could include an Internet host address, e-mail, or mailing address. To limit fraud, items purchased by the user should only be delivered to this address.

PK_U The user's public key. Used to verify the user's digital signature on a commitment to a new PayWord chain.

E   The date the certificate expires.

I_U Optional information. This could include credit limits per vendor, user-specific details, or broker details.

In order to verify a broker's signature on a certificate, a vendor must securely obtain that broker's public key, PK_B, in some way. How this is done will be specific to an implementation and is not discussed in the PayWord scheme.

Since identified certificates with a user identifier and address are used, no anonymity is provided.

7.3.2 Revoked certificates

A broker might maintain blacklists of certificates that have been revoked, much like the certificate revocation lists in SET. A user's certificate would be revoked if his or her secret key was lost or stolen, as this would allow others to generate PayWord chains under their name. It is the responsibility of a vendor to obtain any revoked certificate lists from a broker.

7.3.3 PayWord chains

A *PayWord chain* represents user credit at a specific vendor. It is a chain of hash values. Each PayWord (hash value) in the chain has the same value, normally 1 cent. Other values are also possible as described in Section 7.3.4. To generate a new PayWord chain, the user performs the following steps, as illustrated in Figure 7.19:

1. Decide on the length, N, of the chain. A PayWord chain of length 10 will be worth 10 cents if the PayWord value is 1 cent. The chain value should be greater than the amount one is likely to spend at a vendor that day. Unused PayWords in a chain can be safely discarded. Since they represent user credit, no value is lost.

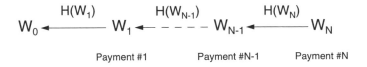

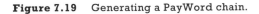

Figure 7.19 Generating a PayWord chain.

2. Select a random number, W_N, called the root of the hash chain, since the rest of the chain will be derived from it.

3. Perform N repeated hashes of W_N. Each hash value forms one PayWord. SHA could be used as the hash function.

4. The final chain will be: $\{W_0, W_1, W_2, \ldots, W_N\}$.

7.3.4 Commitment to a PayWord chain

Since PayWord is a credit-based scheme, the vendor and broker need to know to whom the spent PayWords belong so that the user's account can be charged appropriately. The user is authenticated by signing a *commitment* to a PayWord chain. The commitment will authorize the broker to redeem any PayWords from the committed chain. It allows the vendor to be confident that he or she will be paid for PayWords accepted from the user.

A commitment to a PayWord chain has the form:

$$Comm \quad = \quad \{V, C_U, W_0, E, I_{Comm}\}\ SK_U$$

The commitment is signed with the user's secret key. The fields have the following purpose:

V	The vendor at which the committed PayWord chain is valid. A PayWord chain is vendor-specific.
C_U	The user's PayWord certificate, as described earlier. Used to verify the user's signature and to verify authorization from a broker.
W_0	The final hash, or anchor, of the PayWord chain. Identifies the chain and allows PayWords to be verified as belonging to that chain.
E	The date on which the commitment expires. This limits the length of time both users and vendors need to store information about the state of a PayWord chain.
I_{Comm}	Additional information. This could contain the length, N, of the chain. It could also define the value of a PayWord. Typically, each PayWord will be worth 1 cent, but other chain values might also be useful. The upper limit to the value of a PayWord will depend

on the risk a vendor or broker is prepared to accept. The broker might recommend an upper limit within a user's certificate. PayWords with value greater than $1 may have too much risk associated with them.

7.3.5 Spending PayWords

When users encounter a vendor from whom they wish to purchase goods, they generate a new PayWord chain and a commitment. The commitment is then sent to the vendor, as shown in Figure 7.20, to show the user's intentions of spending PayWords there.

To make a 1-cent payment, the user then sends the first PayWord (W_1) to the vendor. This is verified, as shown in Figure 7.21, by taking the hash of the PayWord W_1. If the PayWord is valid, the hash should match the anchor of the chain (W_0) found in the commitment. This works because only the user could possess the valid W_1 PayWord. It is computationally difficult to generate a value that would hash to W_0 due to the nature of one-way hash functions. Thus, even knowing W_0, an attacker or a cheating vendor cannot generate valid PayWords in the chain.

To make a further 1-cent payment, the user will send W_2. The vendor then compares the value obtained by taking the hash of W_2, $H(W_2)$ to the previous valid PayWord (W_1) received. If W_2 is valid, then the values will match, as shown in Figure 7.22.

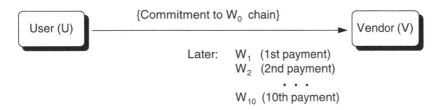

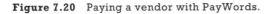

Figure 7.20 Paying a vendor with PayWords.

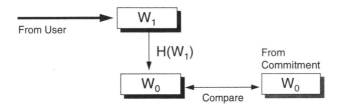

Figure 7.21 Verifying the first PayWord.

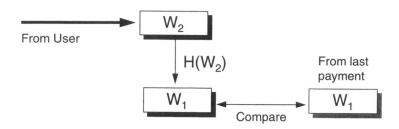

Figure 7.22 Verifying further payments.

7.3.6 Variable-size payments

Payments of values greater than one cent can be made by sending Pay-Words further down the chain, without having sent skipped-over Pay-Words. For example, to make a 3-cent payment after having spent W_2, the fifth PayWord, W_5, can be sent. This is shown in Figure 7.23. The actual payment message consists of a PayWord and its index into the chain:

$$P = (W_i, i)$$

This allows the vendor to know how many hashes should be performed. In this example, the vendor must perform three repeated hashes on W_5. The user's name may also have to be included in the payment message to allow the vendor to identify the user, depending on implementation details. The vendor is responsible for recording the last valid PayWord in a chain accepted from a user.

The broker does not need to be contacted during a payment. The Pay-Words can be quickly verified locally by the vendor. After the initial commitment, the actual size of the payment message, P, sent is small, which further improves communications efficiency. As with many electronic payment systems, there is no guarantee that the purchased item will be delivered by the vendor.

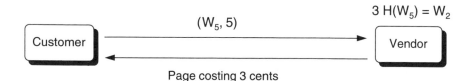

Figure 7.23 Making a payment greater than 1 cent.

Users maintain unspent PayWords until they have finished spending at the vendor or until the commitment for that PayWord chain has expired. A user need only store the root of the hash chain, W_N, since all the other chain values can be derived from this. A vendor should keep each user's commitment and last valid PayWord received. Even after redeeming a spent chain, the vendor should retain a commitment that has not expired to prevent replay attacks.

7.3.7 Redeeming spent PayWords

To receive payment a vendor redeems PayWord chains with the appropriate broker, perhaps at the end of each day. For each chain, the vendor must send the following, as shown in Figure 7.24:

 ▸ The signed user commitment for that chain;

 ▸ The highest indexed PayWord spent.

The broker verifies the highest PayWord, W_l, by performing L hashes on it. The value obtained must match W_0 in the user's commitment if W_L is valid. If the user's signature and W_L are valid, the broker debits the spent amount from the user's account and pays the vendor.

7.3.8 Computational costs

The efficiency of the PayWord system is summarized below:

Broker:
   ▸ One signature/user/month (C_U);

   ▸ One signature verification/user/vendor/day (*Commitment*);

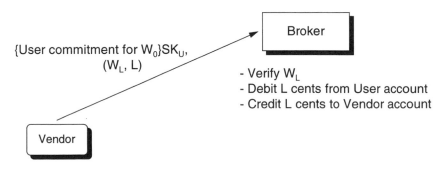

Figure 7.24 Reclaiming PayWords with a broker.

› One hash per PayWord spent.

Vendor:

› Two signature verifications/user/day (*Commitment* and C_U);

› One hash per PayWord spent.

User:

› One signature/vendor/day (*Commitment*);

› One hash per PayWord constructed.

Only the user needs to perform the computation-intensive public-key signature on-line, and then only once per vendor per day. RSA signature verifications are less computation-intensive (see Table 7.4) and are also kept to a minimum. Hash functions are computationally cheap and are performed once per PayWord by all parties. The broker could perform certificate generation and PayWord redemption off-line for efficiency. PayWord is most efficient for repeated micropayments to a specific vendor.

7.3.9 Extensions
It may be desirable to be able to use PayWords of different values at the same merchant within a short space of time. This could be done by extending the commitment to contain the anchors of several different chains. The PayWords would have different values in each separate chain, and these values would be specified in the commitment. The payment message would then have to identify which PayWord chain was being used as well as the PayWord index.

A commitment could be used as a simple electronic check to make a macropayment. Instead of including the anchor of a PayWord chain, the commitment would specify the amount to pay the vendor. The commitment, like an electronic check, is signed by the user.

7.3.10 Remarks
PayWord uses efficient hash functions to minimize computational and communications costs for a payment transaction. A payment verification requires only one hash computation, and the vendor need only store the highest payment hash received.

PayWord minimizes communication costs for a payment transaction. Unlike the Millicent system, a broker does not have to be contacted for a new vendor payment nor is there any need for scrip change or the return of unused vendor-specific scrip to the broker. However, PayWord's credit scheme provides more opportunity for user fraud than Millicent, especially if a user's secret key is compromised.

7.4 *i*KP micropayment protocol

The authors of the *i*KP [6, 7] suite of protocols have developed a credit-based micropayment scheme [8] that can be used in conjunction with 3KP but does not depend on it for making micropayments (Section 4.7 provides a detailed account of the *i*KP protocol). The scheme is based on the creation of a chain of hash values [9, 10] using a one-way function. A strong one-way function (F) is such that given a value (x) it is easy to compute $F(x)$. But given a value (y), it is computationally infeasible to find x such that $y = F(x)$. Using such a one-way function F, a customer chooses a random value X and computes a chain of hash values using the following:

$$A^0(X) = X$$
$$A^{i+1}(X) = F(A^i(X))$$

The values $\{A^0, ..., A^{n-1}\}$ are referred to as *coupons*. These coupons enable the customer to make n micropayments of fixed value (val) to a merchant. The customer forwards A^n to the merchant together with the value (val) per coupon and the total number of coupons n using an arbitrary macropayment system. The micropayments are performed by successively revealing $\{A^{n-1}, A^{n-2}, ..., A^0\}$ to the merchant. The merchant can verify this in turn as it is he or she that possesses A^n.

$$A^n(X) = F(A^{n-1}(X))$$

For example, say $n = 100$. The customer releases the coupon A^{99} for the first item to be purchased. The merchant can verify this as $A^{100}(X) = F(A^{99}(X))$. The customer releases subsequent coupons $\{A^{98}, A^{97}, ...\}$ for each additional payment made to the merchant.

Conceptually, a hash chain in the *i*KP micropayment protocol is identical to one used in the PayWord scheme, but different terminology and numbering has been used in the specification of each.

7.4.1 μ-3KP protocol

The basic payment model used is the same as in 3KP. It consists of a customer (C), a merchant (M), and an acquirer gateway (A), each of which possesses a public-key pair. This provides for verification of the authenticity of each of the participants and nonrepudiation of messages between them. Figure 7.25 shows the message flows that are used in the initial authentication of a customer to a merchant which binds that customer to a specific hash chain. This is done by sending a Credit-Request message signed with the secret key of the customer. Once the merchant has obtained authorization for the customer from the acquirer, the customer can start making micropayments. Note that, as before, the customer and merchant agree upon the description and value of the goods prior to initiating the μ-3KP protocol.

The merchant accumulates the coupons deposited by the customer until the last coupon in the chain is reached or until the merchant is satisfied that the merchant has accumulated enough coupons to warrant sending a Clear-Request to the acquirer. (Note that there is no maximum lifetime for coupons.) There is a tradeoff between clearing intermediary coupons, in which case the merchant may suffer from multiple clearing charges and waiting for all coupons to be deposited by a customer, whereby the merchant may lose some amount of interest. The merchant

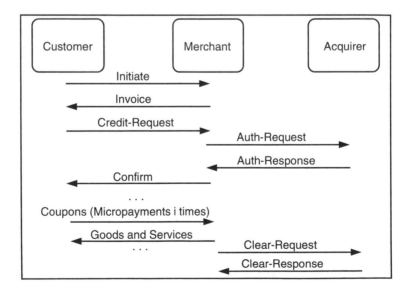

Figure 7.25 Framework of μ-3KP protocol.

receives a Clear-Response message back from the acquirer indicating whether the payment has been accepted or rejected.

There are two possible behavior patterns that may be observed among users of micropayment protocols:

- Customers that engage in repeated micropayment transactions with a merchant (e.g., downloading multiple Web pages from a server);

- Customers that engage in a single transaction with a particular merchant.

The latter requires a trusted third party (TTP) such as a broker to accumulate the micropayment transactions from a number of users and forward it to the merchant to make the protocol economically feasible.

7.4.2 Repeated micropayments

In circumstances in which a customer is going to have a long-term relationship with a merchant, it is economically feasible to establish a direct macropayment relationship with that merchant. The customer chooses the "root" of the hash chain X. The customer calculates a chain of hash values (n coupons) $\{A^0, A^1, \ldots, A^n\}$ using a one-way function such as MD5 or SHA, and then initiates the μ-3KP protocol for credit verification from the merchant.

Before taking a detailed look at the protocol exchanges, we explain the meaning of the various quantities exchanged by the entities in the system (see Table 7.5). These individual quantities are usually combined to form composite fields, as shown in Table 7.6.

The basic message flows, depicted in Figure 7.25, are as follows:

- *Initiate:* The customer initiates the payment transaction by sending to the merchant his or her identity (CID), the anchor of the chain of hash values (A^n), the value of each coupon (val), the total number of coupons in the chain (n), a random number (SALT$_C$), and her public-key certificate (CERT$_C$). This information is sent to the merchant in cleartext.

- *Invoice:* The response from the merchant contains the merchant's identity (ID$_M$), the transaction identifier to uniquely identify the transaction, the date, and a nonce. These fields are transferred as part

Table 7.5

Individual Quantities Occurring in μ-3KP

Item	Description
CAN	Customer's account number (e.g., credit card number)
ID_M	Merchant ID; identifies merchant to acquirer
TID_M	Transaction ID; uniquely identifies the transaction
DESC	Description of the goods; includes payment information such as credit card name and bank identification number
$SALT_C$	Random number generated by C; used to randomize DESC and thus ensure privacy of DESC on the M to A link
$NONCE_M$	Random number generated by a merchant to protect against replay
DATE	Merchant's current date/time
Y/N	Response from card issuer; YES/NO or authorization code
R_C	Random number chosen by C to form CID
CID	A customer pseudo-ID that uniquely identifies C; computed as CID = $H(R_C, CAN)$
V	Random number generated by merchant and used to bind the Confirm and Invoice message flows
V'	Second random number generated by the merchant and used to bind the Auth-Request and Clear-Response message flows

Table 7.6

μ-3KP Composite Fields

Item	Description
Common	Information held in common by all parties, A^n, n, val, ID_M, TID_M, DATE, $NONCE_M$, CID, $H(DESC, SALT_C)$, $H(V)$, $H(V')$
Clear	Information transmitted in the clear, ID_M, DATE, $NONCE_M$, $H(Common)$, $H(V)$, A^n
SLIP	Payment Instruction, n, val, $H(Common)$, CAN, R_C
EncSlip	Payment Instruction encrypted with the public key of the acquirer, $PK_A(SLIP)$
$CERT_X$	Public-key certificate of X issued by a CA
Sig_A	Acquirer's signature in response to Credit-Request message flow, $SK_A[H(Y/N, H(Common))]$
Sig'_A	Acquirer's signature in response to a Clear-Request message flow, $SK_A[H(Y/N, Sig_A, V', A^{n-i})]$
Sig_M	Merchant's signature, $SK_M[H(H(Common), H(V))]$, $H(V')$
Sig_C	Cardholder's signature, $SK_C[H(EncSlip, H(Common))]$

of Clear. The merchant and customer share some information such as the amount and description of the goods, which is known as Common. The merchant creates a message digest on Common and a random number (V). The merchant forms a digital signature (Sig_M) on the two digests and includes this in the Invoice. This allows the customer to verify that the customer and the merchant agree on the details of the transaction.

- *Credit Request:* The customer sends a request to the merchant that contains the total number of coupons (n), the value of each coupon (val), and the customer's account number in SLIP. The SLIP is encrypted with the public key of the acquirer to form EncSlip. The customer then forms Common and creates a message digest on it. This should match the one sent by the merchant in Invoice. The customer creates a digital signature on EncSlip and H(Common) to form Sig_C. The customer sends EncSlip and Sig_C to the merchant.

- *Authorization Request:* This is a request from the merchant to the acquirer to authorize a payment transaction. The merchant creates a digital signature Sig_M. The merchant forwards Clear, the randomized hash of the goods description ($H(\text{DESC}, \text{SALT}_C)$), the encrypted slip (EncSlip), the signature of the customer (Sig_C) and the merchant's own signature (Sig_M) to the acquirer. The actual transfer of money is initiated at a later date using the Clear-Request message flow.

- *Authorization Response:* The acquirer sends a signed response that contains a positive or negative indication. A positive response gives the merchant guarantee of the customer's credit limit.

- *Confirm:* The merchant forwards the acquirer's signed response to the customer as well as the first random number V. The inclusion of V in Confirm proves to the customer that the merchant has accepted the authorization response.

- *Micropayments:* The customer can then make multiple micropayment transactions until such time that the customer has purchased all the goods that he or she requires or has exhausted his or her supply of coupons for the merchant. The customer may have to supply the transaction identifier (TID_M) with each micropayment so that the merchant can associate a coupon with a particular hash chain.

• *Clear-Request:* The merchant asks the acquirer to perform a payment. In our case, it consists of a number of micropayments. When the merchant receives the last coupon in the chain (A^0) or decides to deposit the coupons (A^j) collected so far, he or she composes a Clear-Request message. The merchant then calculates the total payment due, which is $n - j$ times the amount of each coupon (val), and sends this along with the last coupon (A^{n-j}), the second random number (V'), and the signature of the acquirer (Sig_A). The merchant, sends the Clear-Request message to the acquirer. The acquirer can verify the hash chain and processes the request as a regular *i*KP transaction. The amount to be cleared may be different from the amount authorized.

• *Clear-Response:* This is a signed response from the acquirer to the merchant indicating whether the payment transaction was successful or not. It contains a positive or negative response as well as a digital signature (Sig'_A) on the second random number (V'), the total number of coupons (A^{n-j}), and the acquirer's previous signature (Sig_A).

Figure 7.26 shows the detailed message exchanges that take place when making repeated micropayments to the same merchant.

7.4.3 Nonrepeated micropayments
In many cases, when a user is initially browsing a merchant site, he or she may make one or a small number of micropayment transactions. This may not warrant the overhead of establishing a macropayment context between the customer and the merchant. In such circumstances a TTP in the form of a broker is introduced who acts as an intermediary and collects micropayments on behalf of merchants from customers. The volume of transactions processed by the broker is large enough for a macropayment context to be established between the broker and the merchants. The protocol steps are as follows:

• The customer establishes a micropayment relationship with the broker. The customer also establishes a shared session key with the broker (K_{CB}). The latter is not part of the μ-3KP protocol.

• When the customer wants to make a purchase from a specific merchant, the customer sends a coupon $A_{CB}^i(X)$, the name of

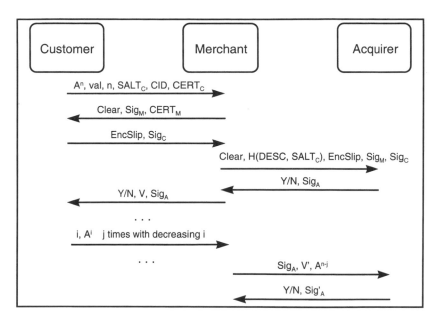

Figure 7.26 µ-3KP protocol.

the merchant (M), and the description of the goods (DESC) (see Figure 7.27). In the context of the Web, the DESC could be a URL. The fields of the message are encrypted using a previously established session key shared between the customer and the broker.

▸ The broker translates the customer's coupon into a coupon for the merchant $A_{BN}^{K}(X)$ and adds the customer's name and the description of the requested goods. The broker encrypts the fields of the message with the session key shared between himself and the merchant. The encrypted message is either sent directly to the merchant or to the customer, who transparently forwards it to the merchant.

▸ The merchant sends the goods to the customer.

Using a broker as an intermediary provides no additional security gains. It does, however, simplify the transaction complexity at the merchant's site as the merchant-broker relationship will usually be a longer lasting one than one with individual buyers. Therefore, more micropayments can be performed per macropayment relationship.

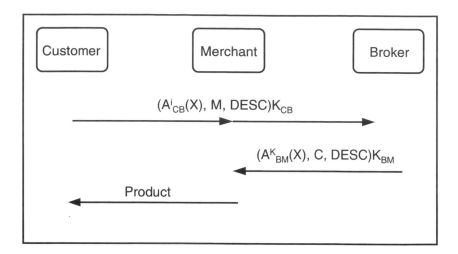

Figure 7.27 Nonrepeated micropayments.

7.4.4 Remarks

The μ-3KP protocol aims to provide all the benefits of a micropayment system with the added security of nonrepudiation of messages between all entities involved in the process. The initial authentication of a customer to a merchant requires a number of message flows, which adds to the overall cost of the transaction. The protocol also requires the establishment of a full certification hierarchy. Compared to other micropayment protocols, the μ-3KP protocol seems to be an expensive option.

7.5 Hash chain trees

A hash chain is linear in form, with each hash value having a single child value derived from it by applying a hash function, until the required chain length is met. More generalized nonlinear data structures may also be derived using hash functions, and used to improve efficiency aspects within a micropayment scheme.

A tree is a data structure with a single root node to which a number of children nodes are attached by connections called *branches*. Each node may in turn be the parent of one or more other child nodes, forming a structure that looks like a branching tree. Nodes which have no children are called the leaves of the tree, while the other nodes are referred to as internal nodes. With a binary tree each internal node has two children. A tree is said to be balanced if all the leaves are at the same depth, or same distance, from the root node. Figure 7.28 shows a tree structure where the tree root is at the top of the figure, and the children nodes are attached below this.

A hash chain tree is a tree structure that is derived using hash functions, and where the nodes are hash values. A hash chain tree may be derived from the root where each node is formed by hashing the parent node value. Different hash functions, one for each branch, can be used to form a number of children from a single parent. Alternatively, the tree may be formed in reverse from the leaves by concatenating the children nodes and hashing the combined value to form each parent node. The hash chain tree generalizes the hash chain, since a hash chain is a tree where each node has only one child.

We now examine two micropayment schemes which use hash chain trees in order to improve payment efficiency. The first, PayTree, derives the tree structure from the leaves. PayTree reduces the number of signatures that must be generated when using hash chains at a number of different merchants. The second scheme is the Unbalanced One-way Binary Tree (UOBT), where the tree is derived from a single root. UOBT reduces the computation that must be performed by the payer.

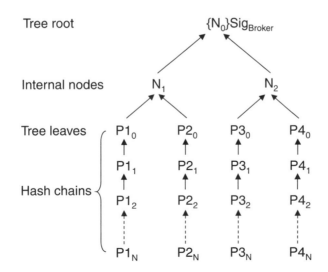

Figure 7.28 PayTree structure with hash chains attached to tree leaves.

7.5.1 PayTree

PayTree [11] is a hash chain tree structure for micropayments proposed by Jutla while working at the IBM T. J. Watson Research Center, and by Yung while working at CertCo. It is based on earlier work by Merkle [10], who used hash chain trees to perform efficient repeated authentication, a technique which became known as the Merkle authentication tree.

One of the key ideas of micropayments is to minimize the use of computationally expensive public-key signatures. PayWord and ikP micropayments showed that each hash chain must be signed to form a commitment before payment can occur. In an environment where payments are made to multiple independent merchants, this can result in a new signature for every merchant visited. PayTree reduces the number of signatures required by allowing multiple hash chains to be signed with a single signature. This is done by linking the chains together through the hash chain tree.

To generate a PayTree the payer creates a specific number of hash chains. Each hash chain will be spent at a different merchant, as with PayWord and iKP micropayments. The final hash value, or anchor, of each separate chain forms a single leaf within the PayTree structure, as shown in Figure 7.28. For example, with the P1 hash chain, the chain is derived from $P1_N$ and the final hash value in the chain, $P1_0$, forms the first leaf of the PayTree. With a binary PayTree the leaves are paired into groups of two, and hashed together to form a parent node. For example, $P1_0$ and $P2_0$ are concatenated and then hashed to form internal node N_1. In turn, the internal nodes are grouped into pairs, joined and hashed. In this way nodes N_1 and N_2 are hashed together to form the PayTree root node N_0. The root of the tree is signed, with an RSA signature, by a broker.

While the user will generate the PayTree nodes, only the root node is revealed to the broker, with whom the user has an account. The secret chain values, later used in payment, never leave the user's machine before they are spent. The broker signature indicates that payment hashes accepted from the PayTree can be redeemed from the broker. By signing a PayTree, the broker extends the user credit, the amount of which could be limited by specifying the maximum value for all chains, as part of the tree signature.

The size of the tree used will be a tradeoff between storage and computation. A larger tree will require extra storage, to store the payment chain roots and some internal nodes, while it will lower the overall computational cost due to a single signature sufficing for a greater number of merchants. A smaller tree will need less storage space, but will contain less hash chains resulting in more signatures since more trees will be needed for the same number of merchants.

When making payments a separate chain, attached to a PayTree leaf, is used at each different merchant as with normal hash chains. For the first payment the payment chain anchor is sent to the merchant, as with a regular chain commitment. However, the PayTree root signature and the parts of the tree which link the leaf through the tree to the tree root must also be sent. Using this, the merchant will verify that the chain anchor forms a leaf of the tree, and that the tree has been signed by the broker. The extra node values that need to be sent in order to show that the leaf belongs to the tree form what is referred to as the *tree authentication path*, and the number of nodes in the path will depend on the tree size. For example, assume that a user wishes to spend the P1 chain from the PayTree shown in Figure 7.28 at a new merchant. The value $P1_0$ is sent, along with $P2_0$, N_2, and the signed N_0 tree root to the merchant. To verify that $P1_0$ belongs to the tree, the vendor concatenates it with $P2_0$ and performs a hash to get N'_1. The vendor then concatenates N'_1 with N_2 and hashes to get N'_0. Finally the vendor verifies that the PayTree signature is a valid broker signature on the derived value N'_0:

$$H(P1_0, P2_0) = N'_1$$

$$H(N'_1, N_2) = N'_0$$

Verify that N'_0 equals N_0 in $\{N_0\}Sig_{Broker}$

If all these conditions are met, the merchant can be assured that the broker has approved the user to spend payment hashes from the P1 chain. Payments are made by releasing hashes from the P1 chain as with other hash chain payment schemes.

When another new vendor is encountered, the new chain P2 will be used. The necessary authentication path and tree signature will be sent to this vendor. In this way, another broker signature on the P2 chain is not needed, as the same original tree signature is enough to show that the broker has approved the chain. The signature is verified without needing to reveal any of the secret values from any of the chains.

While PayTree reduces the computational cost by removing the need for a new signature for each chain, it does increase the communications and storage overheads. The first payment will require extra bandwidth to transmit the authentication path. A tree of depth m requires $m+1$ nodes to authenticate a leaf as part of the signed tree. For example, a balanced binary PayTree with 128 leaves has a depth of seven, and will therefore require eight node values to be sent. Since one of these nodes is the hash chain anchor itself, only seven extra node values must be sent. Using a hash function such as SHA, which produces a 20-byte hash, this will result in an additional 140 bytes to be sent for the first payment. However, the vendor must also store not only the last received hash and the tree signature, but also the authentication path.

The user must also store sufficient information to be able to regenerate the tree. This will require the secret roots of each hash chain. The index of the highest spent value in each chain must also be recorded to allow a user to return to a vendor and resume use of a partially spent chain. In both cases this information would need to be stored by the user anyway if regular broker-signed hash chains were used.

In terms of fraud, since the hash chains are not vendor-specific, double spending of a PayTree is possible with post-fact detection. However, vendors may also collude to double spend or redeem a chain spent at another vendor thereby incriminating an honest user. No extra monetary value can be obtained since the broker will keep track of redeemed chains and will refuse the double redemption. An extension has been proposed to allow the user to dynamically make each chain vendor-specific at the time of purchase, thereby preventing vendor collusion. However, the method used to tag each chain to a specific vendor significantly increases the storage costs, especially for the user.

The contribution of PayTree is that instead of a digital signature generation per vendor, for a new hash chain commitment, the computational cost has been amortized to a single signature for many vendors. This "amortized signature" makes PayTree more suitable for payments to many vendors, a characteristic of the MicroMint scheme which is described in Section 7.6. The saving in computation comes at the cost of increased storage and transmitted data, due to the need to verify the tree authentication path.

7.5.2 Unbalanced One-way Binary Tree (UOBT)

One drawback of PayTree is that the secret roots of each payment chain, from which the chains and the tree itself are derived, must be stored by the user. UOBT [12] is a hash chain tree scheme that overcomes this problem by deriving the tree and all chains from a single-tree root value. The user need only store this single value, from which the entire UOBT can be reconstructed. The UOBT was designed to reduce the computation that must be performed when calculating hash chain values for payment. It is the result of work performed by Yen and Ho at the National Central University in Taiwan and by Huang at ECOM Universal, also in Taiwan.

In essence a UOBT consists of a "backbone" hash chain, derived from the tree root, with further hash chains being derived from each value in the backbone hash chain. Consider the UOBT depicted in Figure 7.29, where hash chains of length 20 are used. $P20_{20}$ is the root of the tree from which the backbone hash chain, with values from $P19_{20}$ to $P2_{20}$ and $P1_{20}$, is derived. Each value in the backbone chain is formed by applying the $h1$ hash function to a parent node to form a child node, connected by a left branch to the tree. Each value in the backbone chain forms a secret root value for another subchain. For example, the value $P2_{20}$ is the root of the P2 chain, which consists of the values $P2_{20}$, $P2_{19}$, and so on until the anchor of that chain, $P2_0$, is reached. Each of these subchains is derived using a different hash function $h2$, in order to be able to derive two different children from a single parent node. Popular hash functions such as SHA and MD5 can be used as the $h1$ and $h2$ hash functions. Rather than use two different hash functions in deriving the UOBT, a single function may be used by applying different prefix data with the value to be hashed when constructing the backbone and subchain parts of the tree.

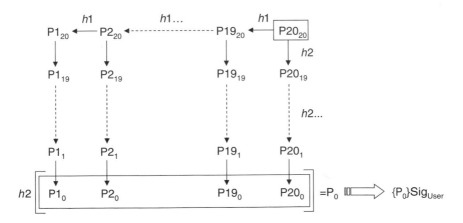

Figure 7.29 Unbalanced one-way binary tree.

With UOBT each subchain forms a series of right branches in the tree, while the backbone chain values continue forming left branches. In Figure 7.29 the logical right branches are depicted as vertical lines while the logical left branches form horizontal lines. Since each value in a UOBT has at most two children nodes, and since each node in a subchain has only one child, the tree structure forms an unbalanced binary tree. It is one-way due to the use of one-way hash functions which allow branches to be traversed in one direction only, given a certain node value.

A payment chain must be signed in order to show that the signing entity is assigning value to hashes in that chain. In the PayTree scheme the tree structure was used to link together multiple payment chains using a single signature. An alternative method of achieving this is to directly link each chain together using a signature on a hash of the concatenated chain anchors:

$$\{h2(P1_0, P2_0, ..., P19_0, P20_0)\}Sig_{User}$$

This is the approach used in UOBT. It has the disadvantage that all the anchors of each chain must be sent to a vendor in order to verify the signature, thereby increasing both communications and storage overheads.

While the multiple payment chains in a PayTree were designed to be spent at many vendors, the UOBT structure is spent entirely at a single vendor. For the first payment the signed chain anchors and the first payment hash, $P1_1$ from the P1 subchain, are sent to the vendor. Since the P1 chain anchor forms part of the UOBT signature, as shown in the equation above, the vendor can be confident that hashes spent from this chain are redeemable at the broker. In order to prevent double spending, a vendor identity could be included with the UOBT signature making the tree specific to that vendor.

Following payments are made by releasing subsequent hashes from the P1 chain. After this hashes are released from the P2 chain. Again, the vendor can check that the P2 chain forms part of the UOBT since the P2 chain anchor is signed as part of the tree signature. Each subchain is spent in turn, with the final payment hash released being the root value of the UOBT tree, in this case $P20_{20}$.

On small devices with limited storage, such as a smart card, all the values of a normal hash chain cannot be stored. Before making a payment, the hash function must be applied repeatedly to the chain root to obtain the next hash value to spend. On average the number of hashes performed for a chain of length n is $(n-1)/2$. Therefore if a user spends a hash chain of length 400, the average computational overhead per payment, excluding the initial signature, will be 199.5 hashes.

By using a UOBT the number of hashes will be reduced, since the user will only need to calculate part of the backbone chain and part of the current subchain being spent. The backbone chain acts as an efficient index to the current subchain, removing the need to recalculate values in other unspent subchains in order to reach the next unspent value. If a UOBT is used with a backbone chain length equal to the length of each subchain, it can be shown that the average computational overhead is only $n^{\frac{1}{2}} - 1$, where n is the total number of values in the UOBT, and $n^{\frac{1}{2}}$ is the square root of n. Using a configuration in which the subchain is a different length than the backbone chain yields a result that is less efficient than this. A UOBT with a backbone chain of length 20, with each subchain also consisting of 20 hash values, will contain a total of 400 spendable hashes, the same as a hash chain of length 400. However, the average payment cost for such a UOBT will only be 19 hashes, compared to 199.5 hashes for a normal chain. The computation per payment for the vendor will remain at one hash as with a normal chain, because the vendor only needs to verify that the current payment hashes to the last received value.

The contribution of UOBT is a computational efficiency improvement for the user for hash chain payments from $O(n)$ to $O(n^{\frac{1}{2}})$. This efficiency gain comes at a cost of increased communication for the first payment, since all subchain anchors must be sent to the vendor to verify the UOBT signature. The vendor must also store the subchain anchors until enough of the UOBT has been spent so that they may be derived from other received payment hashes.

7.6 MicroMint

MicroMint [4] is a second micropayment scheme designed by Ron Rivest and Adi Shamir who also developed the PayWord scheme. It is based on a unique form of identified electronic cash that requires no public-key cryptography. MicroMint coins can be spent efficiently *at any vendor* without the need to contact a bank or broker for verification at the time of purchase.

The security level provided is less than that of PayWord, but allows MicroMint to be more efficient for micropayments made to many different vendors. While some small-scale fraud is possible, large-scale fraud is designed to be computationally difficult.

7.6.1 The MicroMint model

Within the MicroMint system, coins are minted by a broker, who then sells them to users, as shown in Figure 7.30. A broker might maintain user and vendor accounts that can be settled using a macropayment scheme. A user can spend the coins at any vendor. Double spending is possible since no check is performed to see if a coin has already been spent, at the time of purchase. However, a broker records which coins were issued to a user. Double spending will be detected, after the fraud, at the end of the day when vendors redeem spent coins with a broker. Users whose coins are repeatedly double spent will be *blacklisted* and expelled from the system. Fraud prevention is discussed in Section 7.6.8 in more detail.

7.6.2 MicroMint coins

In macropayment electronic cash schemes, such as Ecash and NetCash, an electronic coin is usually digitally signed by the bank to show that it is authentic. However, to sign and verify every coin in this way in a micropayment scheme would be too computationally expensive. Instead, MicroMint adopts a scheme that makes it very computationally difficult

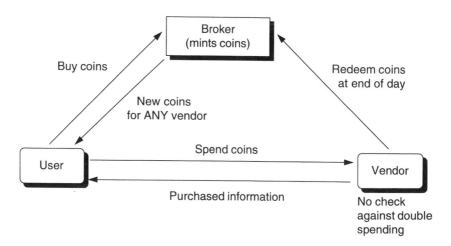

Figure 7.30   Entities within the MicroMint system.

for anyone except the broker to mint valid coins. However, it is quick and efficient for anyone to verify a coin.

A MicroMint coin is a *k-way hash function collision*. A one-way hash function or message digest maps a value x to a value y of specified length, as described in Chapter 3:

$$H(x) = y$$

A hash function collision occurs when two or more different values of x map to the same value of y:

$$H(x_1) = H(x_2) = y$$

It is usually hard to generate two values that map to the same value of y (two-way hash function collision).

A k-way hash function collision occurs when k different input values map to the same output value of y:

$$H(x_1) = H(x_2) = H(x_3) \ldots . = H(x_k) = y$$

If k is set equal to 4 ($k = 4$), a MicroMint coin will be a four-way hash function collision, as shown in Figure 7.31.

Each coin is worth 1 cent, and the coin, C, consists of the four input values that collide to the same value y when the hash function is applied:

$$C = \{x_1, x_2, x_3, x_4\}$$

7.6.3 Verifying a coin
A coin can be easily verified by:

▸ Performing four hashes on each x_i to obtain the same y value:

$$H(x_1) = H(x_2) = H(x_3) = H(x_4) = y$$

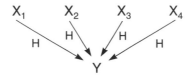

Figure 7.31 A four-way hash function collision.

- Ensuring that each x is different. Otherwise, the x values could be set to be the same value, and they would then obviously map to the same y value.

- Verifying a coin only proves that a coin is authentic. It cannot be used to detect double spending. To do this, the broker needs to maintain a copy of each coin already spent to check against.

7.6.4 Minting coins

To mint a coin involves finding multiple values of x that hash to the same value of y. Within MicroMint, each value of x is restricted to be the same length (m bits). The hash function used will define the length of y (n bits). The hash function will map every x value onto some y value ($H(x) = y$). Since y is n bits long, there are 2^n possible y values.

The procedure can be thought of as throwing a ball (x) into one of 2^n bins (y values). When four balls ($k = 4$) land in the same bin, a valid coin has been minted, as shown in Figure 7.32. This is because four different values of x (four different balls) have hashed to the same y value (landed in the same bin).

Balls are thrown at random and cannot be aimed at a specific bin. That is, we don't know to which y value a certain x value will hash before we perform the hash function. If there are many bins (a large value of n), then many balls will have to be thrown before four will happen to land in the same bin. When this happens, the first valid coin has been minted. The computational costs of minting coins are discussed in Section 7.6.5.

It takes less throws to mint the next coin because many of the bins will already have some balls in them. Thus, it is computationally

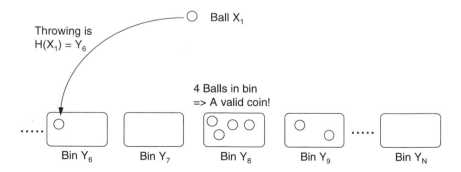

Figure 7.32 MicroMint coin minting analogy.

expensive to mint the first coin, but minting more coins after that becomes progressively cheaper. This makes it difficult for an attacker to economically forge coins. The broker can buy special hardware to perform the hashing, and, by minting a large number of coins, will be able to produce coins cheaply, much like a real world mint.

7.6.5 Computational costs

The number of hashes (throws) needed on average to produce the first coin (k-way collision) is

$$T = 2^{n(k-1)/k}$$

where n is the length in bits of the hash value y. The value k is the number of x values that must hash to the same y value to produce a coin.

Putting $k = 4$ (four balls per coin), $n = 48$ (2^{48} bins), then

$$T = 2^{48(4-1)/4} = 2^{36}$$

To generate the first coin therefore requires 2^{36}, or approximately 69 billion ($6.9 \cdot 10^{10}$), throws.

By throwing c times as many balls as T, there will be on average c^k coins (k-way collisions) produced, so cT hash operations produces c^k coins. Therefore, to generate approximately 1 billion ($1.0 \cdot 10^9$) coins, let $c = 178$, $k = 4$, and

$$c^k = 178^4 = 1.00 \cdot 10^9 \text{ (1 billion coins)}$$

The number of hashes required will be

$$cT = 178 \cdot 2^{36} = 1.22 \cdot 10^{13} \text{ hashes}$$

For a billion coins, this comes out as:

$$\frac{1.22 \cdot 10^{13}}{1.0 \cdot 10^9} = 12{,}232 \text{ hashes per coin}$$

Only 12,232 hashes on average are required to generate a valid coin. This illustrates how after an initial large investment the broker can economically mint coins. The time taken to generate coins will depend on the hash function used, the number of coins required, and other parameters discussed in later sections. The designers suggest some possible current technology that could be used to form the special broker hardware needed in their paper [4].

7.6.6 Multiple coins per bin

The broker should only produce a maximum of one coin from each bin. If more than k balls fall into the same bin, several coins could be made from subsets of the values in the bin. For a bin with five x values, possible coins include:

$$C_1 = \{x_1, x_2, x_3, x_4\}$$

$$C_2 = \{x_1, x_2, x_3, x_5\}$$

$$C_3 = \{x_1, x_2, x_4, x_5\} \text{ and so on.}$$

However, an attacker who obtains any two of these coins can generate the other coins produced from this bin. The value C_3 can be produced knowing C_1 and C_2, for example. For this reason, only one coin should be produced from each bin.

7.6.7 Coin validity criterion

Using special hardware, a broker will be able to calculate a very large number of hashes in a short time period when minting coins. However, to remember the value of each ball and the bin it landed in will require substantial storage space. To reduce this requirement without having to reduce the number of hashes performed, part of the coin's hash value y can be required to match a specific pattern. If there is no match, the coin can be discarded as invalid. When coins are being verified by vendors or users, this additional validity requirement will also have to be checked.

A hash value y is divided into two parts, the high-order bits a and the low-order bits b:

$$y = a, b$$

The broker chooses a value z that is equal in length to a. The choice of z could be random, and should be kept secret while the coins are being minted. For the coin to be valid, a (the high-order bits of y) must match z:

$$a = z \text{ for a good coin.}$$

Those values of x that do not map to a y value that satisfies this criterion can be discarded, and their values need not be stored. By varying the length of a (the part of y that must match a pattern z), the broker can control the number of thrown balls that will have to be remembered and that will become valid coins. However, as the storage requirement decreases, less coins will be produced for the same computational effort. Therefore, more computation will have to be performed to produce an adequate number of coins.

7.6.8 Preventing forgery

A broker takes the following steps to prevent large-scale forging of coins:

- *Special hardware:* The broker invests in hardware that gives a computational advantage over attackers. The hardware might consist of special-purpose chips that can compute hash values quickly. The broker can ensure that good hash values (y) require many computations to discover, by increasing the length of a ($y = a, b$) required to match some pattern z.

- *Short coin validity period:* Coins are given a short lifetime of one month. This gives an attacker less time to try and compute valid coins. Unused coins are returned to the broker at the end of each month.

- *Early minting:* The broker will start minting coins one month ahead of their release. Coins for use in June will be minted during May. The broker has much more time than an attacker to mint coins.

- *Coin validity criterion:* The broker will reveal a new coin validity criterion at the start of the month when the new coins are released. Forged coins cannot be generated until this is known. The coin validity criterion can either be the value z, which the hash values must match, or it could define H to be a new hash function and keep z the same.

- *Different bins (y values):* The broker does not compute all possible coins, only enough for that period's needs. It is likely that some forged coins may map to different bins than those used by the broker. By remembering the bins used by that batch of coins, a broker can detect forged coins coming from other bins. A bit array (an indexed list of 0s or 1s), with one bit (a single 0 or 1) for each bin (y value), can be used for this purpose. To record a bin y as having been used, a 1 is placed at position y in the array. Those bins that were not used will have a 0 at the appropriate index in the array.

- $k > 2$: If coins are two-way collisions, it is easier to compute valid coins. The value of k should be greater than 2. Putting $k = 4$ seems to work well in theory.

- *Extensions:* Further extensions are possible to make forgery more difficult. These are discussed in Section 7.5.11.

7.6.9 A MicroMint purchase

A purchase simply consists of sending the coin(s) along with the purchase request to a vendor, as shown in Figure 7.33. Since each coin is worth 1 cent, the exact amount required can be paid, and no change is necessary.

No encryption is used within MicroMint and the communications channels are not secure. Coins can be stolen and intercepted in any of the steps shown in Figure 7.30. If this is a problem, the user/broker and vendor/broker communications can be encrypted using agreed-upon encryption keys. How this is done is an implementation issue and details are not provided in the MicroMint scheme. The encrypted solution is not suitable for the communications link between a user and an unknown vendor. It would require expensive public-key encryption and certificates to secure the link. Instead, the MicroMint coins can be extended to become user-specific, as described in Section 7.5.11. This makes the spending of stolen coins more difficult.

7.6.10 Double spending

No check is performed at the vendor against double spending. If the coins are valid, the purchased item is returned. However, since MicroMint

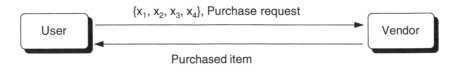

Figure 7.33 A MicroMint purchase.

offers *no anonymity*, the broker will detect doubly spent coins only when the vendor redeems them. Both user fraud and vendor fraud are possible. Vendors might try to redeem coins already spent at other vendors. The broker may not be able to distinguish whether a user or vendor is committing the fraud.

The broker records the user to whom coins are issued and the vendor from whom those coins are received, then keeps track of how many doubly spent coins are connected with each user or vendor. *Repeat offenders* are blacklisted and denied further access to the system. The designers feel that some small-scale double spending is acceptable. They propose that a broker not pay a vendor for an already spent coin. This might discourage cheating vendors from selling already spent coins.

7.6.11 Extensions

A number of extensions and variations are proposed to increase the security and usefulness of the basic MicroMint scheme. These include:

- *Hidden predicates:* By only allowing certain balls (*x* values) to become part of a valid coin, forgery can be further limited. The *x* value must have certain properties initially known only to the broker. These properties, called *hidden predicates*, can be announced by a broker after the coins have been released. Unless all the *x* values that make up a coin obey these hidden predicates, the coin is not valid. Since the broker will know what the hidden predicates are when the coins are minted, it is not necessary to waste time calculating the hash of an *x* value that does not obey them.

  A hidden predicate might require that a low-order bit of *x* be equal to some function of the higher order bits. It should be difficult to work out from examples. A broker could define a series of hidden predicates on a month's coins and reveal a new one each day. Valid coins would obey the required predicate, while many forged coins might not. A vendor can verify that a coin is valid by checking that it obeys the predicate published by the broker.

- *User-specific coins:* Coins can be related to the identity of a user. A vendor can then check to verify that the person spending the coins is the correct user linked to those coins. This ensures that stolen coins cannot be spent by most users.

One way of implementing this is to assign each user to a small user group. The broker will give a user U of that group coins that hash to the group identity:

$$h2 \ (\text{Coin}) = h2(U) = \text{GID}$$

where Coin = (x_1, x_2, x_3, x_4) and $h2$ is a different hash function, than that used for validating coins, which produces a short output, perhaps of length 16 bits. The short $h2$ output represents a user's group identity (GID), and only coins which hash to the correct GID will be given to the user. The group that a user belongs to is derived by applying $h2$ to the user identity U. A vendor can authenticate a user U and check that the GID of the coins matches the user's group.

- *Vendor-specific coins:* To reduce the chance of fraud, coins can be constructed so that they may be redeemed by a small group of vendors only. This may prevent vendors selling already spent coins to other vendors or users. To create vendor-specific coins involves a more complicated method than user-specific coins, where the definition of what forms a coin is made more complex.

- *Coins for multiple months:* It is possible for the broker to mint some of the coins for several different months at the same time. The process can be done at a lower computational cost than minting for one month alone. Since the broker can now effectively mint coins faster, the process can be slowed down by making them harder to mint. This can be done by increasing the length of the hash value y and the validity criterion z.

  To concurrently mint coins for several months, the broker decides on different values of the validity criterion z for upcoming months. A new value of z will be announced each month as new coins are released. When minting, if a ball turns out to be a good ball for one of the months, by meeting the criterion for any month, then it is stored. This will result in coins for several different months being minted simultaneously.

- *Different-valued coins:* Coins could be worth different values, according to predicates on the x values. These predicates might be announced at the start of the month and could be verified by anyone.

Unlike some of the other micropayment schemes examined, MicroMint is optimal for small payments at many different vendors. It proposes a unique form of identified electronic cash suitable for micropayments.

Coins are generated using hash function collisions and no public-key cryptography is required. Since each MicroMint coin must be stored, the storage requirements at all parties will be greater than other micropayment schemes, which may be restrictive if a smart card is used. In addition, if a number of coins need to be sent to pay for a specific amount, the communications bandwidth used will be greater than other schemes where only a single token, such as a hash chain value, need be sent regardless of the purchase amount. Finally, as with some of the other credit-based micropayment schemes examined, double spending is possible with post-fact detection.

7.7 Probability-based micropayments

In the previous micropayment schemes each and every payment is processed by the vendor and later verified and redeemed at a broker or bank. To minimize the number of micropayment transactions that must be performed, the probability theory can be applied so that there is a specified likelihood or chance that the payment will be performed. The value of the transaction is equal to the probability of making an actual payment multiplied by the value of that actual payment:

Transaction_value = Probability * Payment_amount

For example, instead of making 1,000 micropayments each worth 1 cent, one might make a $10 payment with a 1/1,000 probability. Most of the time no payment will be made, but approximately every 1,000 transactions, a $10 payment will occur giving an average cost of 1 cent. Over time each party will get approximately the correct amount.

In such a probabilistic payment scheme there is a known probability, corresponding to the transaction value, that the payment will actually be made. The scheme must provide a mechanism for fairly deciding the outcome of a random event with this known probability. In the first probabilistic payment scheme that we examine a coin flip, performed over the network, is used to decide whether payment should be made. The second scheme that is described proposes the use of electronic lottery tickets, each with a specific probability of being a winning ticket and a stated amount to be paid if the ticket wins. Probability-based micropayments eliminate the cost of making the actual micropayment for most transactions, but add the overhead of fairly predicting a random event with known probability.

7.7.1 Bets using coin flips

Wheeler, while working at the University of Cambridge in the United Kingdom, proposed a probabilistic micropayment scheme [13] in which for each transaction the payer makes a bet with the payee. If the payee wins the bet, then an actual micropayment is made to the payee by the payer; otherwise, no payment is made. The transaction value is set by fixing the probability of the payee winning the bet to a specific value, using the earlier equation. The scheme uses a series of on-line coin flips [14], performed between the payer and payee, to provide the betting mechanism with known probability.

With a normal coin flip there is a 50% probability of guessing the correct outcome, heads or tails. Such a coin flip can be performed over a network between a user and a vendor using the protocol shown in Figure 7.34. The vendor chooses a random number R, of which the least significant bit, a one or a zero, represents the coin-flip outcome. It is now up to the user to try and guess the outcome chosen by the vendor. There is a 50% chance that the user will guess the same one-bit value, in which case the user wins the coin flip, and a 50% chance that the user will guess

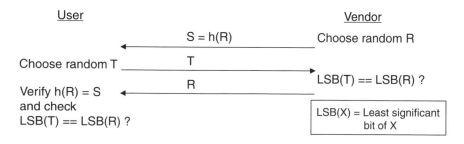

Figure 7.34 On-line coin flip.

incorrectly. The user creates a random number T, of which the least significant bit represents the user's guess.

However, the vendor cannot just send R to the user, who will then reply with T, because this allows the user to cheat by setting T to the correct winning value. The same problem is present if the user sends his or her guess first and the vendor responds. Instead, the vendor commits to the value R by blinding it using a one-way hash function to produce the value S. The hash value $S = h(R)$ is sent to the user, who replies with his or her random guess T, as shown in Figure 7.34. The one-way hash function prevents the vendor changing the value R after he or she has chosen it, since a changed value will not hash to the correct value S. The vendor then reveals R, by sending it to the user who verifies that it was committed to earlier by hashing it. The user wins the coin flip if the least significant bit of T equals the least significant bit of R, which will occur with 50% probability.

To yield a bet with a winning probability of 50%, a single coin flip is used, where only the least significant bits of each party's guesses are compared. To generate bets with different probabilities, multiple coin flips can be used at once, by comparing a number of bits equal to the desired number of coin flips. A number of coin-flip outcomes can be used to obtain a random number within a given range. For example, the outcome of four coin flips can be used to obtain a number between 0 and 15, by assigning a user win to be 1 and a user loss to be 0 in the appropriate four-bit positions. This can be extended with the appropriate number of coin flips to randomly decide the outcome of any probability. For example, multiple coin flips can therefore be used to decide an outcome with probability 17/100, which would represent a 17-cent purchase price with a $1 coin. When required, actual payment can be made using one of the earlier micropayment protocols.

While the protocol requires less actual payments, the communications cost is increased as three messages are sent for each user-vendor transaction, rather than a single message with hash chains. Another problem is that the vendor can increase his or her probability of success by aborting the protocol after he or she discovers an unfavorable outcome in step two. By forcing another new coin flip, the overall probabilities will be changed. Finally, there is no way to prove to a third party that the coin flip took place. A user could use this to deny that he or she owes payment to the vendor. While digital signatures could be used to sign the coin-flip messages, a digital signature per transaction is too inefficient for a micropayment scheme. Rivest overcomes this denial problem using signed lottery tickets based on hash chains, which we now describe in Section 7.7.2.

7.7.2 Hash chain lottery tickets

Rivest proposed the use of electronic lottery tickets as micropayments [15]. The payment is probabilistic since each ticket has a known probability of winning a specified amount. The user will only make an actual payment for winning tickets. As with coin flips, the overhead of processing every micropayment at the bank is reduced to only processing winning payments. The basic idea is to issue a user-signed ticket containing a value that will be used to determine if it is a winning ticket:

$$\{win\_indicator, win\_value\}Sig_{User}$$

The *win_value* is the value that the payee will receive if the payee is given a winning ticket. However, the ticket value for a transaction will be the win_value multiplied by the probability of the ticket winning, as in the earlier equation, since the ticket only wins with fixed probability.

Rivest suggests two types of indicators to decide a winning ticket. With an *external indicator* the ticket *win_indicator* is compared with independently chosen numbers, such as those from a national lottery. The disadvantages here are that neither party knows the micropayment outcome until the external event occurs and the ticket must be held by the vendor until that time.

With an *internal indicator* the guesses from an on-line coin flip (S, T in Figure 7.34) are included as the win_indicator. The vendor can immediately reveal the ticket outcome by revealing the unblinded coin-flip value R. In essence, a digital signature has been applied to step two of the coin-flip protocol so that the user cannot later deny it.

To avoid using a digital signature for every transaction, a single signature can be used to sign a combined sequence of electronic lottery tickets at once. The user and vendor independently generate a hash chain each, labeled as the U and V chains, respectively, as shown in Figure 7.35. The vendor sends the anchor of his chain to the user and both chain anchors, U_0 and V_0, are included in the signed-ticket sequence as shown. The value of a winning ticket, win_value, is also included. Win_value is expressed as a positive integer value, representing the number of cents that a winning ticket is worth.

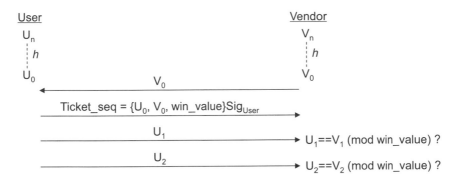

Figure 7.35 Probabilistic payment using hash chain lottery tickets.

As with PayWord, described in Section 7.3, a single hash value is released by the user for each micropayment. Each matching pair of hash chain values, U_x and V_x, form a single lottery ticket within the sequence of tickets. However, the ticket only wins if:

$$U_x \bmod \text{win\_value} == V_x \bmod \text{win\_value}$$

That is, the U_x value modulus the win_value is compared to the V_x value modulus the win_value, to see if they are equal. The probability of a single pair of hashes winning is therefore the inverse of the positive integer win_value (1/win_value). A ticket with a win_value of 1,000 ($10) can be used to make the equivalent of a 1-cent payment, with each hash pair having a 1/1,000 chance of winning.

Effectively the corresponding hash value pairs are acting as blinded coin flips, with the user revealing her coin guess as payment. Hence U_x and V_x correspond to the values T and R, respectively, in the coin-flip protocol. Neither party can change the guess values due to the one-way chain. The results of the current coin flip reveal nothing about the outcome of the next transaction with the next values further up the chain.

Each ticket, or matching pair of hash values, is independent and a ticket sequence may contain any number of winning tickets, although the probability of this will depend on the win_value. The computational cost per payment is similar to PayWord, except for the overhead of the additional vendor chain. However, the bank only needs to process spent chains that contain at least one winning ticket.

Yen and Ku [16] argue that the additional vendor chain adds too much extra computational overhead at the vendor. They envisage the vendor as only storing the root V_n of the vendor chain, and having to perform $(n - x)$ hashes to obtain V_x from the base V_n for each transaction. This results in an extra $(n - 1)/2$ hashes on average per transaction, in addition to verifying the user hash. However, in an efficient implementation the entire chain, or certain key hash values in it, may be cached in memory to avoid such repeated hashing.

To reduce the vendor computation, Yen and Ku greatly decrease the length of the vendor chain so that it is much shorter than the corresponding user chain. Each different user hash U_x in each different payment is now compared to the same vendor hash V_y until a win occurs. The user cannot cheat by foreseeing future outcomes because the value of V_y is not released by the vendor until a win occurs. After a win the vendor uses the next hash preimage, $V_{y + 1}$, until the next win occurs. This saves the vendor from performing unnecessary hashing, even in an efficient application.

Overall, the efficiency of probabilistic payments is similar to other micropayment schemes for both the user and vendor. Due to the probabilities there will be a variability of the amount paid, where an unlucky user will end up paying more than expected. This gambling aspect may reduce user acceptance. The single advantage is that the bank needs to process less micropayments, only the winning ones, although the exact saving will depend on the implementation. This will also add more anonymity as the bank will not see every transaction. However, the saving of some processing, already performed off-line, is not a critical advantage in a micropayment scheme.

7.8 Jalda

Rather than make micropayments by directly passing payment tokens from the customer to the vendor, an alternative approach is to authorize the vendor to incrementally charge the customer's account at a broker, up to a specified maximum amount. The vendor calculates charges in real time and sends a simple charge request, effectively a micropayment request, to the broker. Jalda [17, 18] is an account-based payment system that uses this idea to allow vendors to repeatedly charge customers small amounts as services are consumed. The system was developed by EHPT, a software company headquartered in Sweden, owned jointly by Ericsson (60%) and Hewlett-Packard (40%). EHPT specializes in network billing and payment software for telecommunications network operators, Internet service providers, and financial institutions.

Within the Jalda system, both the customer and vendor must have an account at the same broker, referred to as a payment provider (PP). The user provides the vendor with authorization to make charges by signing a digital contract at the start of a payment session. Given a valid contract, the PP allows the vendor to accept micropayments, by submitting charge requests. At the end of a session, the total value of the charge requests is transferred from the customer's account to the vendor's account. Jalda has similarities with the account transfer systems described in Chapter 5, in that value is moved from one account to another at a central broker. However, unlike these schemes, Jalda is geared specifically toward making ongoing small payments to commercial vendors.

The EHPT vision is that Jalda can be used to allow micropayments from any fixed or mobile Internet access device. For example, the payment provider might be the customer's mobile network operator. Envisioned applications include not only payment for Web services, but also metered payments for IP telephony, streaming video and music, multiplayer on-line games, and payments to other physical devices such as parking meters or vending machines. The Jalda vendor functionality may also be integrated with applications that run locally on a user's PC, so that the software can generate its own charge requests, which are sent to the PP as it is used.

Within the scheme both customers and vendors are issued X.509 public-key certificates by their payment provider, who acts as the CA. All communications with the PP are performed using SSL, with each entity generating digital signatures for authentication. If a credit card is used to fund the customer account at the PP, the credit card payment is digitally signed by the customer, providing a level of nonrepudiation not present with a normal card payment made over SSL. Other options to fund the customer's account include bank account transfers and prepaid cards.

The Jalda payment scheme is illustrated in Figure 7.36. After selecting a product at a vendor Web site, a digital contract is sent by that vendor to the customer over SSL. The contract contains a brief description of the product, the pricing details and conditions, a timestamp, and a unique transaction identifier. It is presented to the customer for

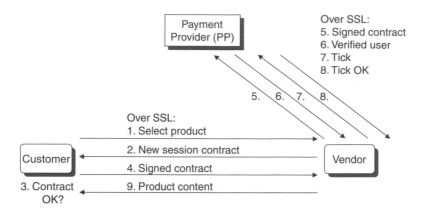

Figure 7.36 Jalda contract signing and payment ticks.

agreement, after which it is digitally signed with the customer's private key before being sent back to the vendor over SSL. The contract proves that the customer agreed to allow the vendor to incrementally charge the user for the specified product, up to the specified maximum amount. The signed contract has similar functionality to an electronic check in that it authorizes the PP to pay the vendor a specified amount from the customer's account. However, the vendor must actually submit the micro-payment charge requests, which should only be done as the customer is provided with the paid-for service, before any money can be debited from the customer's account.

The vendor establishes another SSL connection, this time with the payment provider, and mutual authentication takes place. The customer-signed contract is passed to the PP who verifies it and checks that sufficient funds remain in the customer's account. Accounts may be prepaid or credit based, depending on the PP's policy. The PP sends a response to the vendor, who may start charging the customer for content or service.

As services are used, the vendor will send multiple charge requests, referred to as ticks, to the PP. The same SSL session is maintained, so that the PP can be assured that the ticks are really originating from the vendor. As described in Chapter 4, efficient symmetric keys are used to encrypt messages in an SSL dialogue, after the initial signatures during connection setup. In this case Triple DES, described in Chapter 3, is used as the symmetric algorithm. A tick need only contain the appropriate transaction identifier, as the value of each tick and the user identity may be obtained from the contract using this. The payment provider verifies that the customer has enough funds to pay for the tick, before sending back an acknowledgment to the vendor.

The vendor must be trusted to charge the user appropriately, although fraudulent charging will be limited to the amount specified in the initial contract. This is similar to traditional telecommunications billing where the network operator is trusted to generate accurate charges. Ongoing charging will result in steps 7, 8, and 9 in Figure 7.36 being repeated multiple times. Jalda is on-line, since every tick payment is cleared with the PP, by the vendor, at the time of purchase. This on-line connection will add an additional communications overhead over the other off-line micropayment schemes examined earlier.

When the vendor indicates that user purchasing is complete, the PP will remove the total amount due from the customer's account, deduct a fee, and deposit the remaining amount into the vendor's account. Each product that the vendor is selling must be registered beforehand, with an identifier, description, and price per tick, for that product at the PP. For each product it can also be specified whether that item may be purchased using credit or not, in order to limit the vendor's risk. If necessary a vendor can reverse a transaction at the PP, using the unique transaction identifier. This is termed a repurchase and any amount up to the total transaction value may be refunded.

A number of Jalda implementations already exist, and as the system becomes more widespread, the number of products supporting it is likely to greatly increase. The EHPT Safetrader product provides a Jalda payment provider server, and a set of Jalda application programming interfaces (APIs) that are used by vendors to communicate with this server. The Jalda API module, which is available as freeware, must be integrated with any service for which the vendor wishes to charge. In order to charge for applications that run locally on the customer's PC, the API is integrated into the local software, and the normal vendor-to-PP tick dialogue now takes place between the customer and the PP. However, since the functionality is provided purely in software, it may be possible to remove the payment modules, in the same way that copy protection is removed from commercial software by software pirates. Other Jalda implementations are available in Telia's PayIT and Ericcson's Mobile e-Pay products.

It is planned to add roaming support to Jalda, so that a customer with an account at one PP can buy from a vendor connected to a different PP.

This will be done by establishing roaming agreements between payment providers, in much the same way that roaming agreements are made between mobile network operators to allow mobile users to avail of the services of foreign networks that they roam into. The customer's home PP will need to be contacted on-line, to verify the customer-signed contract before allowing charging to begin.

Jalda provides an alternative approach to micropayments, where vendors send incremental charge requests to a broker with whom both parties hold an account. However, unlike other micropayment schemes, the vendor must be trusted to generate fair-charge requests. The user signatures prove their presence at the start of the session, but not the amount spent. Vendor fraud is limited by the maximum amount present in the contract, and users are not likely to return to vendors with whom they have encountered charging anomalies. The on-line connection for every payment adds the same communications overhead as a traditional macropayment system, but the computation has been greatly reduced by only using lightweight symmetric cryptography for each tick. By requiring registration of every vendor product at the payment provider, use of dynamic pricing is restricted. The PP will also hold a complete record of every item purchased by each user. Overall, the Jalda PP has far more control over the system than other micropayment schemes, a property that is likely to be desirable to network operators wishing to capture a share of every transaction.

7.9   NewGenPay/IBM Micropayments

While Jalda is an on-line payment scheme, in that charging messages are sent to the PP during each purchase, this communications overhead can be removed by allowing the vendor to verify payment off-line, without needing to contact any other party. However, a problem with such off-line payments, which was present in credit-based schemes such as Pay-Word and *i*KP micropayments, is that a rogue user may be able to spend unlimited amounts at every vendor until eventually blacklisted by the broker. A solution which limits the users' overspending ability is for the broker to issue each user a daily spending certificate, which specifies the maximum amount that can be spent at any one vendor. The spending certificate assures the vendor that the user is in good standing with the broker and that the vendor may accept payment orders signed by this user, up to the specified amount.

This approach, utilizing a daily spending certificate, is used in the Mini-Pay [19] system, which later became known as IBM Micropayments, developed at the IBM Research Labs at Haifa, Israel. In early 2001 the research and development team for the original IBM Micropayments project formed NewGenPay [20], an independent company based in Tel Aviv, Israel, to develop and market the payment software. IBM retains a shareholder's interest in NewGenPay and operates a close business partnership with the company.

We now examine the original Mini-Pay protocol, which forms the core of NewGenPay's payment software. As with Jalda, users and vendors have accounts at a broker or PP. Each entity is issued with public-key certificates by the user's provider. However, all parties need not share accounts at the same PP, as a clearing mechanism between PP servers is provided. This allows a user to make payments to any vendor whose payment provider is connected to the clearing network.

Figure 7.37 shows the steps involved in the Mini-Pay protocol. Each day the user is issued with a daily spending certificate, signed by the PP. The certificate can be obtained automatically when the user wallet software is started, or on-demand when the first purchase of the day is made. It specifies the spending limit for the user at any vendor, and will depend on the user's credit and account value at the PP.

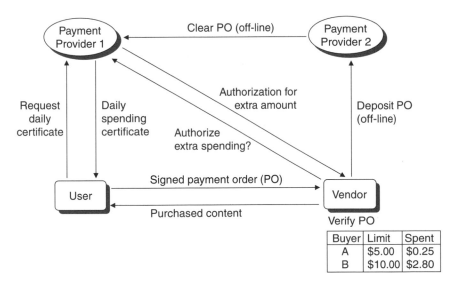

Figure 7.37 Payment in the NewGenPay micropayment (Mini-Pay) scheme.

Within the certificate the user is identified by his or her account number at the PP, and a timestamp indicates the start of the 24-hour period during which the certificate is valid. In essence, the short-lived spending certificate is a form of attribute certificate, discussed in Chapter 3, where the attribute is permission to spend up to the specified amount. At the same time as the spending certificate is received, the PP also informs the user of his or her account balance, and the maximum upper-spending limit extended to that account, that is, the amount that can be spent in total by the user at all vendors that day:

$$\text{daily\_cert\_response} = \{\text{balance, upper\_limit, salt, daily\_spend\_cert}\}$$

$$\text{daily\_spend\_cert} = \{\text{user\_account\_ID, spend\_limit, timestamp,}$$
$$\text{H(balance, upper\_limit, salt)}\}\text{Sig}_{\text{PP}}$$

The Mini-Pay software wallet attempts to prevent the user from spending more than the upper limit amount, although such software cannot provide the same security guarantees as a tamper-resistant device. Since the user needs to be assured that the balance and upper_limit values originate from the PP, they are hashed and signed by the PP, as part of the spending certificate. The hash function blinds these values so that they are not visible to the vendor, unless the user decides to reveal them. The salt is a random value, which extends the length of the data being hashed, so that it is too long for a dictionary attack, where guesses are made, at the balance and upper_limit, to be feasible.

Each vendor with whom the user makes a purchase will verify the spending certificate off-line, without contacting any PP. As purchases are made, the vendor will keep track of how much the user has spent, and provided the spending limit is not exceeded, purchases will be accepted with off-line verification. Each Mini-Pay payment is a user-signed payment order specifying the purchase amount, effectively an electronic check, which is verified locally by the vendor:

$$\text{payment} = \{\text{daily\_spend\_cert, pay\_order}\}$$

$$\text{pay\_order} = \{\text{order\_desc, amount, day\_total, user\_account\_ID,}$$
$$\text{vendor\_account\_ID, timestamp}\}\text{Sig}_{\text{User}}$$

The *day_total* is the total amount spent at the vendor so far that day, and includes the current purchase. As with an electronic check, account identifiers for both the user and vendor, and the current date, are included. For Web applications, the order description includes the purchased Web address, or URL. To allow pricing of Web hyperlinks, the system embeds static pricing information on Web pages, using a micropayment markup language [21] designed by the World Wide Web Consortium (W3C), to which IBM contributed.

If the spending limit is reached at a particular vendor, and the user attempts a further purchase, an on-line authorization is performed with the user's PP, as shown in Figure 7.37. The appropriate PP is identified from the spending certificate, sent during the purchase. The vendor forwards the current payment order to the PP, which will respond with a signed authorization to allow further spending up to a newly specified amount, or a refusal to allow extra spending. While this prevents unlimited overspending, assuming the software spending restrictions can be bypassed, the user can spend the maximum amount at every vendor within the system. If this becomes problematic, any overspending can be prevented by requiring that each user payment order is first signed on-line by the user's PP, thereby producing a certified electronic check. This is also the method suggested for mobile payments within the system, where a signature cannot be produced efficiently by the mobile device. The disadvantage of such an approach is that the PP must be on-line for every single purchase, which will be a bottleneck for frequent micropayments.

In either scenario, vendors deposit signed batches of payment orders to their respective PPs at the end of the day, and these are cleared with the user's PP, through a hierarchy of connected PPs, termed a payments web. A PP need only make a connection agreement with one other PP in order to obtain access to the clearing network, and hence allow their customers to accept payments from parties dealing with any other connected PP.

At the time of this writing, a demonstration payment provider with whom an account, with virtual money, can be opened, is administered by NewGenPay. Payments can be made for several example products, and a software wallet can be downloaded to review and manage purchases, although payments can be effected from a normal Web browser. A demonstration payment provider server for Windows is also freely available.

NewGenPay micropayments, using the Mini-Pay technology, remove the need for an on-line connection to a payment provider during each purchase. However, this can allow user overspending with post-fact detection, although this is limited to a preset amount at each vendor, through use of the spending certificate. The payment overhead is a single user signature and off-line vendor verification. Unlike Jalda, the user signature will give nondeniable proof of agreement to pay the specified amount. However, Table 7.4 showed that generating, and verifying, a public-key signature requires several orders of magnitude more computation than symmetric encryption or hashing. A user signature for every single payment will not only add a large computational overhead for frequent micropayments, but also implies the existence of a global certificate hierarchy, with its own scalability issues.

7.10 Banner advertising as a form of micropayment

In the mid-1990s, as the mass-Internet phenomenon began to take off, some of the most popular sites were those that helped users find information on the Web. These ranged from categorized collections of links to very sophisticated search engines. As these nascent Internet portal sites matured, they needed to find some way to finance their activities and to profit from the service they offered. Had a micropayment method been very widely available at this time it could have filled this gap. Instead, the void was filled by advertising.

Initially, this took the form of static advertisements and page sponsorships modeled on conventional media, but this took no advantage of the unique way in which the Web works, since each time a Web page is fetched, the possibility exists to "serve up" a different advertisement. Any extra information on the users (e.g., what country they are in, what other sites they have visited recently, or what keywords they are searching for) helps to build a profile of the user and can be used to dynamically choose which advertisement to show on the Web page that is presented. Over the years, the industry has standardized a number of standard sizes of ad banners (e.g., 468 × 60 pixels) that fit easily at the top, bottom, or along the side of a Web page. These standard sizes together with information about when and where they appear make up the "currency" of banner advertising.

Customers—those who request the advertisement to be placed—are charged in a number of ways. The simplest way is to count the number of times a banner ad is put in front of a Web user. This is called a *page impression* and is usually priced per-thousand impressions, abbreviated CPM (cost per M—1,000 in roman numerals). Costs can range from $0.50 up to around $40 for 1,000 impressions depending on the level of targeting of where the ads are placed and also on a parameter called the click-thru rate (CTR). This figure is usually given as an estimate and measures how many people who see the ad will click on it to find out more. Another way of charging is to only count the click-thrus. The so-called cost-per-click (CPC) is much higher, usually somewhere between $0.10 and $1.

In a little over five years, Internet advertising grew [22] to become a very large industry with revenues in 1999 of over $4 billion—opinions differ as to whether this growth can be sustained into the future. The flow of money is from the companies that wish to place advertisements through a raft of specialist companies that provide the ad-server infrastructure, ad-placement services, Internet portal operators, and ultimately to the creators of interesting Internet content.

Although it may seem a little contrived to look at Internet advertising as a micropayment method, it has nevertheless become the default way in which creators of Internet content can "sell" their low-value goods to consumers. A single delivery of a banner ad can be viewed as a payment of $0.04 (based on the CPM model at a rate of $40 CPM) to the creator of the Web page on which it is placed. Higher value payments can be made using the CPC method.

7.11 Micropayments summary and analysis

The concept of a micropayment emerged in 1995, and very quickly a diverse range of schemes were introduced. Some of these, such as Millicent, have been designed specifically to cater for the new form of payment, while others, such as $\mu-i$KP, have been designed as an add-on to an existing macropayment scheme. As we have seen, these make use of some novel cryptographic techniques, including the use of fast message digest algorithms to authenticate a message and the use of economies of scale in coin minting.

A key feature of micropayments is to minimize the communications necessary during a transaction and to reduce the number of computation-intensive public-key operations. Millicent uses no public-key cryptography and is optimized for repeated micropayments to the same vendor. Its distributed approach allows a payment to be validated, and double spending prevented, without the overhead of contacting a third centralized party on-line during a purchase. With payments as low as one-tenth of a cent being feasible, it appears to be one of the best candidates for general-purpose micropayments. Its only drawback is that seamless successive payments to multiple vendors are hindered by having to contact a broker for every new party encountered.

SubScrip is similarly optimized for repeated micropayments to the same vendor. However, use of a macropayment to set up a temporary account at a vendor will force the user to spend an adequate amount at that vendor to justify this overhead. It is more suited to replacing short-term subscription services or making micropayments to a regularly visited vendor.

PayWord improves on Millicent and SubScrip by removing the need to contact a third party when making a payment to a new vendor. The need to return some form of change, as with the Millicent and SubScrip schemes, is also eliminated. However, PayWord is a credit-based scheme where a user's account is not debited until some time after a purchase. This provides more opportunity for fraud since a large number of purchases can be made against an account with insufficient funds. The use of user certificates with public-key operations also adds some computational overhead.

The iKP micropayment scheme is unique in that it offers two different solutions: one for repeated payments with the same vendor, and the other for single payments to different vendors. However, the requirement of a full certification hierarchy and several message flows for a transaction make it less efficient than other schemes.

Hash chain trees generalize the hash chain structure of PayWord and iKP micropayments. The tree structure improves computational efficiency, but at the cost of increasing storage and communications overhead. PayTree reduced the signature required per vendor with hash chains, to a single signature for a large number of vendors, making the scheme more suitable for payments to multiple vendors. UOBT reduced the average computation performed by the user when deriving the next payment hash from the hash chain root, and would be beneficial when generating hash payments on smart cards.

MicroMint uses a new form of identified electronic cash to provide a system optimized for micropayments to many different vendors. While it is the most efficient scheme for making these unrelated payments, small-scale fraud is easily possible. Double spending is not prevented, although it will be detected after the fact. In addition, huge computational capabilities are required by the broker to mint coins.

Probability-based micropayments use the novel idea of replacing every micropayment with a fixed chance of making an actual payment. On-line coin flips and hash chain lottery tickets were examined as two methods to implement such probabilistic payments. However, the costs, in terms of computation, communication, and storage, were similar to hash chain micropayments. Therefore, the only advantage of these schemes is that the broker need only process a fraction of the original number of payments, those which are made when the random event outcome favors the vendor.

Jalda provides an on-line charging mechanism for small payment amounts, where a central payment provider maintains tight control over spending. This approach is similar to telecommunications billing, a fact which is not surprising since Ericsson, a large telecommunications supplier, is one of the main contributors. At the time of this writing, Jalda was being deployed in a number of applications around the world, and is likely to have a sizable impact due to the sheer market presence of its backers, Ericsson and Hewlett-Packard.

NewGenPay micropayments arose from the IBM Mini-Pay scheme, where a spending certificate is employed to limit user overspending. While the scheme is off-line, by using a signature for every purchase, it is much more computationally heavyweight compared to any of the other micropayment schemes examined.

Despite all the technical innovations of the above schemes, the most successfully deployed method of allowing small payments over the Internet to date has been through the use of banner advertising, a trend which is likely to continue.

Of the actual micropayment schemes described, Millicent and Jalda are the only systems deployed with real currency, at the time of this writing. User acceptance and uptake of such micropayment systems has been slow, perhaps due to the lack of worthwhile content that is not already freely available in some form elsewhere on the Internet. Similarly merchants have been reluctant to invest heavily in providing quality content until there is a large enough user base to support it. Until this "chicken-and-egg" problem is overcome, and critical mass has been reached in at least one system, micropayments are likely to remain a fringe technology.

Technically, the payment scalability and security problems have been solved. What is now required is a popular-content industry, supported by large technology providers, to rally behind selling content on-line. As an example, the music industry could distribute individual songs, perhaps through an application such as Napster, in return for micropayments, thereby providing the catalyst necessary to spark critical mass. Widespread use of mobile devices may also increase user demand for making small payments, a topic examined in the next chapter. Until such time as critical mass is reached, the Internet advertising revenue model will remain as the dominant method of effectively receiving small payments from each user.

References

[1]   Glassman, S., et al., "The Millicent Protocol for Inexpensive Electronic Commerce," *Proc. 4th Int. World Wide Web Conference*, Boston, MA, December 11–14, 1995, pp. 603–618, http://www.millicent.com/.

[2]   Manasse, M., "The Millicent Protocols for Electronic Commerce," *Proc. 1st USENIX Workshop on Electronic Commerce*, New York, July 11–12, 1995, http://www.millicent.com/.

[3]   Furche, A., and G. Wrightson, "SubScrip—An Efficient Protocol for Pay-Per-View Payments on the Internet," *Proc. 5th Int. Conference on Computer Communications and Networks (ICCCN '96)*, Rockville, MD, October 16–19, 1996, http://citeseer.nj.nec.com/.

[4]   Rivest, R., and A. Shamir, "PayWord and MicroMint: Two Simple Micro-payment Schemes," *Proc. 4th Security Protocols International Workshop (Security Protocols)*, Lecture Notes in Computer Science, Vol. 1189, Berlin: Springer-Verlag, 1996, pp. 69–87.

[5]   Dai W., "Crypto++: A C++ Class Library of Cryptographic Primitives," Version 4.1, January 2001, ftp://ftp.funet.fi/pub/crypt/cryptography/libs/.

[6]   Bellare, M., et al., "*i*KP—A Family of Secure Electronic Payment Protocols," *Proc. 1st USENIX Workshop on Electronic Commerce*, New York, July 11–12, 1995, pp. 89–106, http://www.zurich.ibm.com/csc/infosec/publications.html.

[7] Bellare, M., et al., "Design, Implementation, and Deployment of the *i*KP Secure Electronic Payment System," *IEEE Journal on Selected Areas in Communications*, Vol. 18, No. 4, April 2000, pp. 611–627.

[8] Hauser, R., M. Steiner, and M. Waidner, "Micro-Payments Based on *i*KP," *Proc. 14th Worldwide Congress on Computer and Communications Security Protection*, Paris, 1996, pp. 67–82.

[9] Lamport, L., "Password Authentication with Insecure Communications," *Communications of the ACM*, Vol. 4, No. 11, November 1981, pp. 770–772.

[10] Merkel, R., "A Certified Digital Signature," *Advances in Cryptology—CRYPTO '89 Proc.*, Lecture Notes in Computer Science, Vol. 435, Berlin: Springer-Verlag, 1990, pp. 218–238.

[11] Jutla, C., and M. Yung, "PayTree: Amortized-Signature for Flexible Micropayments," *Proc. 2nd USENIX Workshop on Electronic Commerce*, Oakland, CA, November 1996, pp. 213–221.

[12] Yen, S., L. Ho, and C. Huang. "Internet Micropayment Based on Unbalanced One-Way Binary Tree," *Proc. International Workshop on Cryptographic Techniques and E-Commerce (CrypTEC '99)*, Hong Kong, July 1999, pp. 155–162.

[13] Wheeler, D., "Transactions Using Bets," *Proc. 4th Security Protocols International Workshop (Security Protocols)*, Lecture Notes in Computer Science, Vol. 1189, Berlin: Springer-Verlag, 1996, pp. 89–92.

[14] Blum, M., "Coin Flipping by Telephone: A Protocol for Solving Impossible Problems," *Advances in Cryptology: A Report on CRYPTO '81*, ECE Report 82-04, Dept. of Electrical and Computer Engineering, U.C. Santa Barbara, CA, 1982, pp. 11–15.

[15] Rivest, R., "Electronic Lottery Tickets as Micropayments," *Proc. Financial Cryptography '97*, Lecture Notes in Computer Science, Vol. 1318, Berlin: Springer-Verlag, 1997, pp. 307–314.

[16] Yen, S., and P. Ku, "Improved Micro-Payment System," *Proc. 8th National Conference on Information Security*, Taiwan, May 1998.

[17] EHPT, "A Quick Look at Payments on the Internet," EHPT White Paper, January 2000, http://www.jalda.com/.

[18] Bogestam, K., "Paying Your Way in the Mobile World," *Telecommunications International*, Vol. 34, No. 1, January 2000, pp. 57–58.

[19] Herzberg, A., and H. Yochai, "Mini-Pay: Charging Per Click on the Web," *Proc. 6th International World Wide Web Conference*, Santa Clara, CA, April 1997.

[20] Herzber, A., "NewGenPay Vision: New Generation of Payments,"
      NewGenPay presentation, January 2001, http://www.newgenpay.com/.

[21] World Wide Web Consortium (W3C), "Common Markup for
      Micropayment Per-Fee-Links," W3C Working Draft, Massachusetts
      Institute of Technology, Cambridge, MA, August 1999,
      http://www.w3.org/.

[22] The Internet Advertising Bureau, IAB Internet Advertising Revenue
      Report, 1999 Third-Quarter Results, April 1999, http://www.iab.net/.

CHAPTER

8

Mobile commerce

Trailing slightly behind the mass-Internet revolution came the mobile phone revolution. What had been a very expensive means of communication reserved for wealthy businesspeople became an affordable instrument that is now considered indispensable for a large portion of the population of the developed world. This mass adoption of the mobile phone was led by the Scandinavian countries that were first to reach a stage where more than 50% of the population used mobile phones. They were followed by Europe and Japan. The United States has lagged a little due to the fact that they lacked a ubiquitous digital telephony service based on a single technical standard, but they are rapidly catching up. At the time of this writing, it is estimated that the number of mobile phone subscribers worldwide will reach 1 billion by 2002 and continue to grow thereafter.

With the widespread use of digital mobile phones came the ability to access the Internet from the telephone handset. Since most mobile phones today contain a powerful processor, many megabytes of memory, and a multiline display, it is possible for them to do most things that are possible from a general-purpose workstation. The main differences lie in the fact that the display area is very small, the keyboard has been replaced by a 12-digit keypad, and the network link is considerably slower and more expensive than that available to a user of the fixed Internet. Competing with digital phones as mobile Internet devices are the personal digital assistants (PDAs) such as the Palm Pilot and the Microsoft Pocket PC. These devices are more focused on data services rather than making voice calls and often they use different wireless technologies to connect to the Internet than the cellular voice network.

Collectively, the owners of Internet-enabled phones and wireless PDAs constitute a very substantial user population. Given the nature of the devices, they are likely to be used by a less sophisticated user who may seldom, if ever, make use of the Internet via a fixed workstation. This is one reason why an entire industry is developing to serve their Internet buying needs and promoting the concept of mobile commerce (m-commerce).

Several things are different about an m-commerce transaction than a conventional e-commerce one. First, since many of the phones used will be based on the Global System for Mobiles (GSM) digital telephony standard, users can take advantage of some of the unique security features offered by that technology. Each GSM handset contains a personality device called a Subscriber Identity Module (SIM). This is a smart card that securely holds details identifying the subscriber and his or her profile together with a number of encryption keys that are shared between the subscriber and the network operator offering the subscribers service.

When a user inserts the SIM card into a phone handset and enters the appropriate PIN, the SIM activates, authenticates itself to the cellular network, and negotiates a session key that is used to encrypt the content of any traffic travelling over the air from then on. This authentication and content protection can be very useful in making payments.

The authentication that takes place links a user with an account held by the network operator. For many subscribers, this account will have a name and contact details, and will also represent the fact that the subscriber is billed periodically and has a history of making these payments when requested. For those increasingly numerous subscribers that have prepaid their accounts, the account will probably be anonymous and will have a fixed balance remaining to be spent. This puts the network operator in a very good position to act as a banker in the process of making an electronic payment. An authenticated subscriber can engage in dialogues across the mobile link to instruct the network operator to make payments from the subscriber's account to a third party. Mobile phone operators view their involvement in this process as an important source of income in the years ahead.

8.1 Mobile Internet architectures

The provision of Internet services to mobile users could take several forms. A brand-new wireless network could be built to carry data. This approach has been taken by Ricochet [1] in the United States. Its service is almost indistinguishable from fixed Internet access except that it is done over a wireless link. Other possibilities for radio-link provision in the future include the use of wireless local area network (LAN) or Bluetooth [2] radio technology to provide small wireless cells that could be used by subscribers to gain access to the fixed Internet. Yet another possibility is to use the cellular mobile phone networks built for circuit-switched voice traffic and adapt them to carry data between handheld phone-like devices and the Internet. It is this last possibility that has the most support from the telecommunications industry as a whole.

There are a number of different technologies used in the mobile phone networks across the world, but without a doubt, the digital system that is most highly developed is GSM, which is used throughout Europe, in many parts of Asia, and also in certain parts of the United States (where it is referred to as PCS-1900). When making a phone call in GSM, a dedicated radio channel is reserved between the phone and the base station for the duration of the call. This has a raw bit rate of approximately 16 Kbps.

8.1.1 Carrying Internet data on cellular networks

In making a data call to the Internet, the same channel carries digital data together with some link-management data at rates of 9,600 bps between the mobile handset and an Internet access point connected to the mobile network. Some mobile operators have introduced a facility called High-Speed Circuit Switched Data (HSCSD) that allows multiple channels to be aggregated to offer speeds of up to 64 Kbps, but this has not proved to be very popular.

From the beginning, GSM incorporated a service called Short Messaging Service (SMS)—this allowed users to compose short text messages of up to 160 characters long and launch these into the network for delivery to a mobile user at some time in the future (usually within a few minutes). These messages consume very little of the networks resources, and are typically cheap (and in some cases free) to send. They can be used to deliver data services, but because of the potentially long time lag, they are not suited to highly interactive dialogues.

The future for data transfer in GSM lies with a new service called the General Packet Radio Service (GPRS) [3]. This sends data across the airwaves in packets by sharing a pool of radio channels between all packet-based users in a given cell. It allows relatively high peak data rates. Each *slot* in the channel pool allows 14.4 Kbps and if the maximum number of eight of these were used, speeds of 115 Kbps would be possible. In practice, though, it is likely that initially the access will be limited to one (14.4 Kbps) or two (28.8 Kbps) slots. Since a mobile can remain connected without consuming network resources, the concept of "always-on" Internet will be enabled by this technology.

In the coming years, advancements in radio technology and the adoption of new spectrum bands that make up the so-called third-generation mobile systems should increase the rates that can be delivered via GPRS to 2 Mbps for stationary users and a little less for those who move around.

8.1.2   The wireless application protocol (WAP)

In mid-1997, many of the mobile phone manufacturers were independently developing ways in which the wireless data transfer services outlined in Section 8.1.1 could be used to deliver Internet services to users of mobile handsets. A number of divergent technologies were beginning to appear, and rather than fragment the market, Ericsson, Motorola, Nokia, and Phone.Com (now Openwave Systems) came together in July 1997 to form the WAP Forum—a consortium that would develop the Wireless Application Protocol (WAP) [4].

In WAP, a browser in the handset interacts over the wireless link with a WAP gateway. A variety of new protocols have been developed, mostly derived from Internet equivalents, to make this possible over a wide range of links from SMS to GPRS. From a payment perspective, one important change to the traditional Internet architecture is that end-to-end security effected with SSL is not possible under WAP. Instead, a new protocol called Wireless Transport Layer Security (WTLS) is used to secure the link from mobile handset to the WAP gateway (see Figure 8.1). The messages used in WTLS are functionally identical to those of SSL (and its successor TLS), but some modifications have been

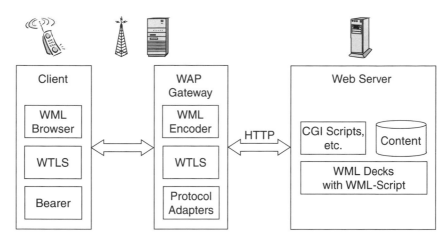

Figure 8.1 The WAP architecture.

made to suit the low-bandwidth link. The certificates used in WAP are expressed in a more compact form than X.509, and the dialogues are structured to send only those certificates that are absolutely necessary. The link between the WAP gateway and the Web server can be secured with normal SSL.

Any GSM phone keeps all the details about the identity of the phone subscriber in a smart card called the subscriber identity module (SIM). These identity details express the relationship between the subscriber and the network operator. The WTLS borrows from this concept and has specified the use of a wireless identity module (WIM) [5], which holds details on the identity to be used for Internet transactions. The WIM holds items such as the WAP certificate and associated private key. It is a logical entity, and can be integrated into the same smart card as the SIM—this combination is referred to as a SWIM card. Alternatively, it can be incorporated into an additional smart card, or implemented in software in the mobile handset.

8.1.3 Japan's iMode service

WAP is being promoted primarily by European mobile phone manufacturers and network operators, and after an initial wave of enthusiasm, the consumer response has not been as good as was initially hoped. At the time of this writing, an alternative system, referred to as iMode, introduced in Japan by NTT DoCoMo in February 1999, is generating considerable interest.

The iMode system is proprietary to NTT DoCoMo and has been used across the packet data service that is available on its Personal Digital Cellular (PDC) mobile phone networks. Since it is packet based, it offers always-on Internet access. From a payment perspective, the iMode gateway [6] is much more transparent than its WAP equivalent and SSL sessions can be formed between the browser on the mobile handset and any normal Web server. This effectively means that the range of payment options available is very similar to that which one could expect on the fixed Internet.

8.2 Industry consortia

Just as the WAP initiative was an attempt by the major mobile equipment manufacturers to standardize the mobile Internet, the Mobile electronic Transactions (MeT) initiative is designed to do the same for m-commerce. It was formed by Ericsson, Motorola, and Nokia in April 2000.

The initiative is at an early stage, and at the time of this writing, they have produced an overview white paper [7] that views the mobile phone as a Personal Trusted Device (PTD). This PTD will incorporate WAP and enable access to WTLS to allow client and server authentication as well as document signing. The intention of the MeT consortium is to develop documents incorporating existing standards to describe how the PTD will register for mobile services, execute those services, and address the consistency of the user interface on the mobile device.

The financial services industry also has an interest in mobile transactions and a number of leading banks, including Deutsche Bank and UBS, have come together with mobile phone manufacturers such as Siemens, Nokia, and Ericsson to help define how financial transactions will be done over wireless links. This organization, which was formed in May 2000, is called the MOBEY Forum [8] and will liaise between technical standards makers and the financial services industry.

8.3 Mobile network operator as banker

One of the simplest methods of effecting payment with a mobile phone capitalizes on the fact that a payment relationship has already been established between the network operator and the phone user. In 1997, Telecom Finland [9] teamed with Hartwall—a company that operates a large collection of drink vending machines. The vending machines display a premium-rate telephone number. When a user wants to purchase a drink, he or she dials this number on his or her mobile phone. The phone network operator will register the transaction on its customer's phone bill and pass a message to the vending machine to dispense one item. This system can, in principle, also work with prepaid telephones with the transaction being debited from the remaining telephone call credits.

A more sophisticated example of operator-mediated payment is the MobilSmart system operated by Swedish mobile operator, Telia, in association with Postgirot in 1997, which allows users to pay electricity bills. Here the user interacts with his or her mobile handset using an application program residing in the SIM and developed with the assistance of a software development environment called the SIMToolkit [10]. A specific PIN number must be entered to activate the application. Thereafter, the destination account number, amount payable, and payment date are entered. The SIMToolkit application packages all of this information into a "short message" and sends it to the network operator's messaging center. There it is passed to a Postgirot system, which makes the payment charging the amount to the mobile phone bill.

In terms of content delivery, if the mobile operator is the conduit through which the content is delivered, this can be used to levy charges for the content via the user's phone bill. In the case of the NTT DoCoMo iMode service, companies wishing to be paid for content can charge subscription fees—a typical fee might be $1 to $5 per month—to access this. Since all the traffic comes through a single gateway, DoCoMo can regulate access to these paid-for sites and for a fee of 9% will deduct the subscription fees from the user's phone account.

8.4 Third-party account-based mobile payment systems

Within any one country or geographical region there are usually a small number of competing mobile network operators from which to choose. A mobile subscriber selects one of these as his or her provider of mobile services. While this does not pose a problem for making mobile calls, since all operators usually offer similar coverage areas, it will restrict the subscriber to using the mobile payment method provided by that operator, at least for payments charged to the user's phone bill. It is not in the interest of competing local mobile operators to make roaming agreements, which would allow their subscribers to use the services of their competitors. A consequence of this is that the mobile subscriber will only be able to use the services of those merchants that have signed up to allow payment to be effected through the particular mobile operator that the user has chosen. Using the example of the vending machine payment in Section 8.3, a situation could arise in which a user would arrive at the vending machine and be unable to use it because the merchant was only accepting payment through a premium-rate number operated by a different mobile network.

To address such a scenario, a number of third-party mobile payment systems, which operate independently of any one mobile network operator, have emerged. The third-party payment provider operates a central transaction server, where user and merchant accounts are maintained. To make a payment the user typically instructs the payment provider to transfer money from his or her account to the merchant's, and after receiving notification, the merchant can provide the requested service. In this way the schemes are similar to the account transfer schemes examined in Chapter 5, with the main difference being the way in which the dialogues are secured between the mobile devices and the payment server, and the way in which transactions are authorized. Indeed, if the Internet protocol stack, along with Web browsing capability, can be provided on the mobile device, as with the iMode system, such Internet account transfer payments can be effected in the mobile realm with little or no modification to the original payment system.

8.4.1   Sonera MobilePay

One advantage of a mobile payment system administered by a network operator is that payments can be charged directly to the subscriber's phone bill. With third-party account schemes, the payment must be obtained from the user by other means. MobilePay [11] is one such operator-independent mobile payment scheme, and is a product of Sonera, a Finnish telecommunications company. It was designed for making physical-world purchases from the mobile device, such as vending machine payments. After registering with the system, payment amounts are debited directly from a user's bank account, or charged to a credit card.

As with the Telecom Finland solution described earlier, the mobile user calls a premium-rate number, which is unique to a specific vending machine. The call is routed to the MobilePay server, and the user is identified using the caller identification feature of GSM. Associated with each number is a fixed purchase price, which is debited from the user's account at the server. For purchases over a certain threshold amount, the server can interactively request a PIN from the user to confirm the transaction. Based on the called number, the MobilePay server then notifies the merchant that payment has been received and the goods can be released. Such notification can be sent by making another GSM call to a merchant mobile device in the vending machine, or over an Internet connection.

More advanced payment dialogues, such as conveying the payment amount, can be composed using SMS messaging. This is used in situations where the payment amount is not known in advance, such as when paying for a restaurant bill. A payment acknowledgement can also be returned to both the payer and payee using SMS.

8.4.2 Paybox

Rather than using premium-rate numbers for fixed-price products, the merchant can dynamically request variable payment amounts from a mobile user, by means of a payment server. While providing more flexibility, this increases the required interaction from the user, and the number of messages that must be transferred per transaction. Paybox (www.paybox.net) is one such operator-independent scheme that takes this approach, and facilitates both physical-world payments and Internet payments for GSM users. Deutsche Bank owns a 50% stake in Paybox, and handles the payment clearing and settlement for its transactions. The company was founded in 1999, with the first payments commencing in Germany in May 2000. While Paybox has been initially targeted at GSM users, there is no reason why it could not be deployed over any digital mobile phone standard that provides secure communications.

Figure 8.2 highlights the steps involved in making a Paybox payment. The scenario considered is a physical-world payment in which a mobile user pays a merchant who also holds a GSM mobile phone. For example, this might be a user paying a taxicab fare. However, for an Internet payment the merchant could equally well be represented by a Web server, with the merchant GSM connection being replaced by an SSL dialogue over the fixed network.

To initiate a payment the user informs the merchant of his or her mobile phone number. A preselected alphabetic alias can also be used instead of a phone number if desired. For a physical-world payment the information is passed manually to the merchant, perhaps by calling out the phone number aloud. With an Internet payment, the number will be

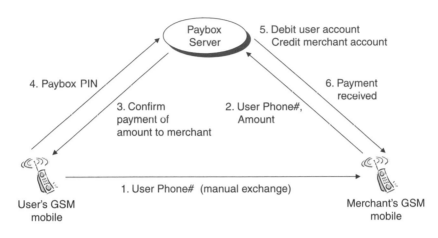

Figure 8.2   Paybox mobile-to-mobile payment.

entered into a Web form, and sent securely over SSL to the merchant Web server.

The merchant then accesses the Paybox server, by calling a toll-free number from his or her mobile, and sends the user's number and the transaction amount to the server, using the phone's keypad. The digits are transferred over the GSM audio channel using the Dual Tone Multi-frequency (DTMF) tones. The server obtains the merchant's identity by using the GSM caller-identification service.

The Paybox server checks the accounts of both the user and merchant to see that they are in good standing order and that no restrictions apply. Subsequently, the server calls the user, and narrates the transaction details to the user over the voice channel. To confirm the payment the user enters his or her four-digit Paybox PIN, after which an audio confirmation is given. Money is transferred from the user's account to the merchant's account, and a payment confirmation message is sent to the merchant.

A Paybox transaction between two mobile phones takes less than 60 seconds. However, due to this transaction time, the on-line dialogues over GSM, and the payment clearing through traditional financial networks, the scheme is not suitable for micropayments.

In the initial rollout in Germany, the payment amount is directly debited from the user's regular bank account, and listed on the user's bank statement. However, other payment instruments, including prepaid accounts, are also planned for use with the system. The merchant's bank account is credited every two weeks with the total payments received. Paybox takes a percentage fee dependent on the average number of transactions.

At the time of this writing, Paybox is available in both Germany and Austria, with expansion planned across Europe. Crossborder payments will be possible, although, as with GSM roaming, this is likely to involve an on-line connection back to the home Paybox server with which the user has an account. The Paybox model is also suitable for mobile-to-mobile payments between users, although this aspect has not yet been emphasized.

8.4.3 GiSMo

With both MobilePay and Paybox, the GSM phone is used as a mobile wallet through which a purchase is initiated and authorized. While direct m-commerce will no doubt flourish, a large user population will continue to make purchases through a fixed computer or Internet access device. As outlined in Chapter 4, a problem with payment card purchases made over the network, is how to prove that it is actually the cardholder initiating the purchase, and not just somebody who has acquired knowledge of the card details. As mentioned at the beginning of this chapter, the GSM SIM is used to authenticate the mobile subscriber to the network operator, and the ability to receive calls on a specific GSM number shows that this authentication has taken place. Therefore, the mobile phone can be leveraged to provide identity verification and transaction authorization for a regular Internet purchase.

If during the Internet purchase a code is sent to the user's GSM phone, and this code is then reentered through the Internet computer, the authenticated GSM user must be present making the purchase. GiSMo (www.gismo.net) uses a GSM mobile device in this way to provide extra authentication and authorization for a purchase initiated from a fixed Internet computer. GiSMo is a subsidiary of Millicom International Cellular, a wireless carrier and operator of cellular networks around the world, with headquarters in Sweden.

To use the system, a customer opens a GiSMo account, linked to an existing bank account or credit card, and is assigned a GiSMo account identifier. The user's mobile phone number is also linked to the account, and used for purchase authorizations. The account identifier is used in the same way as a payment card number when making an Internet purchase. However, if an attacker learns of this number, the attacker will be unable to make purchases without also being able to access the user's mobile phone.

The steps involved in a GiSMo transaction are shown in Figure 8.3. The user browses an Internet merchant's store, and selects to pay for an item using GiSMo. The merchant Web server returns the purchase details to the user, as part of a Web form. The user adds his or her GiSMo account identifier to this form, which is then submitted to the GiSMo server. SSL is used to secure all Internet dialogues.

At the central server the user's mobile phone number is obtained using the account identifier. The server creates a random transaction code and sends this to the user's GSM mobile using SMS messaging. To authorize the transaction, the user must reenter the code obtained on his or her phone, into another Web form on his or her Internet computer, which is then sent back to the GiSMo server. If the correct transaction code is not received back from the Internet computer within a limited time frame, currently two minutes, the transaction is canceled. Receipt of the code proves that the mobile phone user is present during the transaction, rather than just proving knowledge of a valid account identifier.

The GiSMo server debits the user's account and credits the merchant. The server then returns a signed digital receipt to both the user's Internet computer and the merchant. This receipt proves to the merchant that the user has paid, and the goods can be shipped. As with the other mobile

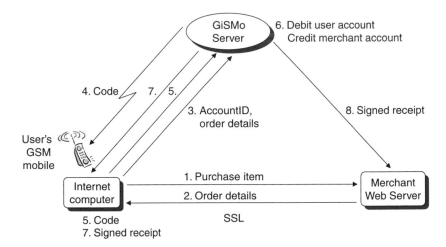

Figure 8.3   GiSMo Internet purchase utilizing mobile for payment authorization.

schemes, the merchant is charged a percentage commission fee on each transaction.

At the time of this writing, GiSMo is being targeted at the European market, and has been deployed in the United Kingdom, Sweden, and Germany. Expansion of the scheme into other European countries is also planned. In many scenarios users will continue to use regular Internet access devices for on-line commerce, rather than trying to navigate complex Web sites using the limited display of their mobile. GiSMo is aimed at such an environment where the mobile is only called into play to authorize the transaction, rather than to browse for the actual purchase.

8.4.4 The Fundamo architecture

One company that has attempted to put a structure on the different variants of account-to-account transfers from mobile handsets is the South African–based Fundamo [12]. Its Fundamo architecture is depicted in Figure 8.4 and is centered around a server that maintains accounts on behalf of its user community. Anticipating the fact that there are likely to be several payment providers around the world, it has planned a Fundamo-to-Fundamo Protocol (F2P) that can be used to transfer amounts between accounts maintained by different providers.

Fundamo envisages a variety of payment scenarios, some of which are similar to those outlined in the GiSMo and Paybox systems, but generalizes this by depicting a Fundamo Payment Protocol (FPP) operating between a variety of mobile devices interfaced by a protocol layer called

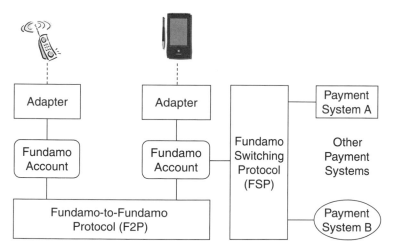

Figure 8.4 The Fundamo architecture.

an adapter to the user accounts. A Fundamo Switching Protocol (FSP) handles situations in which the payments necessitate connections to other existing payment networks (e.g., to charge an item to a credit card).

This architecture is sufficiently general to describe most scenarios in which a mobile device is involved in an e-commerce transaction. For its own part, Fundamo has implemented different components of this architecture in particular implementation scenarios, one of which is similar to the Paybox system outlined earlier.

8.5   Credit card–based systems

Chapter 4 identified the major players in the credit card world and gave an estimate of the number of cards in circulation as well as the total sales in U.S. dollars worldwide. It then went on to describe a number of payment systems that allowed a cardholder to securely transmit card information across an open network such as the Internet. Today there are two main protocols that are used to secure on-line purchases with credit cards: the secure sockets layer (SSL/TLS), and the Secure Electronic Transactions (SET) protocol. Both of these protocols were developed with the assumption that the associated applications would reside on a desktop PC with substantial processing capabilities. Work has to be done to adapt these protocols for current mobile devices, which do not possess the same processing capabilities. In this respect the WAP forum has developed a version of the Transport Layer Security (TLS) protocol for mobile devices, which is known as Wireless TLS (WTLS). Figure 8.5 depicts a generic configuration of the entities involved in a credit card–payment transaction that has a mobile component.

Depending on the capabilities of the mobile device all, some, or none of the payment processing may take place on the device. In accordance with this there may be a Wireless Identity Module (WIM) present on the mobile device or integrated into the device's smart card (SWIM). A gateway/wallet server may be present in the network that will process part of the payment transaction. The consumer will, as before, browse a merchant's Web site and choose a product. The merchant will then send a payment request to the cardholder's mobile device directly or via the gateway server. If the mobile device can complete the transaction on its own, then it will return the payment information directly to the merchant server; otherwise, it will request the gateway/wallet server to complete the payment transaction on its behalf. The wallet server must have

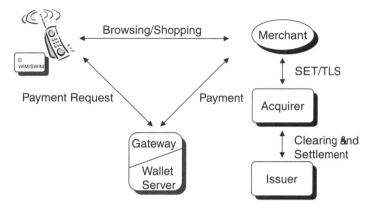

Figure 8.5 Entities involved in a mobile credit card payment.

enough information about the cardholder to be able to process the payment transaction. The merchant will then forward the payment details to the acquirer for authorization. The link between the merchant and the acquirer may be secured either using SET or TLS.

A number of initiatives are currently under way by the major credit card players to develop a common specification for enabling credit card transactions over a wireless interface such as those by Visa [13] and Cyber-COMM [14]. However, at the time of this writing, the most advanced specification that has been available for public review is by the Global Mobile Commerce Interoperability Group (GMCIG), which have released four documents [15–18] which outline its strategy for mobile credit card payments. Interestingly enough, Visa, which is a member of the EMV, CEPS, and SET consortiums, is conspicuously missing from this group.

8.5.1 Mobile SET

SET was designed with the assumption that the main users of the protocol would be consumers on fixed terminals that would have a high-speed connection to the Internet. The user's terminal would be in most cases a commodity PC, which would have the capability to perform complex and processor-intensive cryptographic computations. Also, the availability of a fast network link would mean that large amounts of information pertaining to the payment transaction could be exchanged between the various entities in the system. However, with the huge explosion in the number of mobile users, there is a need to address the issue of performing SET transactions from a mobile device. Most mobile terminals are designed with voice telephony as the main application and usually have very limited data processing capabilities. We now outline three approaches that have been proposed [19, 20] to enable a SET transaction from an off-the-shelf mobile terminal.

8.5.1.1 Handset–based SET wallet

The handset-based wallet approach is equivalent to the standard SET configuration that is used in fixed network transactions. The SET client software is implemented in full on the mobile terminal, and requires the terminal to have enough processing capability to implement a complete SET transaction and the accompanying cryptographic operations. The advantages of this approach are that no modifications have to be made to the original SET protocol and, as the cardholder's public-key pair is held within the WIM, there is no requirement to trust any network entity. However, large amounts of data have to be transferred between the mobile terminal and the merchant over a relatively slow wireless link, which will result in performance degradation. Figure 8.6 shows the SET message exchanges between the entities in the system. These correspond exactly with the messages in a regular SET dialogue between a cardholder on a fixed Internet terminal and a merchant.

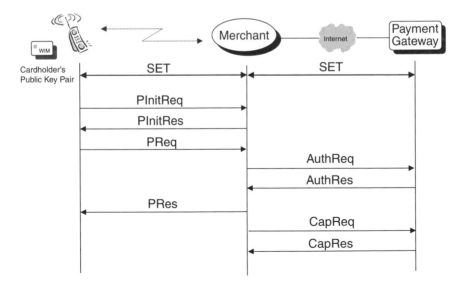

Figure 8.6   Handset-based SET wallet.

8.5.1.2 SET wallet server

The remote wallet server approach takes into account the low processing capabilities of current mobile devices and the associated slow wireless links, and tries to address both issues. The wallet server is a highly secure, trusted entity located in the network that performs the payment transactions on behalf of the cardholder. The SET functionality is now placed in the wallet server along with the cardholder's private-key and public-key certificates. The mobile terminal involvement in the processing of the payment transaction is minimal and the number of messages exchanged over the air interface is limited to two. It triggers the SET transaction at the wallet server by sending a proprietary Payment Request message (see Figure 8.7). Upon receiving such a message, the server engages in a full SET dialogue with the merchant server. The cardholder in effect grants the wallet server authorization to perform payment transactions on the cardholder's behalf. Another advantage of this scheme is that the cardholder can go off-line while waiting for the transaction to be completed.

8.5.1.3 Split-SET

The previous configuration requires that the cardholder place his or her full trust in a remote network entity, the wallet server. The wallet server has access to the cardholder's private key and has the potential to misuse it. Figure 8.8 outlines the split-SET server approach, which is a

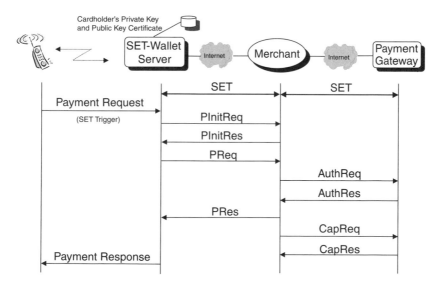

Figure 8.7 SET wallet server.

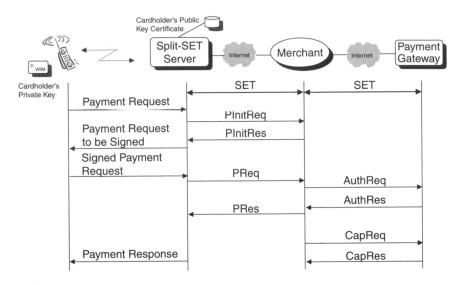

Figure 8.8 Split-SET.

compromise between the previous two solutions, in which the user's private key is kept within his or her WIM, and his or her public-key certificate is placed on the split-SET server, which resides in the network. The signature process required in the SET transaction will be computed on the mobile terminal using the cardholder's private key, while the bulk of the processing will take place on the split-SET server. This implies that we do not require heavy-processing capabilities on the mobile terminal, nor do we need to exchange large amounts of data across the wireless interface. A limited amount of trust is required between the mobile terminal and the split-SET server.

8.5.2 Remarks

As indicated above, the mobile component imposes certain restrictions on the design of the system architecture. A number of solutions proposed in Section 8.5 were designed keeping these limitations in mind. However, with the introduction of third-generation services, one can assume that the current bandwidth restriction will become less of an issue. It is also envisaged that the next generation of mobile devices will have larger displays and greater processing capabilities. This will allow for one to at least compute digital signatures on the device. In time these devices will be able to perform complex cryptographic functions within a reasonable time period. The battery life of a mobile device is also an issue, as more processing on the mobile terminal will result in greater expenditure of the battery. With rapid advances in mobile technology we envisage that these limitations will be overcome and see the mobile handset evolving into a full payment instrument.

8.6 Summary

In this chapter, we have attempted to give an overview of the ways in which payments may be made in the rapidly expanding m-commerce world. This is a difficult task, since so many aspects of this technology have yet to stabilize. While it does seem clear that around 1 billion people will own mobile phones in the very near future, it is not at all clear how these users will access the Internet.

The vision promulgated by the principal mobile phone manufacturers and operators in Europe involves the incorporation of WAP technology into handsets, and the delivery of Internet content through WAP gateways. While this technology choice undoubtedly suits mobile operators, allowing them an opportunity to become a middleman in e-commerce, the initial market reaction to WAP services has been less enthusiastic than predicted. Some attribute this to the low bandwidth available in current second-generation mobile systems and predict that this obstacle will be removed with the emergence of higher bandwidth third-generation systems. Others cite the lack of appealing user services.

In Japan, the NTT DoCoMo-promoted iMode service has proved to be very popular indeed and allows easier access to existing Internet content. Since the gateways are more transparent, all existing methods of payment across the Internet are open to users, as well as some additional ways in which items can be charged to the mobile phone bill. It remains to be seen, though, whether this technology will be popular outside of Japan and supplant the rapidly growing installed base of handsets and gateways based on WAP technology. Many of the payment methods that we have examined in this chapter are dependent on the use of WAP components such as WTLS and the WIM and whether they prosper or not will depend on the success of the underlying technology.

Irrespective of which technology is used for Internet access, the fact that the mobile handset is a personal device is likely to be important. The implicit authentication of a user by virtue of his or her ability to make calls on the mobile device is central to many of the account-based systems discussed earlier. Linking this either to the billing relationship that exists with the network operator or to an account held with a payment provider such as Paybox opens up new payment avenues not available to users of the fixed Internet. These systems, however, do face the same obstacles as account-based systems in the fixed Internet, namely, the chicken-and-egg problem of signing up a critical mass of registered users. Currently, most users of the Internet on mobile devices probably tend to navigate through pages that are quite "local" and this helps ensure that the buyer and seller are signed up with the same payment provider, but this may not persist as the mobile Internet expands its scope.

For credit card–based payments, we have described the progress being made in deploying SET in an m-commerce environment. At one level, the fact that many mobile phones incorporate secure hardware capable of holding public keys and certificates may make SET deployment easier. The "local" scope of the mobile Internet usage may also help in linking SET-enabled buyers with SET-enabled merchants. Nevertheless, the complexity inherent in a SET client makes it less likely that a full implementation will be realized in a handset. The more lightweight variants may have a greater chance of success in the first instance at least.

In the medium-term future, the prospect of third-generation (3G) mobile systems holds out the promise of a single common mobile telephony system for all countries of the world. At the point at which third-generation devices begin to appear, the architecture to be used for Internet access will have stabilized and the global mobile phone network may begin to be as important as the fixed Internet. Other developments in wireless technology, such as the Bluetooth short-range radio system may also be very influential in how users access the Internet from handheld devices. As the technologies change, the payment methods will adapt to meet the changing circumstances.

References

[1]   Metricom Inc., "What's Behind Ricochet: A Network Overview,"
       http://www.ricochet.net/ricochet_advantage/tech_overview/index.html.

[2]   Mettala, R., "Bluetooth Protocol Architecture Version 1.0," Bluetooth
       white paper, August 1999, http://www.bluetooth.com.

[3] Kalden, R., I. Meirick, and M. Meyer, "Wireless Internet Access Based on GPRS," *IEEE Personal Communications,* Vol. 7, No. 2, April 2000, pp. 8–18.

[4] WAP Forum, The Wireless Application Protocol Architecture Specification, April 1998, http://www.wapforum.org.

[5] WAP Forum, Wireless Application Protocol Identity Module Specification, WAP-198-WIN, February 2000, http://www.wapforum.org.

[6] Natsuno, T., and D. Macdonald, "DoCoMo's iMode—Toward Mobile Multimedia in 3G," *Presentation 47th Meeting of IETF,* Adelaide, Australia, March 2000, http://www.ietf.org.

[7] MeT Overview white paper, "The MeT Initiative—Enabling Mobile E-Commerce, Version 1.0," October 2000, http://www.mobiletransaction.org.

[8] Mobey Forum, "Leading On-Line Financial Institutions and Mobile Phone Manufacturers Form Mobey Forum to Drive Mobile Financial Services," press release, May 2000, http://www.mobeyforum.com.

[9] Sonera, "Telecom Finland Invents New Ways to Use Mobile Phones," press release, November 12, 1997, http://www.sonera.fi/english/press/cola.html.

[10] ETSI, Digital Cellular Telecommunications system phase 2+, Specification of the SIM Application Toolkit for the Subscriber Identity Module—Mobile Equipment (SIM-ME) Interface, ETSI Technical Specification TS 101 267, V8.3.0, August 2000, http://www.etsi.org.

[11] Sonera MobilePay, "There's Money in Your Mobile," Sonera presentation, 2000, http://www.sonera.com/mobilepay.

[12] Fundamo, http://www.fundamo.com.

[13] Visa International, "Visa, Nokia and MeritaNordbanken Group to Pilot Mobile Payment," Visa press release, May 1999, http://www-s2.visa.com/pd/eu_shop/presscentre/press_articles/.

[14] Cyber-COMM, "Cyber-COMM SET-Enables Mobile Payments," Cyber-COMM press release, November 2000, http://www.epaynews.com.

[15] Global Mobile Commerce Interoperability Group, "Introduction to Digital Mobile Payments over Open Networks," Version 1.0, http://www.gmcig.org/specifications.html.

[16] Global Mobile Commerce Interoperability Group, "Remote EMV Payments Using a Mobile Device—Architecture Document," Version 1.0, http://www.gmcig.org/specifications.html.

[17] Global Mobile Commerce Interoperability Group, "Remote Wallet Server—Architecture Document," Version 1.0, http://www.gmcig.org/specifications.html.

[18] Global Mobile Commerce Interoperability Group, "Remote EMV/SET Payments Using a Mobile Device—Technical Document," Version 1.0, http://www.gmcig.org/specifications.html.

[19] Europay International, "Mobile-Commerce New Opportunities for SET," October 1999.

[20] Wrona, K., and G. Zavagli, "Adaptation of the SET Protocol to Mobile Networks and to the Wireless Application Protocol," *Proc. European Wireless '99*, Munich, Germany, October 1999, pp. 193–198.

Payment systems: prospects for the future

E-commerce is undergoing huge growth in terms of the volume of goods and services that are being traded on-line. New areas such as B2B and the related business-to-government (B2G) e-commerce are developing as well as the potential for large numbers of people engaging in m-commerce from wireless handsets. Even the most optimistic estimations of e-commerce still place the goods value at less than 1% of the total value of goods and service traded in the conventional economy, so as larger numbers of people come on-line, there is plenty of scope for growth.

In order to bring an on-line transaction to completion, payment must be fully integrated into the on-line dialogues. Just as the complexity of conventional commerce has led to the evolution of many different payment instruments, electronic commerce will also demand a range of electronic payment methods. An on-line transaction between two large companies to buy $2 million worth of raw materials is very different to an individual placing a $1 bet in an on-line casino. The level of risk involved is different, as is the degree of trust that is in place between the transacting parties. In between these two extremes are a multitude of other scenarios, each of which has different characteristics.

In Chapter 4, we saw that credit cards have dominated the electronic payments market in B2C e-commerce. The use of SSL has sufficiently allayed consumer concerns and in the short-term has proved more palatable to consumers and merchants than undergoing the upheaval necessary to get SET up and running. The industry is now stuck between these two choices and is searching for something that will give the security features of SET with the simplicity of SSL. It is likely that such a hybrid will be found that is acceptable to the market. Since merchants are bearing the brunt of the fraud costs, the push to migrate to full SET will not come from consumers.

Electronic checks have been slower to take off. This is partly due to the fact that they involve banks and any initiative would need to secure the backing of all major banks operating in a given region. The FSTC came close to this in the United States, and although consensus was reached, their efforts in electronic checks have not yet progressed past the level of small pilot operations. The Identrus effort is also evidence of global collaboration to bring banks into the on-line trust business. It is likely that the emergence of B2B e-commerce with its large transaction sizes will give a new impetus to efforts in this area. Banks will find a demand from their large business clients to effect high-value bank-mediated transfers of funds easily and efficiently. Similar demand will be experienced in Europe and Asia and, to a lesser extent, the developing world. It may be that developments such as Worldwide Automated Clearing House (WATCH) may eventually lead to a situation in which individuals and organizations transacting on the Internet can easily move funds to and from any country in the world.

In cases in which a community of users can be persuaded to sign up with a single on-line payment provider, much of the complexity of checks and interorganization clearing and settlement can be eliminated, allowing easy account-to-account transfers of funds. It may be that these new payment systems providers can be more agile in responding to customer needs and may supplant banks for certain classes of payments. This is particularly appropriate in countries whose banking infrastructure is less developed than, say, the United States. There are, however, a very large number of companies seeking to become the universal payment provider in this space, and a shakeout is inevitable.

In conventional commerce, the use of cash is very important and one would expect that this need would persist in the on-line world. Digicash's Ecash, while technically very highly developed, failed to capture a sufficiently large base of users to be commercially successful. The company has refocused its efforts and now offers a range of payment products, some of which are clearly descended from its flagship cash payment method. The banks and financial institutions have pursued a path of developing smart-card–based electronic purses. These work quite well in conventional commerce where a single bank can issue compatible cards and readers to a population of customers and merchants in the same geographic region. Since the concept of geographic region is less relevant in the Internet world, gaining acceptance of a payment standard cannot be achieved in the same way. The advent of global standards such as Mondex and Visa CEPS may increase the chances of success of these systems on-line. Their success, though, is still predicated on the widespread availability of smart card–reader hardware on commodity Internet workstations.

In the late 1990s, it seemed as though micropayments would usher in a whole new industry where companies could offer information services and other low-value content to consumers and accept micropayments of very small amounts in return. We have outlined several technical systems that make this possible in Chapter 7. While Internet portal sites have developed, offering a whole host of ostensibly free information and services to consumers, they have not chosen to use any of these methods. Instead, the void was filled by on-line advertising. It seems that it was easier to talk on-line advertisers into paying for ad placement than it was to convince users in their millions to sign up to a micropayment scheme. The use of real micropayments, though, is clearly more flexible and allows a much clearer link between the content delivered and the amount paid. It may be that when new markets develop for multimedia content—such as streamed audio—these techniques will have a resurgence.

At the time of this writing, m-commerce is undoubtedly the most active area in electronic payments. As telecommunications manufacturers and network operators seek to define the shape of the mobile Internet, startup companies are busy coming up with new ways to make payments on-line. One very large area of uncertainty is the degree to which the mobile Internet will resemble the fixed-line Internet. If it does, then most of the payment systems described in earlier chapters will work equally well in a mobile environment. If, as is the case with WAP, a gateway is used to mediate all dialogues, then a whole new set of payment solutions will be required. One element that is missing from the m-commerce debate is a compelling list of products and services that consumers will wish to buy as they move from place to place. There are a large number of companies offering candidate payment systems for m-commerce. As the form of the Internet becomes clear and the patterns of usage become more obvious, a shakeout can be expected in this area, too.

In Chapter 2, we gave an overview of the size and structure of the current conventional payment systems market. Clearly, if electronic methods were to supplant even 1% of conventional payments, it would represent an enormous industry worldwide. The unstoppable growth of the Internet and the tidal wave of electronic commerce that follows in its wake indicate that they will capture considerably more than 1%. It is this impetus that will continue to inject dynamism into the industry in the years to come.

About the authors

Donal O'Mahony received his B.A., B.A.I., and Ph.D. degrees from Trinity College, Dublin, Ireland. After a brief career in the computer industry at SORD Computer Systems in Tokyo and IBM in Dublin, he joined Trinity College in 1984 as a lecturer in computer science. He is a coauthor of *Local Area Networks and Their Applications*, published by Prentice-Hall in 1988. At Trinity College, he coordinates a research group working in the areas of networks and telecommunications. Within this group, projects are ongoing in a wide range of areas, including electronic commerce, network security, and mobile communications technology. He spent 1999 as a Fulbright Fellow at Stanford University, California, before returning to his present position as senior lecturer in computer science at Trinity College. Dr. O'Mahony has acted as an independent consultant to government and private industry organizations across Europe, and to the United Nations on a wide variety of projects involving strategic networking issues. His e-mail address is Donal.OMahony@cs.tcd.ie.

Michael Peirce holds B.A. (Mod.) and Ph.D. degrees in computer science from Trinity College, Dublin. His doctoral thesis concerned the design of multiparty electronic payment methods for mobile communications. Papers and articles relating to his work on network payment schemes have appeared in academic journals, conference proceedings, and the popular media. Dr. Peirce has presented to international audiences tutorials focusing on electronic commerce, financial cryptography, and network payment. He is a member of the Networks and Telecommunications Research Group (NTRG) at Trinity College where he pursues research in network security and electronic payment systems. His e-mail address is Michael.Peirce@cs.tcd.ie.

Hitesh Tewari earned his B.A. (Mod) and M.Sc. degrees in computer science from Trinity College, Dublin. His M.Sc. thesis was on electronic payment systems and made use of secure cryptographic protocols in association with control information to check key usage by individuals. He is currently working as a lecturer at Trinity College. He is an active member of NTRG. His current research interests are in mobile communications, ad hoc networking, and security protocols. His e-mail address is Hitesh.Tewari@cs.tcd.ie.

Index

Multimedia Database Management Systems, Guojun Lu

Practical Guide to Software Quality Management, John W. Horch

Practical Process Simulation Using Object-Oriented Techniques and C++, José Garrido

Secure Messaging with PGP and S/MIME, Rolf Oppliger

Security Fundamentals for E-Commerce, Vesna Hassler

Security Technologies for the World Wide Web, Rolf Oppliger

Software Verification and Validation for Practitioners and Managers, Second Edition, Steven R. Rakitin

Strategic Software Production with Domain-Oriented Reuse, Paolo Predonzani, Giancarlo Succi, and Tullio Vernazza

Systems Modeling for Business Process Improvement, David Bustard, Peter Kawalek, and Mark Norris, editors

User-Centered Information Design for Improved Software Usability, Pradeep Henry

Workflow Modeling: Tools for Process Improvement and Application Development, Alec Sharp and Patrick McDermott

For further information on these and other Artech House titles, including previously considered out-of-print books now available through our In-Print-Forever® (IPF®) program, contact:

Artech House	Artech House
685 Canton Street	46 Gillingham Street
Norwood, MA 02062	London SW1V 1AH UK
Phone: 781-769-9750	Phone: +44 (0)20 7596-8750
Fax: 781-769-6334	Fax: +44 (0)20 7630-0166
e-mail: artech@artechhouse.com	e-mail: artech-uk@artechhouse.com

Find us on the World Wide Web at:
www.artechhouse.com